Way Up
NORTH in DIXIE

Way Up NORTH in DIXIE

A BLACK FAMILY'S CLAIM TO THE CONFEDERATE ANTHEM

Howard L. Sacks and Judith Rose Sacks

SMITHSONIAN INSTITUTION PRESS
WASHINGTON AND LONDON

Some of the discussion presented here appeared in "Way Up North in
Dixie: Black-White Musical Interaction in Knox County, Ohio,"
American Music 6, no. 4 (Winter 1988): 409–27. Used by permission.

Copy Editor: Aaron Appelstein
Supervisory Editor: Duke Johns
Designer: Kathleen Sims

Library of Congress Cataloging-in-Publication Data
Sacks, Howard L.
    Way up north in Dixie : a black family's claim to the
Confederate anthem / Howard L. Sacks and Judith Rose Sacks.
        p.   cm.
    Includes bibliographical references and index.
    ISBN 1-56098-258-6
    1. Afro-Americans—Ohio—Music—Social aspects. 2. Snowden
family. 3. Emmett, Daniel Decatur, 1815–1904. Dixie. 4. Ohio—
Race relations. 5. Minstrel shows. I. Sacks, Judith Rose. II. Title.
ML3556.S2   1993
780'.92'2771—dc20
    [B]   92-39328

British Library Cataloguing-in-Publication Data is available

Manufactured in the United States of America
00 99 98 97 96 95 94 93   5 4 3 2 1

♾ The paper used in this publication meets the minimum
requirements of the American National Standard for Permanence of
Paper for Printed Library Materials
Z39.48-1984

Except where otherwise noted, all photographs are from a private
collection. For permission to reproduce these illustrations, please
correspond directly with the authors; to reproduce any other
illustrations, correspond directly with the sources, as listed in the
individual captions. The Smithsonian Institution Press does not retain
reproduction rights for these illustrations individually, or maintain a
file of addresses for photo sources.

*To the memory of Irving Rose and Helen Balis Sacks,
who taught us to love books, and to Hannah Rose Sacks,
who inspires us always*

I wish I was in de land ob cotton,
'Cimmon seed an sandy bottom,
Look away—look 'way, away Dixie Land.
In Dixie land whar I was born in,
Early on one frosty mornin;
Look away—look 'way, away Dixie Land.

CHORUS
Den I wish I was in Dixie, Hooray, Hooray,
In Dixie's land, we'll took our stand,
To lib and die in Dixie,
Away, away, away down south in Dixie,
Away, away, away down south in Dixie.

Old missus marry Will de Weaber,
William was a gay deceaber;
When he put his arm around 'er,
He look as fierce as a forty pounder.

His face was sharp like a butchers cleaber,
But dat did not seem to greab 'er;
Will run away missus took a decline, O'
Her face was de color ob bacon rhine. O'

While missus libbed she libbed in clover,
When she died she died all ober;
How could she act such a foolish part, O'
An marry a man to break her heart. O'

Buckwheat cakes an stony batter,
Makes you fat or a little fatter;
Here's a health to de next old missus,
An all de galls dat wants to kiss us.

Now if you want to drive 'way sorrow,
Come an hear dis song to-morrow;
Den hoe it down an scratch yer grabble,
To Dixies land I'm bound to trabble.
                              —"Dixie's Land" (1859)

Contents

Acknowledgments ix

Introduction: Searching for Dixie 1

1. 'Cimmon Seed and Sandy Bottom 25
2. The Snowden Family! Are Coming! 57
3. I Am Sitting Sad and Lonely 94
4. Ohio's Not the Place for Me 124
5. I Wish I Was in Dixie 153

Epilogue: A Clinton Quadrille 189

Appendix: A Sampler of the Snowden Family Band
  Repertoire 209

Notes 211

Index 253

Acknowledgments

Many individuals and institutions deserve our thanks. A Faculty Development Grant from Kenyon College and a Fellowship for College Teachers and Independent Scholars from the National Endowment for the Humanities supported much of our research. At Kenyon a summer seminar in American studies funded by the Lilly Foundation provided a first forum for the issues we explore here. Reed S. Browning, Dena J. Epstein, Archie Green, Peter Kolchin, Peter M. Rutkoff, and Nicholas Spitzer offered helpful comments on early proposals for the project.

At the heart of our work are the community members who keep and share the Snowdens' story. First and foremost, we are indebted to Marie Moorehead and her late husband, Myron (Bud). Their hospitality and enthusiasm for our work inspired us throughout the years we visited with them. Dan Bartlett, Jean Bartlett, George Booker, Jim Burgess, Rose Cole,

Dwight Greer, Mildred Greer, Stella Lee, Jean Irwin McMillan, Joseph Greer McMillan, Andrew Lewis, Gabriela Lewis, Bessie Payne, James Payne, John Payne, the late Vera Payne, and Isabelle Wintermute all contributed to our portrait of the community's musical history. In Maryland, William Diggs told us much about Charles County black history, and Kathleen Snowden provided additional information on black life in Frederick County.

We received invaluable research assistance at numerous institutions. In Ohio we thank the staff of the Knox County Historical Society, Knox County Clerk of Courts, Knox County Recorder, National Road/Zane Grey Museum, Ohio Historical Society, Olin Library of Kenyon College, and the Public Library of Mount Vernon and Knox County. In Maryland we are grateful to the staff of the Enoch Pratt Free Library, Historical Society of Frederick County, Inc., Maryland Hall of Records, Maryland Historical Society, and the Southern Maryland Studies Center of Charles County Community College.

Sarah L. Barley at the Southern Maryland Studies Center, F. William and Bette Fetters at the Knox County Historical Society Museum, Bill Myers at the Ohio Historical Society Museum, Elizabeth Reeb at the National Road/Zane Grey Museum, and J. Richard Rivoire deserve our special thanks for regularly assisting us in obtaining documents and photographs for our research. Ellice Ronsheim and Donald Hutslar helped to identify the age and media of photographic images in the Snowden and Greer collections. Clifton C. Crais, Henry Drewal, John Janzen, Robert Farris Thompson, Patricia A. Urban, and John Michael Vlach offered their ideas on the likely origins of Lew Snowden's ivory-bead watch fob. Micah D. Rubenstein reconstructed some Dan Emmett tunes for us on his keyboard synthesizer. Virgil Shipley and Kelly Wilder photographed original materials from private collections.

Individuals who helped with various research tasks include Amy Chenoweth, Gary Fitzgerald, Barbara Kuhns, Kathryn Reed-Maxfield, Margaret Mary Sidlick, John G. Wilson, and Tony Ziselberger. Barbara Knox painstakingly transcribed the Snowden correspondence. Sharon Duchesne kept her patience and good humor as she prepared both the preliminary and final versions of the hard copy and disks. We thank Jack Finefrock for his ideas about marketing the book. Special thanks goes to John J. Macionis for alerting us to the Snowden gravestone, which got us started.

We benefited greatly from our reviewers' critical comments. Joseph

T. Wilson brought his wide-ranging scholarship and sensibilities to bear on our research and writing. James Horton suggested important ideas we might explore in discussing the life of free blacks in the North. We also thank our friends and colleagues, from a range of disciplinary backgrounds, who commented on individual chapters: Rita Smith Kipp, Lori Hope Lefkovitz, William B. Scott, Ric S. Sheffield, Paul Sidlick, and Gregory P. Spaid.

At the Smithsonian Institution Press, Daniel Goodwin and Ruth Spiegel shared their enthusiasm for our manuscript from its earliest stage. Mark Hirsch inspired us to reshape the final manuscript both structurally and substantively. Duke Johns managed the production process with professionalism and goodwill. Aaron Appelstein, our copy editor, improved the book with his meticulous, sensitive handling of our words and ideas.

Introduction

Searching for Dixie

In a large, well-tended graveyard overlooking Mount Vernon, Ohio, rests a pioneer of American blackface minstrelsy, Daniel Decatur Emmett. Emmett's epitaph bears testimony to what in the popular imagination was his most valued contribution: "Daniel Decatur Emmett (1815–1904), whose song 'Dixie Land' inspired the courage and devotion of the Southern people and now thrills the hearts of a united nation." The marker was erected twenty years after Emmett's death, funded in part by traveling minstrels visiting Mount Vernon who believed a suitable monument should honor one of their own who contributed so significantly to American culture.[1]

Three miles north of Emmett's grave is another cemetery, small and obscure, beside an old clapboard church. Among the graves are those of the Snowdens, one of the first black families to settle in rural Knox County, Ohio, in the early nineteenth century. One marker in that cemetery,

Ben and Lew Snowden playing fiddle and banjo from the second-story gable of their home in Clinton, ca. 1890s. Ohio Historical Society, Columbus.

erected in the year of the American bicentennial by the black American Legion post, commemorates two Snowden brothers, Ben and Lew. On their common stone is an inscription that expresses the understanding of four generations of local African Americans: "They taught 'Dixie' to Dan Emmett."[2]

Both gravestones bespeak a song of great significance to the nation and reflect controversies that have followed this song from its birth to the present day. "I Wish I Was in Dixie's Land," as it was first titled, debuted to the public on April 4, 1859, and almost immediately became America's most famous song. Only two years later, the *New York Clipper*—trade paper of the theatrical world—described the song as "one of the most popular compositions ever produced. . . . [It] had been sung, whistled and played in every quarter of the globe." Even today, more than a century later, nearly everyone can construct an identifiable bit of the tune and recall its stirring refrain: "Away, away, away down South in Dixie." And that ain't just whistling "Dixie."[3]

"Dixie" was introduced as the finale to a performance by Bryant's Minstrels, engaged for a run at 472 Broadway, New York City. Dan Emmett—who first performed the song and is its acknowledged composer—played the violin with Bryant's organization, but he was also an expert banjo player, fifer, and dancer. Emmett had left his rural Ohio home to join the circus in the early 1830s and soon entered the theatrical world of New York. In his long career he gained fame as an outstanding composer, musician, theater manager, and founder of the first professional blackface minstrel troupe.

Authorship of "Dixie" soon became the subject of contention. The controversy began over copyright, as several publishers rushed to produce sheet music for the new hit until Emmett finally sold exclusive rights to Firth & Pond. In 1872 the *Clipper* commented, "[Emmett's] claim to the authorship of 'Dixie' was and is still disputed, both in and out of the minstrel profession." By the time of Emmett's death in 1904, no fewer than thirty-seven would-be composers, all white men, had come forward claiming the song.[4] A generation later, cultural historian Constance Rourke attributed black origins to Emmett's compositions but acknowledged that "controversy has in fact gathered around the entire question of the composition of 'Dixie,' and Emmett has been denied even the smaller glory of transcription or adaptation."[5]

To most contemporary listeners, "Dixie" conjures images of the antebellum South because of its historical association with the Confederacy.

When Southern states seceded from the Union in 1861, they adopted "Dixie" as their national anthem. A monument on the site of Jefferson Davis's inauguration as president of the Confederate States of America at Montgomery, Alabama, proclaims that "Dixie was played as a band arrangement for the first time on this occasion"; so momentous was the event that historians thought to preserve the bandleader's bonnet in the state archives museum.[6] New lyrics were composed celebrating the Confederacy, whose soldiers marched into battle to the strains of "Dixie" played on fife and drum.[7]

Today, the song is no less a source of pride to some Southerners. Some years ago, while strolling through the French Quarter in New Orleans, we were drawn to a bar by the exuberant sounds of the house band. Upon hearing a familiar tune, the bartender tugged a cord to unfurl a huge Confederate flag, and the patrons rose to their feet as the band played "Dixie." For the rebel proud to drape the Stars and Bars on his humble barn near Macon or Cincinnati, and the Son or the Daughter of the Confederacy yet crusading for the Lost Cause, "Dixie" conjures Southern and white entitlement, if not racial enmity.[8]

But to other Southerners, "Dixie" is a hateful reminder of generations of segregation, an auditory code cheering racial oppression. Since the 1960s black students at Southern state universities have protested the song's performance at football games and have in some cases been successful in eliminating it from the halftime repertoire, which traditionally has included "Dixie" along with the alma mater and the national anthem. As recently as 1989, *Jet* magazine noted the protest of the song by three black state senators from Georgia, Arthur Langford, Horace Tate, and Gary Parker; they left the Georgia chamber when the song was sung by Miss Georgia Sweet Potato Queen—incidentally the niece of a white Georgia senator, Walter Ray.[9]

Contemporary scholars of American music view the song as a racist fiction. Music critic Sam Dennison offers this typical reading of "Dixie":

Consanguinity of "Dixie" and racism is inherent in the original purpose for which the song was written. Association with the Southern Confederate cause emphasizes its racist mold as both words and music assumed meanings far beyond anything conceived by Emmett. Today, the performance of "Dixie" still conjures visions of an unrepentant, militantly recalcitrant South, ready to reassert its aged theories of white supremacy at any moment. . . . This is why the playing of "Dixie" still causes hostile reactions.[10]

In a discussion of the interaction of white and black musicians, the American-music critic Tony Russell (who is English) comments, in his characteristically flip style, "When whites did make records about blacks they tended rather to be comfortably commercial couplings like *Run, Nigger, Run* and *Dixie*, which, with its affirmation of the southern values of home pride and nigger-hating, would ensure for the band a warm welcome in any port-of-call."[11]

For good or ill, "I Wish I Was in Dixie's Land" expresses something of America's changing character and consciousness. After more than a century and a quarter in the popular repertoire, "Dixie" thrills some and humiliates others. Largely because of its rich variety of meanings, "Dixie" refuses to lie peacefully in that trunk of Victorian sheet music forever consigned to the attic. It grabs at our popular culture in ways both subtle and overt, and it continues to shape the identity of the blacks and whites in its community of origin.

Americans first heard "Dixie" in the minstrel show, which, along with the circus, was the most popular form of entertainment in nineteenth-century America. Although the roots of blackface minstrelsy extend deeply into European theatrical history, the American minstrel show can be traced to a single event. In January 1843 four entertainers—Dan Emmett, Frank Brower, Dick Pelham, and Billy Whitlock—found themselves without work in the midst of a disastrous theatrical season in New York. All were "Ethiopian delineators"—white actors who blackened their hands and faces and performed music and dance in what they claimed was the manner of plantation slaves. Since the 1820s individual blackface entertainers had performed in circuses and in theaters between acts of plays, and a few such actors became quite famous—for example, Thomas "Daddy" Rice for his wild dancing character of Jim Crow. But Dan Emmett, an entertainer in search of a gimmick, came up with an idea that was to transform the American stage: Perhaps if this ensemble of *four* musicians presented an entire evening's entertainment in blackface, he reasoned, they could generate more interest than they could as individuals in parts of other shows. The next night, calling themselves the Virginia Minstrels, Emmett, Whitlock, Brower, and Pelham presented their idea to the public.

Seated in a semicircle on the stage, the minstrels offered songs and instrumental selections played on fiddle, banjo, tambourine, and bones, interspersed with comedic dialogue by Brower and Pelham, who were seated at either end (the "endmen"). The first part of the evening's entertainment closed with a "stump speech," featuring nonsensical oratory on a topic of the day, delivered in an exaggerated speech style meant to represent "Negro" dialect. Part two of the show proceeded in much the same manner, closing with a "walk-around"—music and dance from the entire company, set in a plantation scene.

Immediately successful, the Virginia Minstrels soon left the States for a performance tour of England. They won only modest acclaim abroad, however, and broke up midtour. But in their absence numerous new minstrel troupes had formed in the States to meet a ready public. By the mid-1850s ten New York theatrical houses continually featured minstrel shows, and traveling minstrel troupes had begun to perform in small towns throughout the West.[12]

The minstrel rage continued unabated until the turn of the century, when the genre's fast-paced mixture of humor, music, and dance evolved into the new forms of burlesque, vaudeville, musical comedy, and the variety show. Even today minstrelsy's theatrical formulas, characterizations, and music infuse every form of American entertainment. A few examples will suffice here to make the point: radio and television portrayals of blacks, from "Amos 'n' Andy" to "The Jeffersons," often reworked minstrelsy's stock characterizations; Ed Sullivan's mix of opera divas and plate jugglers and puppet mice replayed late minstrelsy's extravagant varieties; and the zany films of the Marx Brothers were structured like minstrel skits, complete with the walk-around ending. As late as 1985 we were able to attend what was billed as an "authentic minstrel show" at an elementary school near Bellville, Ohio, about fifteen miles north of Mount Vernon. Gone were the blackface and any overt plantation imagery; overall, the show simply provided a venue for local entertainers. But the second half, replete with "Southern melodies" and punctuated by the humor of four men dressed in clownish costumes and multicolored "Afro" wigs, was reminiscent of the show Emmett conceived nearly a century and a half in the past.

Beyond the occasional amateur performance, minstrelsy has had a pervasive impact on American music. Many of the songs Dan Emmett brought to the minstrel stage are still American favorites: "Old Dan Tucker," "Turkey in the Straw," and, of course, "Dixie." As traveling entertainers performed in theaters and halls throughout small-town America, local musicians learned and subsequently performed these tunes in their own communities. Minstrelsy also popularized the banjo among whites in locales as diverse as the southern Appalachian mountains, Ireland, and South Africa.[13]

The Original Negro Minstrels, Organized by Uncle Dan Emmett

Postcard of Dan Emmett's Virginia Minstrels, the first blackface minstrel band in America. Sold in Mount Vernon in the early 1900s, the card represented black- face artists with grotesque exaggerations of African American features and ex- pressions. Bones, fiddle, banjo, and tambourine were the classic minstrel band instruments. Private collection.

Minstrelsy is most notorious, however, for its social consequences. In dehumanizing blacks, antebellum minstrelsy excused slavery and those who profited by its continuation. Ironically, the minstrels' portrayals of slaves as childlike and in need of care satisfied abolitionist paternalism as well. Minstrel shows belittled the physical appearance, intellectual capac- ity, social institutions, and culture of African Americans. The Jim Crow character, for example, was a rough, savage man prone to violence and mischief. He epitomized the antithesis of respectability as defined in Anglo-American culture—industriousness, responsibility, and self-con- trol. A second classic character of the minstrel stage, Zip Coon, affected the manners and dress of Northern whites, but audiences were supposed to find him funny and inferior precisely because of his affectations. En- countering African Americans—and, later, various European ethnic groups—as the brunt of minstrel humor, white audiences could affirm their own sense of cultural superiority in an era of increasing multicultural tension and contact.[14]

The undoubted racism in minstrel characterizations, songs, oratory, and dance poses a challenging question: How can such materials be racist and yet authentically derived from African American culture, as the minstrels claimed? Minstrels, products of the new popular culture in the mid-nineteenth century, had much to gain by announcing their expertise in plantation arts. Their audience was Northern whites who found blacks interesting, for two reasons: blacks generally were unknown and therefore exotic, and they were increasingly the subject of concern as civil war approached. But the identification of certifiably African American sources of minstrelsy remains elusive, as music historian Dena Epstein notes concisely: "The whole question of the relationship of black folk music to Negro minstrelsy is a knotty one, still to be disentangled."[15]

Some scholars accept the minstrels' claims of authenticity, viewing the early minstrels essentially as folklorists or anthropologists whose site of fieldwork was the Southern plantation and whose population under study was slaves. Other writers observe that since most of the early minstrels were Northerners, they would have had little opportunity to interact with plantation folk, and therefore early minstrelsy was entirely devoid of authentic black content. Others who reject minstrelsy's basis in black arts focus on the genre's racism as evidence that white minstrels had little or no contact with blacks; familiarity, they reason, would have made the formation of such demeaning and grotesque images impossible. As different as these interpretations sound, they all carry a troubling blind spot, namely, a focus on blacks in the South and nowhere else as models for blackface artists.

Robert Toll, in his careful examination of the minstrel show, *Blacking Up*, poses the debate aptly: "Although primarily Northern and white, the Virginia Minstrels and their many successors claimed to be authentic delineators of black life. But were they?"[16] Perhaps nowhere else on earth are the questions surrounding minstrelsy more graphically adduced than in the Snowdens' burial plot in rural central Ohio. Literally etched in stone there is something terribly rare in American musical history: the connection of an individual white minstrel with particular black musicians whose art might have been reshaped for the minstrel stage. And no less a figure is identified than Dan Emmett, founder of the genre and acknowledged composer of its most famous song.

"Dixie" conjures images of the South and was first performed in the North, but the song's origins rest in the association of African Americans and European Americans in the western frontier. There, people of diverse backgrounds met and created communities and a common culture very different from those of the Old South and the growing urban population centers.

Knox County, Ohio, was established in the first generation of frontier settlement. The Northwest Ordinance—the federal government's first piece of legislation, in 1787—provided for the distribution of land north and west of the Ohio River and for its eventual incorporation as states into the Union.[17] The prospect of Indian warfare deterred white settlement into the region's interior until 1794, when federal troops under the command of the revolutionary war hero General "Mad" Anthony Wayne defeated Indian forces at the Battle of Fallen Timbers, some one hundred miles north of Cincinnati. In the following year, Wayne counseled with representatives of the region's Indian nations at Fort Greenville and signed a treaty defining Indian lands as those northwest of a boundary crossing the mid-section of Ohio. The Greenville Treaty line would eventually serve as the northern boundary of Knox County, named for Henry Knox, secretary of war at the time of Wayne's Indian campaign.[18]

By 1800 the first settlers had reached the banks of Owl Creek, an area long frequented by Indians who favored its beauty and natural abundance. This community on the frontier included Americans of African descent from the very first; the character of their experience, however, differed greatly from that of whites.[19] By the time of Knox County's incorporation in 1808, the population included its first black resident, Enoch Harris. Enoch—"Knuck"—worked with horses, conducting the duties of a stable hand with considerable care. He was likely a jockey, too, as horse racing was a favorite amusement in the community.[20]

Members of the first generation of African Americans to come west in the 1820s, Thomas Snowden and Ellen Cooper had traveled to Knox County as members of white households. Ellen was a child of ten, Thomas a young man of twenty-three when they separately left slavery for freedom in Ohio. Born on a plantation in the Nanjemoy district of Charles County, Maryland, Ellen had grown up in the very heart of black America. By the time of her birth in 1817, blacks had been the numerical majority in the region for more than a generation. Significantly, the range of activities and age categories of slaves on the wealthier estates supported the development of black communities, vital forces in fostering a distinctive black culture while mediating the privations of enslaved life. In the accounts of early white travelers to southern Maryland, we find evidence of rich and vibrant African American traditions. Commenting on the musical and verbal displays of slaves in Nanjemoy, for example, Nicholas Cresswell in 1774 described a slave's stringed instrument as a *banjo*—the first recorded use of this word now so familiar in our lexicon of American folk instruments.[21]

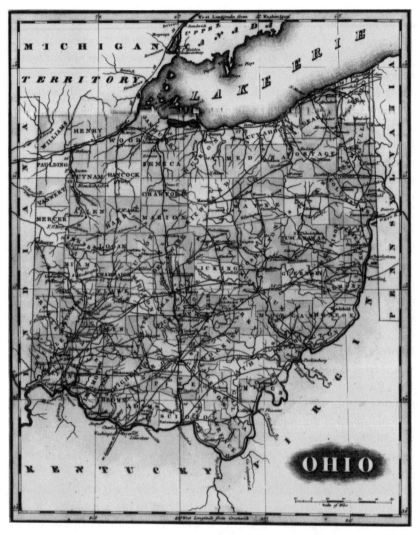

Map of Ohio, 1825. The Northwest Ordinance opened lands for settlement north and west of the Ohio River. Knox County, in the center of the state, remained partially a wilderness into the 1820s. Ohio Historical Society, Columbus.

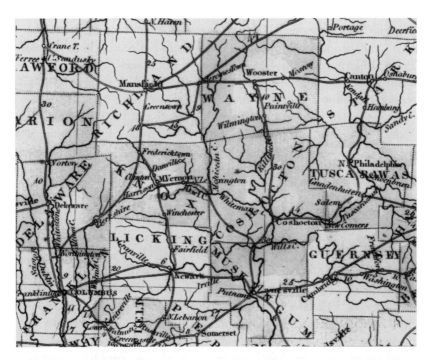

Detail of central Ohio, 1825. Located along a stagecoach route linking the National Road to the Ohio interior, Mount Vernon won a measure of prosperity in the first generation of frontier migration. Ohio Historical Society, Columbus.

Thomas and Ellen Snowden's marriage was the first to be recorded among blacks in Knox County. Settling in the village of Clinton, just north of Mount Vernon, the couple farmed a small parcel and raised a family. Of their nine children, seven would survive childhood: Sophia, Benjamin, Lewis, Martha, Phebe, Annie, and Elsie. Illiterate themselves, the Snowden parents lived to see their children attend school alongside their white neighbors and master reading, writing, and recitation. The Snowden family made their living by farming, but they were best known as the "Snowden Family Band": talented composers, singers, dancers, and instrumentalists. Traveling regularly to farming communities roughly within a seventy-five-mile radius, the band also played within their home county for both white and black audiences. In contrast to the elaborate advance work by minstrels and other professional entertainers, the Snowdens used word of mouth and a simple handbill to gather their audiences at churches, community halls, family reunions, and picnics.

The Snowdens started out performing as a family ensemble in about 1850, and two sons, Ben and Lew, were still performing into the early 1900s. Elderly residents of Knox County, blacks and whites, reminisce about visiting the Snowden house, where Ben and Lew performed on fiddle and banjo from a second-story gable modified into a stage. Black touring bands were rare—and ephemeral—before the Civil War. No other African American string band approaches the Snowdens in longevity, spanning from antebellum times to living memory.

The Snowdens' public life was shaped most directly by the twin social forces of sentimental culture and race. Sentimental culture offered nostalgia and narrow prescriptions for behavior as responses to widespread changes in American social life occasioned by the rise of industrial society. Death, love, friendship, home, women's virtue, temperance, and Christian piety were subjects of nostalgic interest. Particularly a matter of public debate was womanhood, defined increasingly in terms of the domestic and moral spheres. Destined never to fully embody sentimental ideals because of their race, Ellen Snowden and her daughters responded to these cultural messages with a mix of acceptance and resistance informed by their distinctive experience as African Americans. If odes to olden times and tracts on religion were important to this family, so were the speeches of Frederick Douglass and the news coverage of John Brown's raid.

In part, the family's experience of race relations was defined by the demographics of settlement in the county. Like Thomas and Ellen Snowden, a majority of Knox County's first black residents resided with whites who had journeyed to Ohio from the Upper South and mid-Atlantic states. In 1820 Knox County's first census identified only two black households of the twenty-two blacks listed; most individuals appeared as a single thin stroke in the "Free Persons of Color" column following the tally of the white household members. Upon her arrival in Knox County in 1827, Ellen Cooper was the only person of color within ten miles, a good day's ride on horseback.[22] Only when increasing numbers of African Americans migrated north after the Civil War could Mount Vernon's blacks establish a viable community, built on the foundation of the African Methodist Episcopal Church.

Thomas and Ellen Snowden and their children were of necessity in constant contact with their white neighbors, and a significant degree of intimacy defined their relationships. The Snowdens exchanged song lyrics and gossip and flower seeds through the mails, taught white farmhands how to play the fiddle and sing the most popular songs of the day, and held regular open-air concerts on their farmstead. Just about everybody—playmates and pharmacists, chicken breeders and attorneys—knew the Snowdens as fine musicians, beyond their everyday activities in the school, the church, and the farming economy.

Intimacy between individual blacks and whites did not, however, mitigate the profound discrimination blacks faced in the West. Contemporary historian William Loren Katz comments upon the images and realities of black life on the frontier:

> It has been one of our enduring myths that the western lands offered people—all people—an escape from the inhibiting social customs and mores of the East, that the frontier environment was a stage upon which each performer would be judged by his performance, not his ancestry, sex, color or wealth. It has been assumed that social and geographical mobility was the frontier's hallmark. But the black person who came west, whether slave, slave runaway or free man, found neither social mobility, geographical mobility, social acceptance, nor an absence of inhibiting customs or laws. He often found that he could not even enter a western territory or state because their earliest laws prohibited the migration of black people. When he could, the black settler found white settlers clinging with the tenacity of a slaveholder to the folkways, mores and legislation of the East and South.[23]

Music may have helped the Snowdens cross the color line, but it did not render them immune to the incidents of prejudice and discrimination that were the common fate of black Americans.

Early in this century, sociologist W. E. B. Du Bois observed that African Americans experienced a divided self, caught between an inner striving for authentic self-expression and the oppressive expectations of a racist society:

> It is a peculiar sensation, this double-consciousness, this sense of always looking at one's self through the eyes of others, of measuring one's soul by the tape of a world that looks on in amused contempt and pity. One ever feels his twoness,—an American, a Negro; two souls, two thoughts, two unreconciled strivings; two warring ideals in one dark body, whose dogged strength alone keeps it from being torn asunder.[24]

To balance their need for personal and cultural integrity with an equally strong need for community acceptance, the Snowdens employed a complex strategy of alternately accommodating whites' expectations, resisting these expectations, and affirming their cultural heritage. Ellen Snowden, the family head after Thomas's death in 1856, emerges from oral and written accounts as a forceful woman vitally concerned with achieving personal and family respectability. Perhaps the most poignant evidence of Ellen's efforts is her role in the relationship between her son Ben and his white friend Nan Simpson. Theirs was a sad and doomed interracial love affair, undone finally by Ellen's continual interference. The cost, tragically, was no less than the perpetuation of the Snowden name.

Dedicated to resisting racial and economic discrimination, the Snowdens staked their claims in the local judicial system. Only days after the Fifteenth Amendment extended the right to vote to African American men, Ben Snowden brought suit in court against township officials who had denied his voting rights in a local election—possibly the first such challenge by an African American. And the widowed Ellen Snowden, who could sign her name on a complaint only with an *X*, successfully sued for damages when whites denied her the opportunity to plant crops.

Music was their strongest social voice, however, and it was in their performances that the Snowdens most fully articulated their connection to black cultural heritage. Their instrumentation matched that of Southern black string bands in the antebellum era, the same instruments whites adapted to use on the minstrel stage: fiddle, banjo, guitar, triangle, and bones. Mindful of popular taste, the Snowdens selectively built a repertoire that was pleasing and current but that avoided songs with demeaning racial themes or dialect. They also performed traditional African American sacred songs. In making music, whether privately in their own parlor or up in the gable for the public, they connected to—perhaps conjured—lost family members, black kin and friends in Maryland, and, more broadly, the shared culture of black Americans.

Music is a particularly clear window into the complexity of American social life and race relations. The interplay of African American and Anglo-American musical traditions has yielded most of America's distinctive musics: rock and roll, rhythm and blues, country music, jazz, ragtime, and minstrelsy. The fiddling of Ben Snowden and the banjo playing of Lew Snowden epitomize this interplay. The fiddle, a European classical and folk instrument, was typically mastered by blacks in slavery who played for their own amusement and for that of their masters. The banjo originated in Africa, starting its life as a long-necked gourd in the savanna. Even the earliest documentary accounts of slave life in the United States are replete with notes and drawings of this "exotic" instrument.[25]

The coming together of fiddle and banjo also captures the integration of two distinct musical cultures. Complex melodies characterize European aesthetics. Those melodies comprise precise pitches arranged within strict metric patterns. That is why when we are taught rhythm in elementary school, we are told to count. In vocal music the Western European tradition stresses the solo singer performing text-heavy messages. African music, in contrast, reflects the tonal character of languages spoken on the African continent. The pitch and tone with which a word is spoken determine the meaning of the word itself. African drums, modeled on the tonal quality of language, are played at a variety of pitches to convey messages. Short, tonal phrases communicated by these "talking drums" were an effective means of communication among people who had familiarity with local events, so much so that Southern slaveowners banned the drum out of fear of slave insurrection.[26]

But if one lesson of American music is that it springs from African roots as well as European, another is that the respective sources have benefited unequally from this cross-fertilization. A long line of white musicians have made their careers by imitating black aesthetics and performance characteristics, and it has been whites who have reaped most of the rewards. A story about the legendary record producer Sam Phillips says it well: Recording black and white musicians in Memphis on his Sun label in the 1950s, Phillips dreamed aloud, "If I could find a white man who had the Negro sound and Negro feel, I could make a billion dollars." When a young truck driver by the name of Elvis Presley walked into the Sun studios in 1955, singing covers of rhythm and blues hits he listened to on black radio stations in the South, Phillips came close to realizing his dream. Phillips, and others before and since him, had the genius to follow a formula well known in the entertainment business since Dan Emmett's time: "white singers + black style = pop bonanza."[27]

This legacy of cultural appropriation and stereotyping, from minstrelsy onward, poses a difficult question of identity for African Americans: What symbols can African Americans retrieve from a history marked by centuries of enslavement and oppression, of co-optation and distortion? Cultural groups actively create an identity, a history, by examining their collective past, elevating and carrying forward some elements and subordinating others. New forms may be created—dances, holidays, songs, and the like—that conform, in varying measures of authenticity, to older elements of the culture. Evidence of this process is plentiful among Americans of diverse ancestry: the rise of choreographed clogging teams in the 1950s in western North Carolina (a nontraditional blend of square dancing and solo, freestyle mountain dance) or the practice of ethnic organizations to spend a great deal of time and money re-creating costumes and dances of the "old country" while forgetting foodways or poetry traditions. Culture is built selectively; what is discarded tells just as much as what is kept.

The banjo perfectly symbolizes this dilemma: a genuine African American musical instrument, the banjo is yet to be salvaged from its abuse as a demeaning stereotype on the minstrel stage. Are we to regard Lew Snowden, one of the last few African Americans who continued to play the banjo, as an embarrassing relic or as the carrier of an important tradition, if one fraught with unfortunate associations? Popular minstrel hit, proud anthem of the South, hated symbol of racism—can "Dixie" also be understood today as a valid expression of African American experience?

Although we tend to think of banjos and songs as stable entities, sometimes we need to see and hear such things anew. The black community of Mount Vernon, Ohio, offers "Dixie" for this sort of retelling. For them it speaks of the familiar and authentic experience of those who, like the Snowden parents, left the black South for the mixed circumstances of life in the white North.

Ellen and others in her situation must have felt tremendously isolated on the frontier. The contrast between past and current life would certainly have involved a sharp awareness of a loss of black community. If someone like Ellen Cooper Snowden were to make a song inspired by the grief of this loss, it would be the kind of lament we know as the blues. If elements of that song were to express rage and ridicule against the whites who controlled black life, these transgressive sentiments would be masked, following black folk tradition, in language of multiple meanings, "safe" for the ears of uncomprehending whites. We listen to "Dixie," then, for its black voice, its expression of themes of diaspora in the North—generations before the Great Migration made its promises and its disappointments known to the nation.[28]

The idea of "Dixie" as a product of African American inspiration has been a source of pride in the local black community for generations. Vera Payne (1893–1990), the oldest woman we talked to, summed up the belief about "Dixie" in this way: "The man that wrote 'Dixie,' he was in New York at the time, they asked him to write something, he asked the Snowdens." This scenario, emphasizing the family as the source if not necessarily the sole composers, has circulated in Mount Vernon at least since the early decades of the century. Vera Payne first heard about "Dixie" and the Snowdens in 1915 when she moved to Mount Vernon: "That is what they [black community members] told me; that's what they thought."[29]

The story also has been carried for generations among the Greers, the white family that brought Ellen Cooper out of slavery in Maryland to Knox County in 1827. Emigrating from County Antrim, Ireland, to Maryland in the early 1820s, Mary Greer and her seven children had stayed with relatives in southern Maryland, on the farm of Ellen's birth, for several months. With the tobacco economy weakened, the Greers decided to join another branch of the family in Ohio. James Greer was among that party venturing west, and his great-grandson Joseph Greer McMillan recalls hearing about the musical partnership between the Snowdens and Dan Emmett from his grandmother and other family members: "They told the story often; it was something they were proud of."[30] Family pride was sufficient to warrant including the story on the opening page of their family history: "After the Greers had settled in Knox Co., Ellen [Cooper] stayed with them until she married Tom Snowden, an entertainer whose musical gifts inspired Daniel Emmett to write 'Dixie.' The Snowdens had 9 children and remained friends with the Greers through the generations, known as their colored cousins."[31]

For black residents of the county, and some whites as well, the Snowdens are important well beyond their connection to one famous song. Some of the most cherished memories among the elderly are recollections of picnics and concerts at the Snowden homestead, where Ben and Lew Snowden played their fiddle and banjo dance music. Whites and blacks alike recall the family as fine people, beyond their musical talents; for black residents the Snowdens are legendary as cultural heroes in a community history that has yet to fully acknowledge its black contributors.

The authors first heard about Dan Emmett and the Snowdens on a local radio talk show. Mount Vernon celebrates its favorite son each year with a three-day festival, "Dixie Days." Nearly every small town in Ohio hosts a summertime festival—Fredericktown's Tomato Festival, Circleville's Pumpkin Festival, Utica's Ice Cream Festival—that includes commercial promotions, contests, exhibits, and stage entertainments. As Dixie Days nears each year, the local newspaper typically publishes stories on Emmett or on life in Emmett's time, and radio shows also pick up on the "Dixie" theme.

During this particular show, about 1976, someone called in to take issue with the idea that Dan Emmett wrote "Dixie," attributing it instead to two black men whom Emmett knew, Ben and Lew Snowden. The fact of authorship, the caller went on, was inscribed on their gravestone. A rousing debate followed for some thirty minutes, and the noon hour approached with no resolution of the issue in sight. Shortly before the program closed, however, the moderator introduced the apparent authority on the subject, Isabelle Wintermute, who had joined the program by phone at the moderator's request. The late H. Ogden Wintermute had published a laudatory biography of Dan Emmett and was a noted collector of Emmett materials, among his many antiques.[32] Isabelle Wintermute, known throughout the region as the organizer of a series of fine antique shows and a member of one of the society families in the town, assured the audience that Emmett's repute was well deserved.

Our interest was rekindled a few years later when we came across an article in a file of folders on Knox County subjects in the Mount Vernon Public Library. Written in 1950, "How 'Dixie's' Composer Learned about the South" included pictures of Ben and Lew Snowden.[33] Then, in 1982, we received a call from a friend who, while walking the dog near his farmhouse, had stumbled upon a small graveyard. He described having seen a gravestone that said something about teaching "Dixie" to Dan Emmett. We realized what he had uncovered, so the next day we visited the Snowden graves and then set out to find the Snowden homestead.

We drove down Clinton Road, about a half mile from the county fairgrounds, where sulky drivers regularly practice with their trotters, just as Lew Snowden had a century before. Pulling into a driveway where three fellows were shooting a tin can out of a tree with their .22 caliber rifles, we explained what we were looking for. One remembered seeing something about the Snowdens in a special bicentennial commemorative section of the newspaper, which he had kept, and he headed indoors to retrieve it.[34] We discovered that one of the other two men was related to John Baltzell, a local fiddler. Baltzell had been a partner of Emmett's after the old minstrel had retired from show business to Mount Vernon in 1888.[35] Finally we were told, "The only old house left around here is that one," they said, pointing across the street.

The woman answering the door of that house confirmed with some pride that this was indeed the Snowden house. The wood siding had been covered with aluminum, and the open gable had been closed in, but the walnut woodwork and framing were original. The owner, a schoolteacher named Rose Cole, was related by marriage to one of the long-established African American families in Mount Vernon, the Bookers. Virtually all of the African Americans in this community belong to three major family groups, with a great deal of overlapping, and the Bookers are part of this network. We later discovered that her father-in-law, George Booker, a retired mail carrier, had seen the Snowdens perform and even had a photo of himself as a boy with the elderly Lew Snowden. Rose volunteered, "But if you really want to know about the Snowdens, you should talk to Marie Moorehead next door." Rose took us next door and furnished an introduction.

Marie Moorehead and her husband, Bud, were gracious hosts, and our common interest became the basis for a lasting friendship.[36] Marie, born in 1907, is a graduate of Wilberforce University; Bud received a master's degree from The Ohio State University and worked in Mount Vernon as a storeroom supervisor. Marie's grandfather, William Turner, had cared for Ben and Lew in the last years of their lives, and Marie recalled seeing them as a young girl during visits to the Snowden home. Her uncle, Clyde Turner, a music teacher and a collector of Indian artifacts and antiques, received the family's effects when Lew died in 1923. Clyde and then Marie had been careful to preserve the Snowden family materials, which she brought out to us that June afternoon. Arrayed on the coffee table and across the floor were the Snowdens' instruments—a banjo engraved "L. D. Snowden," flute, and tambourine—and their sheet music collection, replete with comic, sentimental, and minstrel songs. There was the scrapbook of the Snowden girls, composed of poetry and recipes, feminist tracts, and news accounts of John Brown's hanging clipped from the popular press. A family photograph album depicted the Snowdens' music making, their friendships, and their passage from childhood to death. And from a narrow brown box emerged sixty-four letters to and from the family spanning from 1836 to 1900, from slavery to freedom.[37]

These rare materials inspired us to reconstruct the experiences of a remarkable family and their world. They offer primary evidence of the kinds of exchanges that birthed not only minstrelsy but so much else in American expressive culture. Letters, in particular, capture relationships as few other documents can. As statements to friends and acquaintances, lovers and associates in business, correspondence conveys the details of

Musical Snowdens Were Known by Local Woman

By RUTH DIXON

Incidents and dates concerning the life and times of Mount Vernon's own Dan Emmett, and the Snowden Brothers — song and dance men Benjamin and Lewis — can dim with the passage of time.

And this information was of little help in the presentation's world premier production in early October in the Memorial Building.

Luckily, a 'Mount Vernon couple, Mr. and Mrs. Myron E. Moorehead, could supply many facts ... confirm many events for the upcoming musical play incorporating the years 1830 to 1907.

The four - night presentation of Dixie Corporation will include sketches on Emmett, the Snowdens and the Civil War period.

The Mooreheads live at 25 Clinton Rd., next door to the green - shingled house which the Snowdens called home in the 1800s. The shingles now cover the open stage built into the upper portion of one side of the house at 26 Clinton Rd.

Time - browned pictures of the performing Snowden family, invitations they received to sing and play their banjo, violin and tambourine at school outings and state and county fairs, and the instruments themselves are in the care of the Mooreheads.

"My grandfather, William Turner, was guardian of the Snowden brothers," Mrs. Morehead said, "and my uncle, Clyde Turner, looked after Lew, is Snowden when he was old and ill.

"The pictures, invitations and musical instruments were passed down to me through my family this way."

Mrs. Morehead remembers

she and other children would at times gather at the Snowden home when her uncle lived there and she saw the two brothers perform during impromptu song fests.

Looking through the mementos made fragile with time, she pointed out sheet music belonging...

One of the sheets was dated 1898. Others carried dates of 1904, 1905 and 1907. Titles were "My Creole Sue," "An Old Sweetheart of Mine," and "When the Moon Shines Bright." The L. C. Penn Music Co., 14 S. Main St., published the 1904 music called "Our Christmas Annual."

Mrs. Morehead said the mother, Eleanor Snowden, was "devoted to the boys, and always traveled with them ... sitting right on the stage with them."

The Snowden family scrapbook revealed the family's taste for elegance and the arts, Mrs. Morehead said. Pages were filled with copies of paintings, steel engravings and Godey prints, and sentimental prose and poetry.

Godey's Lady's Book, a periodical founded in 1830, was the first American woman's magazine and dealt largely with fashions and etiquette.

The brothers were also fond of sulky races and saved race programs from fairs. One, dated 1895, was from Smyrna Fair, in Harrison County. Letters they kept, now difficult to read because of the fading ink, included news of horses and their times in races.

A horsehair bridle, with its intricate braiding, is one of the Snowden mementos Mrs. Morehead has saved.

And now something new has been added to the Morehead

home which stores the treasured souvenirs of the past, but this article is on the corner of the lot on which the home is built.

A city street sign proclaiming the roadway next to the home to be "Snowden St." was finally put in place last week. According to Courthouse records which time has not yet dimmed, the sign should read "Snowden Rd.," Mrs. Morehead said.

Her father, Charles Turner, had the road built in 1958, she said and laughed, but it took 10 years for the sign to go up.

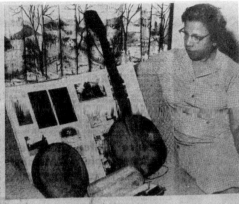

MEMENTOS OF PAST—Scrapbook with pictures and clippings of 19th century, and musical instruments equally old, recall memories of Snowden brothers, for Mrs. M. E. Moorehead. Banjo's elegant silver rim is etched with name, L. Snowden. (News Photo)

Marie Moorehead in a 1968 Mount Vernon News *article focusing on her collection of Snowden memorabilia. She inherited the family's instruments and other items from her uncle, Clyde Turner. Marie's grandfather, William Turner, was the guardian of the elderly brothers Ben and Lew in the 1910s and 1920s.*

everyday life. Unlike diaries, which record similar detail, letters are a part of social life itself. In contrast to more formal, public documents, letters reveal directly the joys and concerns of those who write them.

In the absence of materials from "ordinary" lives so removed in time, researchers of American music have relied on the examination of minstrel lyrics or bits of antebellum plantation lore for traces of the social relationships that shaped minstrelsy's form and content. Examined as texts, these materials provide only indirect evidence of the actual exchanges between blacks and whites. Robert Toll has termed materials like those in the Snowden collection, in contrast, "virtually the only sources for the popular thoughts and feelings of the past, . . . 'new' kinds of documents that challenge scholarship to expand its analytical and conceptual tools":

> The problem, of course, is sources. Average people rarely kept diaries, wrote letters, or authored books. But they were far from inarticulate. Swapping stories, singing songs, laughing at jokes, and retelling their history, they shared their folk culture with their friends and neighbors. They also joined with strangers in crowded theaters to shape the performances of professional entertainers whose major goal was to please as many people as possible. If scholars can learn to use the surviving records of these folk and popular expressive forms, they can gain at least partial access to the vehicles that spoke for and to average Americans.[38]

We take as our starting point key items from the Snowden collection: a letter to Ellen from her father, Henry Cooper, still in slavery; the family's performance handbill; the lyrics of an original song; and the Snowden scrapbook. We unpack these artifacts, searching for clues to the character of the Snowdens' social lives and the personal meanings they extracted from their experiences. To these materials touched by the Snowdens' hands, we add other documents available in the public record: wills, court proceedings, newspaper articles, census records, and county histories. Here we find additional details about the Snowden family and capture the broader events that touched upon their lives. The accumulated research of scholars contributes further evidence on black life in the West and popular culture in the nineteenth century. But in contrast to aggregate historical accounts, which often lump together unrelated sets of people and circumstances, we endeavor to tie historical circumstances directly to the biographies of a particular family, transforming "history" from an abstraction to lived experience.

But the Snowdens exist not merely as historical artifacts. They live— alongside Dan Emmett—as part of the collective memory of a particular community. The story is kept and told by Marie Moorehead, by the participants in call-in radio shows about local history, and by elderly people who recall having seen the Snowdens perform so many decades ago. In the village of Greer in northeastern Knox County, Dwight and Mildred Greer remember that their great-great-grandfather Robert brought Ellen Cooper to Knox County; nearly a century later, they recall, Ben and Lew would stay with Robert's descendants in their final days as traveling musicians. When Mount Vernon resident Jim Burgess saw our query in the newspaper asking about the Snowden family, he called to relate that his great-grandfather had brought Thomas Snowden to Mount Vernon in 1825 and had sold him the land in Clinton where Thomas built his house after marrying Ellen Cooper.[39] The stories these people told us provide another important source of information about the Snowdens, Dan Emmett, and "Dixie." It is in the fit between oral history and recorded documents that we gain the most complete telling of the story behind "Dixie."

Many scholarly disciplines have informed our approach. Issues in music history first stimulated our interest in the Snowdens. A generation of modern historians has helped us appreciate the need to understand our nation's past not only in the actions of its elites but through the experiences of all participants. The disciplines of black and feminist studies have impressed on us the importance of giving voice to those who, past and present, have been marginalized by the institutions of our society. From folklore we gain respect for the stories transmitted with care and pride across generations and for the ways in which a community may construct its identity in the telling.

In our primary focus on the social relationships and feelings that motivated the creation of "Dixie," our approach is fundamentally sociological. We reflect sociology's angle of vision in linking the everyday experiences of the Snowdens to the broader political, economic, and cultural conditions that framed their lives. We attempt, in the final analysis, what C. Wright Mills expressed as the essential task and promise of the sociological imagination: "to grasp history and biography and the relations between the two within society."[40]

We are motivated, too, by our own experiences living and playing music in this area for twenty years. The venues in which we play are substantially the same as those in which the Snowdens performed a century ago. We are reminded of the role they played as musical resources whenever we get a telephone call asking for the lyrics to a forgotten song or where to repair a banjo or guitar. We have become firm believers in paying attention to what goes on just beyond the back porch and in listening to local stories for what they convey about issues fundamental to our society.

The story suggested by the gravestones remains a part of the community's public imagery to this day. For many years a part of the annual Dixie Days celebration was a play entitled *The Birth of Dixie* that included among its characters Dan Emmett and the Snowdens. The Snowdens' musical contribution to the community appears along with Uncle Dan's in the most recent county history.[41] On Mount Vernon's north end stands the Dan Emmett Grange, near Emmett's place of retirement and just a few blocks from Snowden Road. Entering McDonald's, one first encounters a large glass partition engraved with the score of "Dixie." And we think of those two gravestones when we see, in a downtown storefront, the home-grown T-shirts decorated with a Confederate flag and the words "'Dixie' was written by a Yankee."

1. 'Cimmon Seed and Sandy Bottom

I wish I was in de land ob cotton,
'Cimmon seed an sandy bottom,
Look away—look 'way, away Dixie Land.
In Dixie land whar I was born in,
Early on one frosty mornin,
Look away—look 'way, away Dixie Land.
                    —"Dixie's Land" (1859)

In the last days of winter 1836, Ellen Cooper Snowden received a letter from her father, Henry Cooper, who lived in bondage at Smith's Point in the Nanjemoy district of Charles County, Maryland. Smith's Point, the place of Ellen's birth, was the thriving tobacco farm of Alexander Greer, a wealthy Irish emigrant who owned Henry Cooper and thirty-four other men and women of color. Nine years had passed since the child Ellen Cooper had left slavery on the Greer farm for life in free Ohio, long enough for her to have become a wife and mother:

Dear Child, I was happy to hear by Coln [John] Greer that you and Family was through the blessing of the Supreme being enjoying one of the greatest blessing bestowed on us by our Creator that of health. only that which is incident to persons in your situation. Coln Greer informed me that you

Charles County, Nanjemoy, Smith's Point Feby 14th 1836

Dear Child, I was happy to hear by Coln Greer that you and Family was through the blessing of the Supreme being enjoying one of the greatest blessing bestowed on us by our Creator that of health. only that which is incident to persons in your situation. Coln Greer informed me that you were confined when he left home having lately had an Heir and I am in hopes this will find you and Thomas likewis your dear child enjoying still the gift of your maker good Health. I am happy to say that through my all Bounteous Redeemer that I am enjoying as large a portion of the blessing of health as any one of my years could possibly expect and more than we poor frail mortals deserve. Sophia has lately had a Daughter and has been very un=well ever since but not dangerously so. Thos and Harry are both well and presents their love to you and Thos hopes you are and will do well. Sophia's daughter Ellender request her love to be given to you and her Uncle Thos your old master is as well as any one in his stage of life could posibly expect and all your old fellow servants are in as good health as could be expected. At present you will give my love to Thomas and tell him I hope he will do every thing in his power to render you and himself comfort=able here and happy hereafter. Old master is I hope preparing to meet his Heavenly master as he devotes much time to Religious duties in his family. Coln Greer still presses me in case I should survive master to move to Ohio. but time will only determine that event. Now through the power of God I remain your loving Father till death you must not fail to write me as soon as the Coln returns and you get this short and imperfect Epistle how you all are. and remain your loving Father, Henry Cooper

Henry Cooper's 1836 letter to his daughter Ellen Cooper Snowden, carried to her in Ohio by Colonel John Greer.

were confined when he left home having lately had an Heir and I am in hopes this will find you and Thomas likewis your dear Child enjoying still the gift of your maker good Health. I am happy to say that throug[h] my all Bounteous Redeemer that I am enjoying as large a portion of the bless- ing of health as any one of my years Could possibly expect and more than we poor Frail mortals deserve—Sophia has lately had a Daughter and has been verry unwell ever Since but not dangerously so. Thos and Harry are both well and presents their love to you and Thos hopes you are and will do well. Sophia's daughter Ellender request her love to be given to you and her Uncle Thos. Your old master is as well as any one in his Stage of life could posibly expect and all your old Fellow Servants are in as good health as could be expected at present—you will give my love to Thomas and tell him I hope he will do every thing in his power to render you and himself comfortable here and happy hereafter—Old master is I hope preparing to meet his Heavenly master as he devotes much time to religious duties in his Family. Coln Greer still presses me in case I should survive master to move to Ohio. but time will only determine that event. Now through the power of God I remain your loving Father till death you must not fail to write me as soon as the Coln returns and you get this short and imperfect Epistle how you all are. and remain your loving Father, Henry. Cooper[1]

Blacks and whites, young and old, family and friends, master and servants—the people named in Henry Cooper's letter defined the contours of life at the Greer place, where Ellen was born in 1817. So dear to Ellen were Henry's words that, though she could not read, she kept this trea- sured letter for the rest of her life—for nearly sixty years—as a tangible connection to the people and place of her youth.

The Nanjemoy district of Charles County lies in southern Maryland, bounded on the west and south by the Potomac River. Smith's Point, jut- ting into the river like a tiny peninsula, served as a ready dock for the many vessels traveling to and from the nation's new capital some fifty miles to the north. The bottom land off Smith's Point, like much of the area, was low and sandy, well drained by the numerous creeks—Nan- jemoy, Chicamuxen, Mattawoman—flowing into the Potomac. Tobacco grew on these slopes, fields punctuated by the planters' manor houses and elegant gardens.[2]

Nineteenth-century travelers on the Potomac regularly praised the locale's charms in their journals. A traveler bound for Savannah, Daniel W. Lord, commented in February 1824: "This is a most beautiful river; wide and straight; in some places, on very clear days, you can extend your

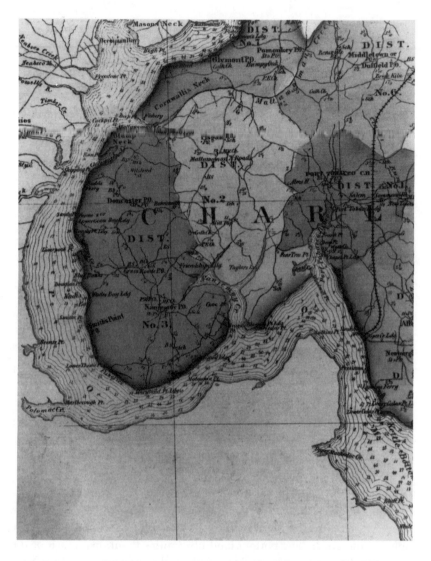

Detail of a map of Charles County in southwestern Maryland, 1872. Smith's Point on the Potomac River, the site of Alexander Greer's farm, was the childhood home of Ellen Cooper. Maryland Historical Society, Baltimore.

vision to objects thirty or forty miles distant. To delineate half the beauties, here visible, a painter's skill would be necessary."[3]

But to others the landscape was tainted by the condition of slavery that bound them to this land. Like Ellen Cooper Snowden, the famed abolitionist Frederick Douglass was born in Maryland's tobacco country in 1817. As the product of an enslaved person close to Ellen in place and time, Douglass's autobiography spoke to Ellen's circumstances.[4] For Douglass the sight of ships on the water evoked a feeling of pain more than serenity:

> Those beautiful vessels, robed in purest white, so delightful to the eye of freemen, were to me so many shrouded ghosts, to terrify and torment me with thoughts of my wretched condition. I have often, in the deep stillness of summer's Sabbath, stood all alone upon the lofty banks . . . and traced, with saddened heart and tearful eye, the countless number of sails moving off to that mighty ocean. The sight of these always affected me powerfully. My thoughts would compel utterance; and there, with no audience but the Almighty, I would pour out my soul's complaint, in my rude way, with an apostrophe to the moving multitude of ships:—
>
> "You are loosed from your moorings, and are free; I am fast in my chains, and am a slave! You move merrily before the gentle gale, and I sadly before the bloody whip! You are freedom's swift-winged angels, that fly round the world; I am confined in these bands of iron! O that I were free! O, that I were on one of your gallant decks, and under your protecting wing! Alas! betwixt me and you, the turbid waters roll. Go on, go on. O that I could also go! Could I but swim! If I could fly! . . . I am but a boy, and all boys are bound to some one. It may be that my misery in slavery will only increase my happiness when I get free. There is a better day coming."[5]

The presence of African Americans in the tidewater region was tied inextricably to the tobacco economy.[6] By the time of Charles County's establishment in 1658, settlers had discovered a lucrative market for tobacco in England, and tobacco became the staple crop of the region. Planters along the Chesapeake and the Potomac benefited from the easy access for dispatching hogsheads of tobacco to English markets. Despite the vagaries of the tobacco market, tidewater planters relied almost exclusively on the crop until the Civil War, particularly in Charles and other southernmost counties in Maryland.

Tobacco required intensive cultivation throughout the growing season and therefore a large labor force. Most Maryland tobacco planters were land rich, but labor poor. Without sufficient labor few areas of tobacco could be cultivated, limiting profits. Throughout most of the seventeenth century, planters filled their labor need with white indentured servants—typically British subjects who agreed to work in the colonies for a fixed period of time, in exchange for passage to the New World and subsistence during the period of indenture. Following their terms of servitude, those servants who survived often acquired land of their own, refusing to work for their former masters. By 1700, however, planters had difficulty recruiting sufficient numbers of white servants to meet their labor need, prompting planters to turn to another source of cheap labor, African slaves. Maryland and neighboring Virginia soon supported the largest slave traffic on the continent. Although by 1740 the Chesapeake slave population had begun to grow by natural increase, the importation of Africans to the region continued until the revolutionary war.[7]

The population of Africans and African Americans along the Potomac in southern Maryland and Virginia increased steadily throughout the last half of the eighteenth century. In Charles County people of color constituted 51 percent of the population by 1790 and 60 percent by 1820. On the eve of American independence and at the moment of Henry Cooper's birth, the locale including Nanjemoy was the geographic center of black life in America.[8]

Visiting Nanjemoy in 1774, British traveler Nicholas Cresswell made an entry in his journal that provides a rare glimpse into the African American culture of the area. Cresswell applied his own standards—those of the genteel British aristocracy—and found the slaves' artistic expression rude and uncultivated, but his words are valuable as documentation of important aspects of black cultural practices:

> Mr. Bayley and I went to see a Negro Ball. Sundays being the only days these poor creatures have to themselves, they generally meet together and amuse themselves with Dancing to the Banjo. This musical instrument (if it may be so called) is made of a Gourd something in the imitation of a Guitar, with only four strings and played with the fingers in the same manner. Some of them sing to it, which is very droll music indeed. In their songs they generally relate the usage they have received from their Masters or Mistresses in a very satirical stile and manner. Their poetry is like the Music—Rude and uncultivated. Their Dancing is most violent exercise, but so irregular and grotesque. I am not able to describe it. They all ap-

pear to be exceedingly happy at these merrymakings and seem as if they had forgot or were not sensible of their miserable condition.[9]

Cresswell recorded both the hardships African Americans faced in maintaining their community traditions and the vibrancy of their culture. Noting that blacks had few periods of respite and sociability, Cresswell found a people under the stress of domination. Still, singers, dancers, instrumentalists, and song improvisers were at play, performing kinds of music thoroughly foreign to the ears of the European-educated traveler. Cresswell was mistaken when he supposed that slaves achieved a transcendence through music and dance that rendered them "not sensible of" their miserable conditions; far from unaware, the slaves lambasted and denounced their masters in ways deeply rooted in African oral expression.[10] Testifying to his own insensibility with respect to the music he observed, Cresswell admitted, "I am not able to describe it." Certainly, Cresswell could not have imagined that this tradition of social music for dancing and improvisational songmaking would continue for another two hundred years, manifest in such twentieth-century forms as black string band and blues music.

Josiah Henson confirmed Cresswell's observations of Nanjemoy's black cultural life. Born into slavery near Nanjemoy in 1789, Henson, an abolitionist, was reportedly the basis for the title character in Harriet Beecher Stowe's novel *Uncle Tom's Cabin*.[11] In his autobiography Henson recalled that his father participated in local frolics until he received a severe beating for protecting his wife from the advances of a white overseer: "Previous to this affair my father, from all I can learn, had been a good-humored and light-hearted man, the ringleader in all fun at corn-huskings and Christmas buffoonery. His banjo was the life of the farm, and all night long at a merry-making would he play on it while the other negroes danced."[12]

In and around the largest farms, like those of Alexander Greer and other prominent planters along the Potomac, conditions were most conducive to the creation of vital African American communities. There, the number of blacks relative to whites was greatest and the number of opportunities for sociability most frequent. By the 1770s, when Cresswell visited the region (and when Henry Cooper was in his boyhood), the numbers of African American men and women were roughly equal, enabling slaves to marry, start families, and ensure some stability across generations.[13] At her birth Ellen Cooper joined twenty-eight other African Americans on the Greer farm, a black population that remained relatively stable throughout Alexander Greer's forty-year tenure as master.[14] The group included fifteen men and fourteen women of all ages, with seven slaves above the age of forty-five; Ellen was one of fourteen children. Discussing the Chesapeake slave community, Jean Butenhoff Lee notes that "only on plantations with slaves in all . . . age/gender categories could the full range of daily contacts occur, between young and old, male and female, parent and child and perhaps grandparents."[15]

Henry Cooper's letter attested to long-standing ties that existed among the black residents at Smith's Point, supported by bonds of kinship. Although Ellen Cooper Snowden had left the Greer farm nearly a decade earlier, her father clearly expected her to recall "all your old Fellow Servants" who sent their warm wishes to her through this letter; evidently, the black population there had remained fundamentally intact, despite the increasing sale of slaves to the large cotton plantations of the Deep South in the first decades of the nineteenth century. The Harry mentioned in the letter was Ellen's older brother, and Thomas ("Thos"), mentioned in the same breath, might also have been close kin. In the expression of four-year-old Ellender's warm regards to her "uncle" Thomas Snowden, the slave woman Sophia, age thirty-four, seems linked to Ellen as a sister in spirit, if not by birth.[16]

Whatever bonds existed among African Americans in Nanjemoy, slavery severely constrained their lives. For the Coopers, life at Smith's Point was controlled—owned—by Alexander Greer. Greer emigrated from Ireland to America in 1795 when he was thirty-one—fairly old, by eighteenth-century standards, to be building a new life. But by the time of his naturalization as a United States citizen three years later, Greer had married a widow, Sally Massey Stoddert, joining her and her two children to become master of the estate she had inherited, one of the most prosperous in the county.[17]

The Stodderts traced their Charles County ancestry to 1713, when Captain James Stoddert began purchasing more than three thousand acres along Nanjemoy Creek and throughout southwestern Charles County. His grandson, William Truman Stoddert, enlisted in the Continental army in 1776 and served as major of a brigade. William's wartime service, however, left his health shattered, and after marrying Sally Massey, he settled on the estate called "Simpson" on Smith's Point. At his death in 1793 at age thirty-four, William Stoddert owned thirty-two slaves; Henry Cooper,

"Mulberry Grove," ca. 1900. Similar in size and layout to Alexander Greer's farm (no longer extant), this Charles County estate featured a main house, whose original section was built ca. 1760, surrounded by outbuildings where domestic servants carried out many of their chores. Courtesy Society for the Restoration of Port Tobacco.

born in 1774, may have been one among them. Stoddert's property passed to his widow and then to her second husband, Alexander Greer.[18]

In addition to tobacco production, Greer engaged in frequent land speculation and maintained an interest in commercial fishing along the Potomac.[19] Greer operated a largely self-sufficient estate. Seven stock horses pulled his wagons to market with tobacco hogsheads; two mules and six yoke oxen were hitched for ploughing; fifteen milk cows provided dairy products for the household; and thirty-eight hogs, twenty-eight beef cattle, and twelve sheep were meat for the table. His slaves made cider and spun flax for clothing.[20]

Most slaves labored in the fields of Greer's many farms scattered throughout the Nanjemoy district, returning to their quarters at sunset. But Alexander Greer could boast a special sign of status: the ability to maintain seven artisans and domestic servants who attended to the immediate needs of the family.[21] Henry Cooper, father of Ellen, was foremost among this group.

An important clue to Henry's position and that of the others mentioned in his letter is provided in the Greer estate inventory, taken at the time of the master's death in 1839. Greer's executors, fellow planters in the Charles County elite, systematically moved room by room as they recorded the dozen Windsor chairs that seated dinner guests in the mirrored dining room, the delft bowls, and the pair of "handsome" pitchers atop the sideboard. Beyond the house stood several outbuildings, barns, and sheds containing tools, wagons, boats, tack for the horses, a keg of vinegar, two hogsheads of prized tobacco, and discarded furniture.[22]

As much property as the master's thoroughbred horses, the slaves of Alexander Greer were meticulously listed by sex and decreasing age in the estate inventory. Among those named were Sophia and her daughter Ellender, the friends or kin who sent their love, by way of Henry Cooper, to the Ohio Cooper-Snowdens. Seven other slaves were recorded outside the established pattern, anomalous in this otherwise orderly list: Ellen's "old Fellow Servants" Casey, Sarah, Manuel, Stephon, and Tom, and Ellen's own brother and father, known to the executors as Harry Cooper, Jr., and Harry Cooper, Sr.

The unusual listing of these individuals in the inventory suggests that Alexander Greer regarded them distinctively as house servants and artisans. Thomas was listed as a blacksmith, working in the iron shop. Stephon and Manuel might well have cared for Greer's thoroughbred stock. Surnames of African Americans in slavery sometimes denoted their particular crafts, and so the family name *Cooper* may be instructive: the young Harry might have been, like his father, a cooper, responsible for making the hogshead barrels for transporting tobacco to market. Tobacco planters of Greer's generation encouraged the transmission of craft skills in slave families, thereby enhancing the value of younger slaves and ensuring the continuity of the craft; a benefit to the slaves themselves was that the apprenticeship tradition discouraged the breaking up of slave families. On the estate of planter Charles Carroll in 1773, for example, six of the eighteen artisans had learned their trade from fathers and an additional four from other skilled kin: "Joe, twenty-one, and Jack, nineteen, were both coopers and sons of Cooper Joe, sixty three." Frederick Douglass recounted that on the estate of elite planter Colonel Lloyd, the stable and carriage house were "under the care of two slaves—old Barney and young Barney—father and son. To attend to this establishment was their sole work. But it was by no means an easy employment; for in nothing was Colonel Lloyd more particular than in the management of his horses."[23]

House servants and artisans occupied a unique place in plantation society.[24] As Alexander Greer's personal servant, Henry knew a degree of opportunity and privilege unavailable to agricultural workers. House servants often received food from the household kitchen and old clothing discarded from the white family members. Whites valued and depended upon skilled servants and were less likely to sell them off, affording some security. Craft workers might even hire themselves out on their own time, accumulating money to better their condition and that of their family. As longtime, trusted aids, servants sometimes influenced the master's decisions.

House servants' elevated position resulted, in part, from their indispensability. Josiah Henson related the manner in which Charles County body servants attended the very safety of their masters:

> My master's habits were such as were common enough among the dissipated planters of the neighborhood; and one of their frequent practices was to assemble on Saturday or Sunday . . . and gamble, run horses, or fight game-cocks, discuss politics, and drink whisky and brandy and water all day long. Perfectly aware that they would not be able to find their own way home at night, each one ordered his body-servant to come after him and help him home. . . . Quarrels and brawls of the most violent description were frequent consequences of these meetings; and whenever they became especially dangerous, and glasses were thrown, dirks drawn, and pistols fired, it was the duty of the slaves to rush in, and each one drag his master from the fight, and carry him home. To tell the truth, this was a part of my business for which I felt no reluctance. . . . I knew I was doing for him what he could not do for himself, and showing my superiority to others, and acquiring their respect in some degree, at the same time.[25]

Like Henson, house servants and skilled artisans frequently achieved a measure of pride and self-esteem through their work.

A distinctive kind of interracial intimacy prevailed in and around the manor house, facilitated in part by the size of estates in the Upper South. Farms along the Potomac were small in comparison to the cotton, rice, and sugar plantations of the Deep South. In fact, tidewater planters used the term *farm* rather than *plantation* in describing their agricultural enterprises.[26] Slaves on the largest tobacco farms typically numbered several dozen; the largest estates in the Deep South, in contrast, might have as many as several hundred slaves, especially the sugar plantations of Louisiana and the rice plantations of South Carolina.[27]

House servants constantly interacted with the master's family, serving meals, drawing water for baths, fueling the fire in the bedchamber during the night. Adult slave women raised their owners' children, and body servants often accompanied the master on his travels. Writing of plantation life in Virginia, historian Mechal Sobel observes that "blacks were part and parcel of family relations and were actors on the family stage. Their relationships with whites affected not only themselves but also the interrelationships among the whites—husband and wife, father and son, and siblings. All relationships in a slaveowning household involved slaves, and the day-to-day interaction built up the family history."[28]

Social intimacy between household slaves and slaveowners, however, even when it generated some measure of affection, offered slaves no guarantee of an easy life or benign treatment. Unlike field hands who ceased work each evening, on Sundays, and certain holidays, domestic servants were bound to serve whenever called. Older women slaves, such as Casey and Sarah at the Greer farm, bore an overwhelming burden with the work required to maintain a manor house. Artisans might be hired out to work on other farms for periods of up to a year, separating them from family and friends. And unlike agricultural workers, who labored and lived away from the master, domestic servants in the household continually faced maltreatment by disgruntled whites. Frederick Douglass, for example, noted that the sons of master Colonel Lloyd "enjoyed the luxury of whipping the servants as they pleased. . . . I have seen [one] make one of the house-servants stand off from him a suitable distance to be touched with the end of his whip, and at every stroke raise great ridges upon his back."[29]

Planters and their family members considered house servants, like all slaves, property first and foremost. As property, a slave's fate was governed ultimately by his or her productive value and by the customs of aristocratic society regarding the exchange of valued goods. The estate inventory taken of Greer's property at his death graphically confirms this fact: along with the furnishings, crops, and animal stock, all African Americans at Smith's Point were appraised and assigned a market value. Thomas, a skilled blacksmith in the prime of life, was at $850 Alexander Greer's most valuable slave. Ellen's father, then sixty-four, carried a value of only $125 despite his many years of service. Executors valued Ellender, eight years old, at $150, the same as Greer's bay mare. Casey, who likely raised Ellen Cooper and who was sixty-five at the time of her master's death, was given a value of $1.[30]

Linked by a shared fate of enslavement and a common cultural heri-

December Term 1839 —

					$	cts
1	" "	John	"	15 "	550	00
1	" "	Henry	"	8 "	200	00
1	" "	Ben	"	4 "	100	00
1	" "	Wesley	"	18 months	75	00
1	woman	Rachael	"	49 years	100	00
1	" "	Henney	"	50 "	75	00
1	" "	Maria	"	38 "	350	00
1	" "	Sophy	"	36 "	350	00
1	" "	Juliet	"	24 "	450	00
1	" "	Ann(& infant)		23 "	500	00
1	" "	Mary	"	21 "	500	00
1	" "	Martha(& infant)		17 "	500	00
1	Girl	Ellen	"	8 "	150	00
1	"	Jane	"	5 "	100	00
1	"	Betty	"	4 "	100	00
1	Boy	James	"	10 "	350	00
1	woman	Casey	65 "		001	00
1	" "	Sarah	" 75 "		000	25
1	man "	Harry Cooper (Sen)	64 "		125	00
1	Negro man	Mc Manuel	aged 37 years		150	00
1	" "	Stephen	"	50 "	200	00
1	" "	Harry Cooper Jr	40 "		400	00
1	" "	Tom (Blacksmith)		30 "	850	00

Detail of Alexander Greer's estate inventory, recorded at the time of his death in 1839. Henry Cooper and his family were listed separately, below the listing of Greer's field slaves, indicating their position as house servants and artisans. Courtesy Register of Wills, Charles County, Maryland.

tage, Henry Cooper and the other house servants undoubtedly maintained contact with the field slaves at Smith's Point. Historian Eugene Genovese maintains that "house slaves and field slaves did not generally constitute separate and mutually hostile groups; on the contrary, a variety of circumstances, including the exposure of the house servants to much abuse, bound them closely together."[31] Despite their physical separation, field hands and house servants often formed powerful allegiances. Their respective locations enabled servants and field slaves to make distinctive contributions to the relationship. House servants, in constant contact with the master's family and other whites, "were the field slave's most important windows on the outside world and aides in trying to fathom the planter's psyche."[32] Given their strategic location, house servants could warn of the master's plans to sell slaves and on occasion could help them escape. Field hands, in turn, provided house servants with a link to African American culture and a welcome respite from the ongoing scrutiny of whites.

Personal familiarity strengthened the ties between servant and field slaves. Henry Cooper, for example, knew the field slaves Sophia and Ellender very well. Some house servants worked in the fields during times requiring extra labor or as punishment for alleged wrongdoing. As children, field hands played around the big house, forming lasting friendships with slaves in the domestic sphere. Kinship might also link slaves in the household to those in the fields.[33]

Henry Cooper's letter to Ellen speaks to the complex character of his life at Smith's Point, poised between the larger African American community in the quarters and the intimate world of the Greer household. His detailed report reveals both the strong affinity among those in bondage and Henry's intimate knowledge of his master's conduct and state of mind. The assertion that Master Greer anticipated his impending death was in fact correct. The very year Henry wrote his daughter, Alexander Greer composed his last will and testament. John Greer, a major beneficiary in Alexander's will, likely journeyed from Ohio to Maryland to counsel Alexander in the planning of his estate.

But Henry's comments suggest great ambivalence regarding his position. Assuring his daughter that "Your old master is as well as any one in his Stage of life could posibly expect and all your old Fellow Servants are in as good health as could be expected at present," Henry appeared equally solicitous toward the blacks and whites in his midst. Yet a delicious ambiguity graces Henry's subsequent comment about Greer: "Old master is I hope preparing to meet his Heavenly master as he devotes much time to religious duties in his Family." Was Henry hopeful of his master's religious piety or of Alexander's imminent demise? No less than the reuniting of Henry with his daughter and new grandson hung in the balance: "Coln Greer still presses me in case I should survive master to move to Ohio. but time will only determine that event."[34]

Henry Cooper's evident fidelity toward Alexander Greer may well have been a strategy to gain the indulgences of the man who controlled his fate and that of his family.[35] Greer did, in fact, make special dispensations for Henry and his other servants in his will: "I give manumission to my four Slaves to wit, Stephen, Manuel, Little Harry Cooper, and Tom, and one hundred Dollars to be paid to each of them to enable them to commence with." The bulk of Greer's estate, including "my Negro property," was bequeathed to his granddaughter Lucinda Stoddert, with a special stipulation: "And whereas my two slaves Casey and Harry [Henry] Cooper have always behaved to me with particular affection and fidelity, I desire that they may be treated with the same levity and indulgence that they have been accustomed to receive from me, and I further desire that the said Lucinda Stoddert shall pay to the said Harry Cooper the sum of fifty dollars per annum during his life in quarterly payments."[36]

Greer clearly saw himself as a master from whom the Cooper family and the others making up his household staff could expect "levity and indulgence." Within the limitations imposed by the institution of slavery, owners did, of course, vary in their treatment of slaves. Narratives by both blacks and whites report kind masters. The hundred-dollar allowance Greer specified for the four slaves he intended to free would have supported them for a year while they established themselves as freemen. Henry Cooper's fifty dollars, while modest, would have provided some measure of independence. His owner would still be responsible for paying his subsistence, so Henry could use that allowance to buy occasional goods or favors to make his time easier. On rare occasions masters granted special privileges to favored slaves, supporting them in their declining years free of continued service. Greer himself evidently supported an elderly free black man, recorded in the censuses of 1820 and 1830 as a resident of the Smith's Point estate.[37]

However solicitous he may have been, Alexander Greer did not specify manumission of Casey and Henry Cooper, his most trusted servants, for reasons of custom and circumstance. When Greer wrote his will, Henry Cooper was sixty-three and Casey sixty-four, and Maryland had only recently repealed a law banning the manumission of slaves beyond the age of forty-five. Enacted in 1796 to discourage the practice among slave-owners of freeing nonproductive chattel to avoid the cost of their mainte-nance, the law reflected whites' alarm about the increasing numbers of free blacks without support. Despite the law's demise in 1832, white Charles Countians continued to resist manumission of old slaves.[38]

Recent events had further discouraged Greer from freeing his slaves. The 1831 slave insurrection in Southampton, Virginia, rekindled long-standing fears among whites. Joined by forty or so fellow slaves, Nat Turner led an assault on white families that left dead fifty-five men, women, and children. Turner hoped that his actions would stimulate widespread revolt among African American slaves; the immediate effect of the abortive rebellion, however, was a series of harsh reprisals against all blacks in Southampton and beyond.[39]

Whites in Charles County responded swiftly and predictably. At a meeting held in the county seat of Port Tobacco, the citizens of Charles County resolved "to adopt such measures as shall best guard against any attempt at insurrection of the colored population." The chief targets of these resolutions were free people of color, who, in the opinion of those gathered, "were powerfully instrumental in producing and increasing the discontent, disobedience, hostility, and crime, among the slaves, and . . . they are becoming more and more wretched, debased, wicked, injurious to the prosperity, and dangerous to the State, as they increase in number."[40]

Charles County whites resolved to take a series of actions to rid them-selves of this perceived threat. They encouraged the efforts of the African Colonization Society to remove free blacks to Liberia. Free blacks re-maining in the county would be denied the right to lease or hold land, to be employed by whites, to obtain liquor, to associate with slaves, or to move about freely. Citizens pledged to organize neighborhood patrols to suppress gatherings of blacks, free or slave, and control the black popu-lation generally.

Perhaps in response to these resolutions, Alexander Greer amended his will to reverse the manumission of four able-bodied slaves:

> A codicil to my will. Whereas I have in my will manumitted and set free
> my negroes Stephen, Manuel, Little Harry Cooper, and Tom, and whereas
> doubts have arisen whether or not this clause in my will is not against and
> opposed to the law of the Land and void . . . then in that case I thereby
> leave and bequeath the said negroes . . . to my Executors, that the said

Executors . . . shall and will during the life of the said negroes . . . permit
provide and cause the said several negroes to have use enjoy all the rights
privileges and advantages of freemen, as fully and entirely as the law
will permit, and shall cause the said annuity heretofore given to said Harry
Cooper, to be faithfully paid. . . . I hereby leave and bequeath to my said
Executors in like trust all my Blacksmiths tools & any Iron in the shop at
my Death to and for the use and benefit of my said negro Tom.[41]

When Colonel John Greer read aloud Henry Cooper's letter to Ellen
and Thomas Snowden in 1836—two decades before the Civil War drama-
tized the fate of the nation's Henry Coopers and Caseys and Toms—Ellen
could only hope to see her aged father someday on free soil. But Ohio
remained only a dream for Henry Cooper. Slavery forever separated a father from his free daughter who had made her way up north to freedom.

These two disparate worlds—of slavery and freedom, of past and
present—resided in disharmony in Ellen Snowden's heart. Maryland was
the land of slavery, but it was also the place of childhood, family, and
friends; Ohio was the land of freedom, but it was also a place of permanent
exile from everything Ellen had loved in her youth.

Ellen Cooper Snowden's obituary, printed in the Mount Vernon, Ohio,
newspaper in 1894, is instructive about her view of childhood in Charles
County, for it asserted that "she remembered some of the years of her
bondage, which in reality was not bondage, for she never experienced any
of the hardships of her race in slavery."[42] Abolitionist Levi Coffin related
the story of Rose, who escaped slavery on the Underground Railroad, in
terms nearly identical to those of Ellen's obituary: "She had never experienced any of the hardships and cruelties of slavery." Coffin noted that
Rose lived in a comfortable home and was treated kindly by her master
and mistress, who required her to do only the lightest household tasks.[43]

Ellen Cooper spent her youth in and around the Greer house, surrounded by her father, brother, and the other craftspeople and domestic
servants. Ellen's mother was not named in Henry's letter or in other documents related to the Greer household. Deprived of regular contact with
their mothers, slave children typically became the responsibility of elderly
women, who, like the children, were too frail to raise a hoe in the fields.
Ellen was likely cared for by Sarah, age fifty-three when Ellen was born,
and Casey, age forty-three, domestics in the Greer household.[44]

As a child Ellen likely did a variety of chores in and around the house:
emptying chamber pots and fetching water for washstands, filling wood-

boxes for the fireplaces, tending cows, feeding animals in the barnyard, serving guests, and aiding in the care of children younger than herself.[45] Still, childhood held many opportunities for play. Numerous slave narratives have depicted children's lives as free of the rigors of adult slave life. Describing his own treatment as "very similar to that of the other slave children," Frederick Douglass related that "I was not old enough to work in the field, and there being little else than field work to do, I had a great deal of leisure time. The most I had to do was to drive up the cows at evening, keep the fowls out of the garden, keep the front yard clean, and run . . . errands for my old master's daughter."[46] Annie Burton, writing in 1909 of her childhood in slavery, recalled similarly carefree times:

> The memory of my happy, care-free childhood days on the plantation, with my little white and black companions, is often with me. . . .
>   . . . Our days were spent roaming about from plantation to plantation, not knowing or caring what things were going on in the great world outside our little realm. Planting time and harvest time were happy days for us. How often at the harvest time the planters discovered cornstalks missing from the ends of the rows, and blamed the crows! We were called "little fairy devils." To the sweet potatoes and peanuts and sugar cane we also helped ourselves.[47]

For at least some slave children, the castelike distinction of race was dulled in many everyday experiences. Black and white children played together freely, and a pampered slave child might receive special treats along with the master's children. Thus the arrival in 1826 of Alexander Greer's sister Mary Greer and her children offered Ellen a new source of playmates.

Like Alexander Greer before them, Mary and her family emigrated from County Antrim, Ireland, in search of better fortunes in America. Until the family could get firmly established, the Greers stayed at Smith's Point for several months. But new lands for settlement were virtually nonexistent in southern Maryland, and the continued decline in agriculture offered few prospects. Large numbers of residents left Maryland's western shore for opportunities farther west.[48] For Mary and her family, economic advancement seemed more likely in Ohio. Her brother, John Greer, had already established himself as a prominent citizen in Knox County, Ohio, where inexpensive land was still available.

Alexander Greer offered the child Ellen to accompany Mary and her family on their journey. Several factors likely contributed to Alexander's decision, so momentous in Ellen's life. In part, Greer's action was a gesture of kindness toward his own extended family. Substantial slaveowners often provided newly married daughters with a young slave; the offer of Ellen to family members embarking on a new life in the West paralleled that practice. There is evidence, too, that the Greer family had grown particularly fond of Ellen. Ellen's obituary stated that "Mrs. Mary Greer and her family . . . always during her lifetime took special interest in the child Ellen."[49] The Greer family history attributed to Ellen a corresponding affection: "While staying in Maryland, the Greer women had been served by a young slave girl, Ellen Cooper. . . . She grieved so for the family after they had left for their new home that her master freed her and sent her to join them."[50]

The connection between the Greers and Ellen Cooper may have run deeper than mere friendship. Sexual liaisons between masters or their sons and women in slavery were common, usually against the woman's will. Perhaps Henry was husband to Ellen's mother but not Ellen's biological father. A photograph owned by descendants of the Ohio Greers is suggestive in this regard: Four generations of Greers have identified the individuals in this tintype as James Greer, his wife or sister, and the young Ellen Cooper. Although this cannot be the case, since Ellen would have been in her sixties at the time of the tintype, it is perhaps significant that the woman identified as Ellen is remarkably light-skinned. If Ellen were indeed kin to the Greers, Alexander's freeing of her and benign treatment while in slavery might have reflected his own paternity or that of a stepson.[51]

Whatever Alexander Greer's motivation, Ellen's removal to Ohio seemingly was in her best interests. Ellen faced a grim future in Maryland, regardless of Henry's possible influence. As a slave girl fast approaching maturity, Ellen would soon join the other slaves on the Greer farm in arduous labor in the tobacco fields. Worse yet, she might be sold to a poorer farmer as his only slave or to one of the growing cotton plantations of the Deep South, "the greatest of all terrors to the Maryland slave."[52] Alexander Greer did, in fact, buy and sell slaves throughout his tenure at Smith's Point. In the year of Ellen's departure, Greer received $300 for the sale of "one negro man named Hendley about twenty-two years of age, one negro woman named Jenny about thirty-two years of age, one negro woman named Rose about twenty-five years of age, and one negro boy named Nace about eight years of age."[53]

Tintype from the Greer family, which they describe as showing James Greer, his wife or sister (left), and Ellen Cooper (right), ca. 1880. This attribution confirms the close relationship between the Greers and Ellen Cooper. Courtesy Joseph G. McMillan.

The Ohio frontier, however, was not Ellen's homeplace, and Mary Greer's people were not her people. However benign the reasons, Ellen's relocation to Ohio and separation from family and friends were as much extensions of Alexander Greer's control as slavery itself had been. Josiah Henson, witnessing a similar family separation in 1828, expressed the profound cruelty of a system that so arbitrarily dispersed community and kin:

> And now another of those heart-rending scenes was to be witnessed, which had impressed itself so deeply on my childish soul. Husbands and wives, parents and children, were to be separated forever. Affections, which are as strong in the African as in the European, were to be cruelly disregarded; and the iron selfishness generated by the hateful "institution," was to be exhibited in its most odious and naked deformity. I was exempted from a personal share in the dreadful calamity; but I could not see, without the deepest grief, the agony which I recollected in my own mother, and which was again brought before my eyes in the persons with whom I had been long associated; nor could I refrain from the bitterest feeling of hatred of the system, and those who sustain it. What else, indeed, can be the feeling of the slave, liable at every moment of his life to these frightful and unnecessary calamities, which may be caused by the caprice of the abandoned, or the supposed necessities of the better part of the slaveholders, and inflicted upon him without sympathy or redress, under the sanction of the laws which uphold the institution?[54]

Ellen's westward journey began by boat from the landing at Smith's Point. The broad Potomac River afforded the easiest means of transport, since few good roads transversed Charles County. Sandy soil in the lowlands was ill suited to the building of permanent roads, and with their self-sufficient estates and docks along the river, wealthy planters had little cause to subsidize public conveyances.[55] The Greers likely departed for Ohio in the spring, as was common for those journeying west. Leaving earlier chanced the hazards brought on by snow as the party crossed the Allegheny Mountains. At the same time, the trip would take a month or more, and a spring departure would ensure the family enough time to establish their Ohio home and stock up on provisions before winter.

For Ellen the push off from the dock marked her separation from everything known and familiar, a revisitation of the diaspora that had brought her own ancestors from across the waters. Gone was the protection her own father and family might afford her. Whatever personal toughness she had acquired in the first decade of life, Ellen was now vulnerable to the whims of new masters whom she hardly knew. In this respect her fortunes were no better than those of the countless children sold south, an experience captured in a religious lament:

Mother, is massa gwine to sell us tomorrow?
    Yes, yes, yes!
Mother, is massa gwine to sell us tomorrow?
    Yes, yes, yes!
Mother, is massa gwine to sell us tomorrow?
    Yes, yes, yes!
    O watch and pray!

Farewell, mother, I must lebe you.
    Yes, yes, yes!
Farewell, mother, I must lebe you.
    Yes, yes, yes!
Farewell, mother, I must lebe you.
    Yes, yes, yes!
    O watch and pray!

Mother, don't griebe arter me.
    No, no, no!
Mother, don't griebe arter me.
    No, no, no!
Mother, don't griebe arter me.
    No, no, no!
    O watch and pray!

Mother, I'll meet you in heaven.
    Yes, my child!
Mother, I'll meet you in heaven.
    Yes, my child!
Mother, I'll meet you in heaven.
    Yes, my child!
    O watch and pray![56]

People who headed west from southern Maryland typically began along the Potomac and then traveled up the Chesapeake to Baltimore.[57] From Baltimore the party traveled overland on the National Road. By the

1820s the National Road had become the major artery for the flow of people and commerce into the western frontier. Once the Treaty of Greenville secured safe passage for whites in the former Indian territories, settlers swept like a swelling tide into the Northwest Territory.[58]

As America expanded into the wilderness, the National Road was viewed in the popular imagination as a "bond of union" among the states.[59] But for Ellen this journey on the National Road carried a quite different meaning. Freedom was a powerful idea, but its actual character must have puzzled Ellen, who likely sought clues in every black face she saw en route.

Slavery was still very much in evidence along the road as Ellen looked out from the stagecoach: "Negro slaves were frequently seen on the National Road. The writer has seen them driven over the road arranged in couples and fastened to a long, thick rope or cable, like horses. This may seem incredible to a majority of persons now living along the road, but it is true, and was a very common sight in the early history of the road and evoked no expression of surprise, or words of censure. Such was the temper of the times."[60] The sight of slaves being driven to market—like the innumerable caravans of mules, cattle, hogs, and sheep—must have reinforced Ellen's fears, not her hopes. Even in the free states the specter of slavery loomed large. Tavern keepers frequently aided in the capture of fugitive slaves along the National Road, feeling it was their duty as current or former slaveowners.[61] Ellen could have heard any number of stories about runaway slaves, graphically told in taverns along the road:

Early in the morning . . . while a number of wagoners were engaged in feeding and cleaning their teams, as they stood in the wagon yard, a negro passed along the road, and William King, one of the wagoners aforesaid, cried out in a loud voice to Nicholas McCartney, who was then keeping the house, "There goes a runaway nigger." "Are you sure of that?" inquired McCartney. "I am," replied King, whereupon McCartney darted after the negro and captured him a short distance south of the house, the rocks and brush in that locality having impeded the progress of the fugitive. McCartney led him into the house, and informed him that he was going to take him back to his master in Maryland. The negro seemed submissive, and McCartney placed him in charge of one Atwell Holland, his brother-in-law, while he went for a horse to carry out his purpose of taking him back to Maryland. During McCartney's absence the negro ran out of the house, and Atwell and others pursued him. Atwell being more fleet than any of the other pursuers, soon overtook the negro, whereupon he wheeled upon

Holland, drew a dirk knife from his pocket, struck it into his pursuer's heart, and made good his escape. Holland immediately fell to the ground, and expired while being borne to the house by his companions.[62]

Nominally free in the North, African Americans found themselves in continual jeopardy—especially when slaveowners met their former slaves along the National Road:

Among the old wagoners of the road, was Richard Shadburn. He was a native of Virginia, and born a slave, while his complexion was so fair, and his hair so straight, that he readily passed for a white man. When quite young he escaped from his master and struck out for liberty among the enlivening scenes of the great highway of the Republic. On a certain evening . . . a stage coach pulled up in front of McGruder's tavern, and stopped for water, as was the custom at that point. Among the passengers in that coach was the owner of the slave, Shadburn. Looking out through the window of the coach he observed and recognized Shadburn, and calling to his aid a fellow passenger, emerged from the coach with a determination to reclaim his property. Dick was seized, but being a man of great muscular power, succeeded in releasing himself from the clutches of his assailants and fled. The disappointed master fired at Dick with a pistol, as he ran, but he made good his escape. . . . Shadburn never afterward reappeared on the road, and it is believed that he found a home and at last a grave in Canada.[63]

Ellen could observe enormous inequality between blacks and whites even in the condition of freedom. Social convention clearly established blacks as second-class citizens, typically in the service of whites. Stage drivers carried higher prestige on the road than the wagoners who hauled merchandise. Ellen might have noticed that blacks could be wagoners, but they were never drivers. But although wagoners worked together and as a group prided themselves on their abilities, the distinction of color was a source of segregation in the taverns: "Wagoners, white and black, stopped over night at the same taverns, but never sat down together at the same table. A separate table was invariably provided for the colored wagoners, a custom in thorough accord with the public sentiment of the time, and seemingly agreeable to the colored wagoners themselves."[64]

Ellen and the Greers stopped at taverns for meals and lodging and for respite from the wearying journey. Taverns developed reputations based on their whiskey, food, entertainment, and hospitality. Race proved an important determinant of the level of hospitality offered, as Ohio statesman Thomas Corwin, himself a former wagoner, was to discover:

> Corwin was of very dark complexion, and among strangers . . . often taken for a negro. On one occasion, while he was a member of Congress, he passed over the road in a "chartered coach," in company with Henry Clay, a popular favorite all along the road, and other distinguished gentlemen, en route for the capital. . . . The party stopped one day for dinner at an old "stage tavern," kept by Samuel Cessna, at the foot of "Town Hill," . . . twenty-five miles east of Cumberland. Cessna was fond of entertaining guests, and particularly ardent in catering to distinguished travelers. He was, therefore, delighted when this party entered his house. He had seen Mr. Clay before, and knew him. The tall form of Mr. Corwin attracted his attention, and he noted specially his swarthy complexion, heard his traveling companions call him "Tom," and supposed he was the servant of the party. The first thing after the order for dinner was a suggestion of something to relieve the tedium of travel, and excite the appetite for the anticipated dinner, and it was brandy, genuine old cogniac [sic], which was promptly brought to view by the zealous old landlord. . . . When the brandy was produced, the party, with the exception of Corwin, stepped up to the bar and each took a glass. Corwin, to encourage the illusion of the old landlord, stood back. In a patronizing way the landlord proffered a glass to Corwin, saying: "Tom, you take a drink." Corwin drank off the glass, and in an humble manner returned it to the landlord with modest thanks. Dinner was next announced, and when the party entered the dining room, a side table was observed for use of the servant, as was the custom at all old taverns on the road at that time. Corwin, at once recognizing the situation, sat down alone at the side table, while the other gentlemen occupied the main table. The dinner was excellent . . . and while undergoing discussion, Mr. Clay occasionally called out to the lone occupant of the side table: "How are you getting on, Tom?" to which the modest response was, "Very well."[65]

Cessna eventually learned of the joke, with Corwin good-naturedly urging him to feel no mortification. But for Ellen Cooper and others of lesser privilege, unequal treatment along the National Road would have taught much about life in the white North.

After a month of rigorous travel, the Greer household finally settled in the northeasternmost part of Knox County, a section whose broken terrain and "precipitous hills reaching an altitude attaining to the grandeur of mountains" would have seemed very much like home in Ireland's Antrim Mountains to Mary, her three sons, and four daughters.[66] To the eyes of the young Ellen, accustomed to the sweeping vistas and sedate banks of the Potomac, it was a far less hospitable landscape.

The high hills and rocky bluffs along the Mohican River had long formed a secure retreat for dens of wolves and huge numbers of rattle-snakes and venomous reptiles, and the inhospitable character of this countryside contrasted strikingly with the fertile, gently rolling hills else-where in Knox County. With inexpensive and more arable government-leased land available nearby, most people had bypassed this area. Indeed, when the county commissioners established Jefferson Township as a legal entity in 1825—the last of twenty-two townships so designated—its pop-ulation was so small that the community was unable to elect officers and effect a local government. In short, a wilderness greeted the child Ellen Cooper in 1827.

The Greers' choice of location was motivated chiefly by its economic advantages. Better lands beyond Knox County had already been pur-chased and developed, but hardscrabble Jefferson Township was still a good buy. Even armed with warnings about the ruggedness of pioneer life, many immigrants discovered surprising discomfort and frequent misfor-tune. Those familiar with a more settled life often found their new sur-roundings too severe physically and lacking in civility when compared with Great Britain or even the eastern states. Peter Neilson, in *Recollec-tions of a Six Years' Residence in the United States of America*, warned, "I have known several who emigrated to Canada and the United States, who returned to their native country after trifling for a month or two, but could not set their hearts to the clearing business."[67] Travelers generally discouraged would-be immigrants who already had some measure of wealth by noting that the rigors of settlement in the West surpassed its promise of fortune. Isaac Holmes, providing *An Account of the United States* in 1823, counseled, "Those who are in affluence in England, living upon the income or interest of their property, ought by no means to enter-tain the idea of emigrating thither."[68] Having identified the economic and social pitfalls of life in the United States, Holmes went on to suggest more promising opportunities for those of modest means: "But notwithstanding these disasters, many persons have succeeded in the state of Alabama, and in all the Western States, in an astonishing manner. A poor industrious family, that have the means of purchasing or contracting 160 acres of land, (and for this purpose a very few dollars are sufficient,) may go into the woods, and begin their work."[69] Years after Robert Greer came to

Ohio, he received an inquiry from his Irish uncle, Robert Emerson, about the availability of land: "dear Robert I would wish to know how much money it would require to purchase one hundred acres of good land in a good location near your own place. if I thought I could undergo the hardships of the sea I would like to see you all before I would die."[70]

Beyond its economic appeal, Jefferson Township had proved a happy place for Robert's uncle John Greer. John had emigrated in 1800 from his home near Belfast, settling first with the many Scotch-Irish in westernmost Pennsylvania's Washington County. In 1811 he moved farther west to Knox County with his wife and six-year-old son, eventually settling on an improved tract of land two miles north of the village of Danville.[71] A physically powerful man with a vigorous intellect, John Greer became a prominent citizen. At the outbreak of the War of 1812, John served as captain in the local militia, raising a company from the men in the eastern portion of the county; by the end of the war, he had made colonel. Afterward, Colonel Greer distinguished himself by regular public service, assuming numerous offices in the county government. He served in the state legislature's 1830 session and was for many years a justice of the peace, the chief arbiter of disputes in the West. When Jefferson Township first held elections for officers in 1828, the Greer family figured prominently, a pattern that endured for generations.[72]

Ellen Cooper's well-being as she came of age was to some degree ensured by the Greers' status. In 1828 Robert became the first township clerk; in subsequent years he served as township trustee, postmaster, and overseer of the poor. After two years on his family's homestead, on April 16, 1829, Robert married Sarah Severns and subsequently moved to a farm two miles northeast, along the Mohican River. When Robert moved away from the homeplace to live with his wife, Ellen continued to reside with Robert's widowed mother, Mary. Over the next five years Robert acquired an additional 160 acres along the Mohican. Thereafter he went into business for a time, serving as a merchant, before retiring again to farming. In 1836 Robert platted the only village in the township—Greersville.[73]

Martin Welker, in his 1892 *Farm Life in Central Ohio Sixty Years Ago,* provided an intimate portrait of the everyday life confronting Ellen and her Greer companions. Born in 1819, two years Ellen's junior, Welker grew up only five miles away, on the south side of Danville. His father, John Welker, served as a private in John Greer's militia during the War of 1812. John Welker rejected the encouragement of his neighbors to enter public life, but Martin's initiative led him into politics; he became a county judge and later lieutenant governor of Ohio.

Like other local historians who wrote about Ohio after the Civil War, Welker waxed nostalgic for the simple farm life in the West, so different from the rising industrial cities of the East Coast. But instead of an ideological tract, Welker provided a wealth of detail on eastern Knox County in 1830. As the vision of an age peer and neighbor to Ellen, the book uniquely captured the material and social conditions of Ellen Cooper's life up north.

Farming was the principal occupation in the area, involving all family members in the domestic economy. In a description of the clearing of land, Welker recorded a racially charged local idiom for a key farm task: "There being no cross-cut saws, and to save the labor with the ax to cut up the logs, they were burnt into sections by what was called 'niggering,' putting sticks across logs and setting them on fire. These had to be stirred up often to keep them burning. This was called 'stirring up the niggers.' These logs rolled up together in log heaps, and with the brush were burnt up."[74]

The Greers soon planted corn, a staple crop of the region. Corn and wheat provided feed for animals; ground into flour, or distilled into whiskey, they were primary sources of human nourishment as well. Water-powered gristmills, along with sawmills for lumber, were thus among the first cottage industries to mark the landscape of a developing settlement, sparing residents extended, arduous travel. John Greer constructed the first mill on his farm in Jefferson Township in 1832. Welker recalled that youngsters often spent long days awaiting the milling of their family's supplies of grain.

Like her childhood tasks in slavery, Ellen's activities focused on domestic duties. Welker noted of women's duties that "doing house work, sewing, spinning, knitting and weaving, were their principal labor. . . . The mothers and daughters made their own clothing, and mostly that of the men and boys of the family." Central to the domestic economy, women tended to the milking, gardening, care of poultry, and marketing.[75] As a black woman, however, Ellen was constrained by limited resources, by law, and by the customs governing her social mobility. Ironically, Ellen did not receive an education despite her connection to Robert Greer, an accomplished scholar in mathematics and languages and one of the township's first schoolteachers. Never was Ellen closer to the opportunity for schooling, yet she remained illiterate throughout her life.

During her years with Mary Greer, Ellen joined the Methodist Episcopal Church in Danville. Organized at the close of the American Revolution as a movement to pursue English Methodism in the United States, the Methodist Episcopal Church espoused a gospel of "free grace, free will, and individual responsibility" that had particular appeal among settlers seeking new opportunities in the West. Central to Methodist evangelism was the circuit system, in which preachers traveled within a prescribed region, sometimes on horseback, to serve the communities scattered across the frontier. These itinerant preachers, aided frequently by local exhorters, conducted prayer meetings, provided counsel on spiritual matters, ministered to the sick, and distributed books.

Ellen found a warmer welcome in the church than in most other sectors of public life. Here she could feel less a stranger, more at ease, within this community of white farmers. Methodism included nonwhites from its inception; its *Doctrines and Discipline*—the rules and procedures for Methodist living—considered "the buying and selling of men, women, and children, with an intention to enslave them" activities entertained only by those with no real interest in salvation. This document closed with a clear if moderate statement regarding the issue of slavery:

Quest.
What shall be done for the extirpation of the evil of slavery?

Answ.
1. We declare that we are as much as ever convinced of the great evil of slavery: therefore no slave holder shall be eligible to any official station in our Church hereafter, where the laws of the state in which he lives will admit of emancipation, and permit the liberated slave to enjoy freedom.

2. When any travelling preacher becomes an owner of a slave or slaves, by any means, he shall forfeit his ministerial character in our church, unless he execute if it be practicable, a legal emancipation of such slaves, conformably to the laws of the state in which he lives.

3. Whereas the laws of some of the states do not admit of the emancipation of slaves, without a special act of the legislature, the general conference, authorizes each annual conference to form their own regulations, relative to buying and selling slaves.[76]

The itinerant preacher William O'Bryan held meetings in various places in and around Danville in 1832. Log schoolhouses, including the one in the Greers' township, provided a suitable space for religious congregations, and there were frequent invitations to preach in homes. O'Bryan came to the Greer home regularly, recording one such visit in his diary on December 3, 1832: "I called at Mrs. Greor's, rested awhile, and was kindly entertained. There I saw an Irish newspaper, sent from one of her friends, which contained much country news; among other things of the fatality of the Cholera in Dublin. Have Dublin people forgotten it?" On Sunday, February 10, 1833, O'Ryan "spoke at Mrs. Greor's," noting that "as I went on in the morning the birds were warbling, weather mild as an April morning."[77]

Ellen Cooper's life with the Greers involved frequent trips to Mount Vernon, the county seat. The town was the place for all sorts of political and social transactions, and Ellen might well have been responsible for the marketing chores. Perhaps it was on one such occasion that Ellen met Thomas Snowden, a black man who had come to Mount Vernon in 1825 in the company of whites. In that year William P. Burgess made the journey west with his wife, Lydia, and her parents, Jesse and Ruth Plummer, from their home in Frederick County, Maryland.[78] Thomas had likely lived in servitude to William's father, a large slaveholder in the region.

Thomas Snowden was born in 1802 only forty miles from Ellen, but in an environment quite distinct from that of southern Maryland. Originally a part of Charles County, the area that was to become Frederick County in 1748 did not experience significant settlement until some seventy-five years after the first planters had come to Maryland's tidewater and the Potomac's western shore. But the area grew rapidly, and the county seat of Frederick Town soon became second only to Baltimore in population and economic importance. The growth of settlements was so rapid in western Maryland that it became necessary to establish two counties in addition to Frederick within twenty-five years.

Frederick owed much of its prosperity to its diverse economy. The fertile soil and mild climate were well suited to a variety of grain crops that in turn supported fine herds of cattle, sheep, and other domesticated animals. Iron ore, slate, limestone, and copper were mined; and by 1800 two furnaces and two forges produced iron and hollowware. Within a few miles of Frederick Town, settlers established two glasshouses along the Monocacy River despite British restrictions of manufacture in the colonies that might compete with English goods.[79]

Frederick's fortunes and outlook were tied to westward expansion. As early as 1760 the road to Baltimore facilitated trade, eventually becoming the first link on the National Road. Frederick also maintained a lucrative trade with the Ohio Company, which established the first settlement in the

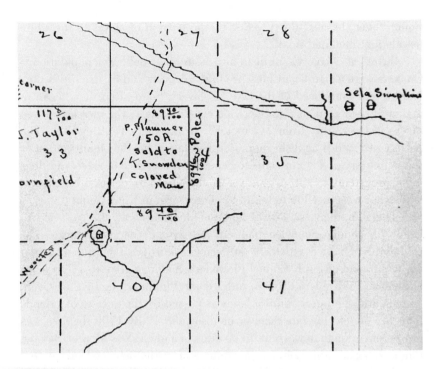

Detail of a plat showing land sold by the Plummer family to Thomas Snowden, 1829. The Plummers and their relatives brought Thomas to Ohio in 1825. His nearest neighbor, Sela (Seeley) Simpkins, was well known as a master fiddler and whistler. Courtesy Knox County Recorder.

Northwest Territory at Marietta. Comparing Frederick County's industry and prosperity with that of other regions in Maryland, historian J. Thomas Scharf remarked that "in the other counties of Maryland the people devoted themselves almost exclusively to the cultivation of tobacco with slave labor, and led, on the whole, a very easy, indolent life."[80]

The small landholders who predominated in Frederick County planted grain crops that did not require continuous cultivation and therefore had little need for slave labor. Slaves did provide labor in the mines and in manufacturing, but the diversity of the economy generally minimized the demand for slaves. The first federal census of 1790 enumerated 3,641 slaves in Frederick County and 26,937 whites. By comparison, Charles County's 10,085 slaves virtually equaled the number of white inhabitants. Although the number of slaves nearly doubled in Frederick

County over the next thirty years, the proportion of slaves to the white population remained small.[81]

Strong antislavery sentiment also assured a small slave population.[82] Quakers were a significant presence in the county, and by the 1760s they had become convinced of the evils of slavery. Soon after, they began to manumit their own slaves, a decision contributing to the increase of free blacks in the county from 213 to 1,777 in the years 1790 to 1820. The Society of Friends actively supported legislation for the emancipation of slaves in Maryland.[83] For some the continued presence of slavery in their midst proved intolerable; a group of Quakers from Frederick Town, Maryland, went west in 1806 to found Fredericktown in Knox County.

The Plummers, senior members of the household that traveled to Ohio with Thomas Snowden, had settled early in Frederick County, establishing their Quaker settlement on Bush Creek in 1743.[84] From an initial 50-acre parcel of land, Samuel Plummer's holdings grew to 1,736 acres located east of Frederick Town. At his death Plummer's many slaves were "retained in the family until a law was passed by the Society of Friends that they should liberate them or be disowned."[85] By 1790 the area was prosperous enough to warrant the creation of a town, New Market. Samuel Plummer's grandson William, in conjunction with Nicholas Hall, platted New Market, located on the Baltimore Road eight miles east of Frederick. Despite its Quaker origins, New Market continued to be a large slaveholding district up to the Civil War.[86]

On October 9, 1834, Justice of the Peace Colonel John Greer joined in marriage Thomas Snowden, age thirty-two, and Ellen Cooper, age seventeen.[87] A year later Ellen gave birth to a son, Oliver, the "Heir" Henry Cooper welcomed in his letter. Inheritors of a Southern experience, the Snowden family now embarked upon a life up north in freedom.

2. The Snowden Family! Are Coming!

We are goin to leave knox County
To lands We Nevre Sean
With nothing But our violins
To make the music ring

fare Well knox conty
fare Well fore a Whyle
fare well knox conty Dear
an friends that on ous Smile
> —Snowden family,
> "We Are Goin to Leave Knox County"

By the time "Dixie" debuted on a New York minstrel stage in 1859, the Snowden Family Band had already gained many friends playing music in towns and villages across rural Ohio. In the summer of 1855, Renfind E. Withrew of Mount Vernon wrote the Snowdens from his new home in Kanawha County, Virginia. He reminisced about their performances and travels, shared experiences of mutual interest, and requested the words to a popular new song by Stephen Foster. Withrew apologized for missing their band during his recent return to Mount Vernon:

Dear Friends
    You must excuse me for not writing to you sooner but were you to
visit A place where you had left but one year previous and find yourselves
blest with an unlimited crowd of friends and relatives. You could then

GRAND
CONCERT!
THE
SNOWDEN FAMILY!
ARE COMING!

The above TROUPE of accomplished, self-taught Colored Musicians, six in number, five regular performers, have the pleasure to announce to the good people of this place and vicinity, that they will give one of their

INIMITABLE, MORAL
AND PLEASANT
ENTERTAINMENTS!

At

On

The performances of this remarkable Family are truly astonishing. All who have heard them agree that they are well worthy the patronage of a generous discriminating public.

THEY HAVE TWO FEMALE VIOLINISTS.

Let all who wish to receive the full value of their money, in the way of amusement, bring out their wives, children and sweethearts, to see the

INFANT VIOLINIST

THE PERFORMANCE WILL CONSIST OF

SONGS FROM THE WHOLE COMPANY
PERFORMANCES ON THE
VIOLIN, TRIANGULAR AND DULCIMER,
WITH
Castinet Accompaniments!
COME AND SEE THE VIOLIN
MASTERED BY FEMALES.

The citizens of Mt. Vernon, recommend to you the Snowden Family. We have known them from their youth up, and they are worthy of all the patronage that can be afforded them. They are highly respected by the citizens of this place and wherever they have performed. Their father was a member of the M. E. Church until his death—the mother is a faithful member of the same church. Let all Christians, Preachers, Lawyers, Doctors, and all good citizens turn out to hear them. They are good and self taught minstrels. Good references given if required.

This troupe hails from Mount Vernon, Ohio, where their father, Thos. Snowden, was an early settler, and with whom they formerly travelled; but Providence having taken him away, they are now traveling under the guidance of their mother, who has accompanied them only since his death. They are not of different families, as many have supposed, but all of one family. The object of their giving Concerts is to secure means to pay the back indebtedness upon their homestead. They have with them hundreds of certificates of recommendation, establishing the character of their performances, which they will be pleased to show to all who may desire it.

Doors open at   o'clock,   -   Concert to Commence at 7 1-2 o'clock,

Admittance 25 Cents. . . . . Children under 12 years 15 Cents.

imagine And pity me I have talked until I am thoroughly exhausted. and if
I should not indite A very good or elegant Epistol you will excuse me wont
you

the rain prevented me from going out to see you monday night as I
had agreed I felt very much disapointed for I am such a lover of music I
have not heard any that so pleased me since

will you be so kind as to copy the song of the old Kentuckey home for
me I want to sing it to some of these old tyrants who hold in bondage
those who are endowed with much better Ability than they but I shall free
my mind to them whenever I have an opportunity

it is late you must excuse my bluntness in closing

you have my good wishes for your future wellfare and prosperity

> May God Bless you from a friend of your race
> Renfind E. Withrew

direct your letter as this is headed please write soon
O how I should love to hear you p[l]ay to night As I fell Somewhat lonely
and sad[1]

In 1860 the Snowden Family Band was sufficiently popular to warrant a unique listing in the federal census: under "Profession, Occupation,
or Trade," the census listed all members of this household collectively as
"Snowden Band."[2] As a category of work in a small rural community in
the mid-nineteenth century, a listing in the field of entertainment was remarkable. Census takers had their own narrow repertoire, rarely straying
beyond the commonplace countings of farmers, milliners, and carpenters.
But this instance recorded an accounting of reputation more than of occupation; farmers by trade, the Snowden family garnered their position in
the community as accomplished musicians and entertainers.[3] In the following decades, the Snowdens still were performing regularly—the 1876
Mount Vernon city directory noted their occupation as "Snowden Minstrels."[4] African American touring bands before the Civil War are virtually
unknown; only a few troupes have been documented, and many of these
apparently survived less than a week.[5]

The band, described in their advertising handbill as "six in number,
five regular performers," comprised the Snowden children. In 1860 Sophia, at age twenty-three, was the oldest; Ben was twenty; Phebe, fifteen;
Martha, thirteen; Lew, twelve; Elsie, six; and Annie, five. Annie, famed as
the "infant violinist," played the fiddle, as did Sophia and Ben. Lew
played banjo, and Phebe danced. At least one Snowden also played the

guitar, a hugely popular instrument for parlor soloists and fiddle accom-
panists.[6]

The patriarch, Thomas Snowden, provided much of the musical inspiration for his family of self-taught musicians. Thomas was a remarkable whistler, a talent he had learned in the South.[7] A mnemonic device, a
shorthand for a tune, whistling was also an important survival skill among
African peoples. In Southern slavery Africans and their descendants
tracked small game by whistling imitatively, and young boys sought out
the older African men to learn their technique.[8] On the streets of Baltimore, African Americans incorporated whistling as part of their labor, becoming known for their distinctive talents:

> Then there was Moses, an old black man who, until 1847, hawked oysters
> and ice cream through the streets, announcing his progress with a whistle
> that "could be heard squares away in snatches between the cry of his
> oysters or ice cream—a curious medley the like of which we may not hear
> again." Moses had a competitor, Whistling Bob, also known as "Bowers
> chief musician," who delivered the *Telegraph* to subscribers and, ac-
> cording to some, exceeded Moses in the skill and volume of his whistling.[9]

Instrumental musicians regarded proficient whistlers as thoroughly
respectable sources for melodies. In African American folklore no less a
figure than Brer Mockin' Bird, a master of imitation, occasionally whistled
a duet with fiddle players in the land of Brer Rabbit, that African American world ruled by survival of the wittiest: "Well, I watch an' I see Br'er
Rabbit take he fiddle from under he arm an' start to fiddlin' some more,
and he were doin' some fiddlin' out dere in dat snow. An Br'er Mockin'
Bird jine him an' whistle a chune dat would er made de angels weep."[10]

The Snowden Family Band featured the violin, the best-loved instrument among European settlers in the colonies.[11] Even the earliest accounts
of travelers through the Ohio wilderness remarked on the fiddling in frontier settlements. In 1808 Fortescue Cuming, making his way through the
territory near Chillicothe, took refuge at Bradleys, "a house of private entertainment":

> Bradley and his wife are about sixteen years from Stewartstown, county Ty-
> rone in Ireland, and have a daughter lately married to a young shoemaker
> named Irons at the next cabin, where I stopped to get my shoes mended. I
> here found a dozen of stout young fellows who had been at work repairing
> the road, and were now sheltering themselves from the increasing storm,

and listening to some indifferent musick made by their host on a tolerably good violin. I proposed taking the violin while he repaired my shoes. He consented and sat down to work, and in a few minutes I had all the lads jigging it on the floor merrily; Irons himself, as soon as he had repaired the shoes, jumping up and joining them.[12]

Fiddle music was a part of nearly every activity deserving celebration from frontier times.[13] Much of the early work of settlement—clearing land, house and barn raising, and harvesting—required collective labor, and the completion of the task was marked by supper and a dance. The preponderance of the fiddle at these events is underscored by the many references to it in local histories and other narratives of the last century. In his 1881 *History of Licking County*, N. N. Hill concluded a lengthy description of pioneer kicking frolics: "When this was done the cabin floor was again cleared and the supper spread, after which, with their numbers increased somewhat, perhaps, they danced the happy hours of the night away until midnight, to the music of a violin and the commands of some amateur cotillon caller, and were ready to attend another such frolic the following night."[14] Dance fiddlers did not make a living from their music, but a fine country fiddler was an important member of the community, as one pioneer Knox Countian would later recall:

The dance was a favorite amusement and was indulged in by old and young. The fiddler of the occasion was the center of attraction of the evening. He regulated and called the dances and was commander in chief. The "French Four," "Money Musk," "Virginia reel," "the Jig" and the "hoe down" were the principal figures danced. The French four usually presented the opportunity to "cut the pigeon wing" which required great activity and practice to accomplish. The dancing of the time required much more muscle to be successful than the present graceful glide or even waltz. "Devil's Dream" and "Fisher's Hornpipe" were the favorite tunes on the fiddle.[15]

African Americans were also playing fiddle on the Ohio frontier. Traveling in 1798 on Zane's Trace—the first path navigable by wagon into the Northwest Territory—Louis Philippe (who later became king of France) stopped at the log tavern of the McIntires in Zanesville. There Louis Philippe spent several days, and "he listened to the strains of the sweet music from the violin of the negro as it floated out over the waters and the wooded hills."[16] The fiddler he enjoyed was Samuel Mess Johnson, familiarly called Black Mess by the earliest of Zanesville's settlers ("Black" was affixed to the name of every settler of distinguishable African descent). Mess Johnson had accompanied John McIntire to the settlement of Zanesville, located at the intersection of the Muskingum River and Zane's Trace.

Like Thomas and Ellen Snowden, Mess had lived in slavery in Maryland. Upon discovering that his master contemplated selling him to a driver who then sold slaves into the Deep South, Mess entered into a plot with a stable hand named Sam, and the pair escaped one night into the mountains on two fast mounts. Wandering in the mountains, Mess and Sam came upon two white men engaged in horse stealing and traveled with them to Pittsburgh, where they boarded a boat and worked their way to Wheeling. Here the white men talked of selling Mess and Sam into slavery—a runaway slave could be sold as easily as a stolen horse—and in retaliation Mess and Sam threatened to report the whites as horse thieves. The four parted company, and Mess and Sam were hired to work on a ferryboat running across the Ohio River at Wheeling to the Ohio shore. There they worked until the next spring, when they hired on with John McIntire to haul his flatboat of goods to Zanesville. Sam subsequently left for Philadelphia, where he was recaptured by his master and returned to slavery in Maryland.

It was the custom in the early days of white settlement to have dancing parties during the long evenings of the fall and winter, and dances like those Louis Philippe attended were frequently held at John McIntire's house. Mess Johnson and neighbor Thomas Dowden furnished the music at these occasions. "At such times Mess was in his glory . . . and no merrymaking could pass off without the aid of [his] fiddle."[17]

From the limited evidence extant, African American fiddlers approached the violin with characteristically African preferences: emphasizing rhythmic rather than melodic qualities, they used an improvisatory rather than a fixed tune structure, and they deployed the instrument as a paraphrase of vocal expression. Black fiddlers of the string band tradition have been documented on recordings only sparsely, yet early recordings present consistent stylistic evidence: these fiddlers used short bow strokes, making for a richly rhythmic sound; their phrasing was individualistic and improvisatory; the tone was husky, almost dry, as if rosin were a scarce commodity (which it may have been for some musicians); and the musicians often engaged in repartee among themselves and with the listeners as they played. Style, more than repertoire, often distinguished black string band fiddling from Anglo fiddling.[18]

Black fiddlers could and did play the fiddle in the same manner as whites on some occasions. Listening to the 1920s Kentucky string band Taylor's Kentucky Boys, for example—exceptional in its time for being an integrated ensemble—one could easily fail to identify fiddler Jim Booker as a black musician. The music itself provides no clues to the musicians' race. Writing about Kentucky fiddle styles of the era, Richard Nevins notes that "the stylistic similarities of Andy Palmer, who was White, and Jim Booker, who was Black, are striking, especially in their approach to syncopation, but it's impossible to say which components of their playing are of White origin, and which of Black."[19]

The Snowdens' distinctively African American instrumentation paralleled that of antebellum Southern plantation bands. The Snowden performances featured "violin, triangular and dulcimer, with castinet accompaniments." When E. D. Root of Pataskala, Ohio, wrote to his Snowden friends with an invitation to visit, he made a point of specifying the instruments he wanted to hear: "please fetch your violins and dulsimer and tambereen tryang and ben fetch his bones."[20] On plantations blacks gathered to play with whatever instruments were available, but some instruments were better suited to African American tastes. Triangles were common, and bones (castanets) fit the percussive role so important in African musics. Among the many references to local bands in the reminiscences of antebellum Southerners, one observer from North Carolina identified instrumentation nearly identical to the Snowdens': "two fiddles, flute, banjo, triangle, and castanets."[21] A flute was among the personal effects of Ben and Lew Snowden, although no written record referred to it; evidently one or more of the Snowdens played it.

Nowhere are the African roots of their music clearer than in the foremost role of the banjo in the family string band. The American descendant of African stringed-gourd instruments, the banjo merged the drum's rhythmic and tonal qualities with the melodic impact afforded by strings. Nineteenth-century black fiddlers played the melody while the banjo accompanied as its rhythmic and melodic counterpart. In the words of John Work, the pioneering black folklorist at Fisk University in the 1940s, "The banjo has several subordinate functions; it may reinforce the melody; it may embellish the harmony; it may accentuate the rhythm, or it may perform all three."[22] The sound of early black banjo playing, like that of early black fiddling, is subject to some speculation, since the recording industry largely overlooked black string band music. Charles Wolfe notes that "the commercial record companies of the 1920s, preoccupied with 'hillbilly' music and 'blues,' effectively ignored [black] bands because they did not fit into stereotyped categories." But when folklorists recorded black string bands in the 1940s, they could determine at least two important features of the older form of banjo playing: a trend toward playing in lower pitches and the use of fretless, not fretted, instruments. Murphy Gribble, for example, a black banjo player from Tennessee, tuned down his banjo strings one and one-half tones for a recording session in 1949.[23] The Snowdens evidently played in this lowered-tuning tradition, and both of the family's banjos were fretless. On their six-string banjo, itself something of an oddity with five regular-length strings and one short one, Lew inscribed the neck with the tuning notes E–A–E–? (illegible, possibly F)–A–B (short string first), the same tuning folklorists termed "antique" in the playing of Murphy Gribble.

> an When Wee reach the nex Station
> apleaS tale Wee Will [tell]
> we haD a varey gooD Dance
> an the muSic pleaS them Well
>
> fare Well knox conty
> fare Well fore a Whyle
> fare Well knox conty Dear
> an frenDS that on ous Smile

Leaving Knox County for several days, the family traveled for a series of one-night stands in the towns and villages to be found every ten miles or so across the rural countryside: "They traveled in a sort of stagecoach carriage, singing and playing along the way. When their destination was reached, supper would be served in the home of a prominent family of the town and they often would remain there for the night."[24] In a letter confirming the variable timetable of the recent Snowden tour, their friend George Root sent his greetings from Harrison, sixty miles east of Mount Vernon: "i supose you have got home buy this time. . . . we have all putt off writing to you so as to bee shure that you may bee at home we thought you may bee gone longer than you expected." Root was anxious to report that their performance in Harrison had been warmly received: "the people

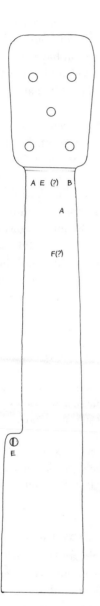

The neck of Lew Snowden's handmade, six-string banjo, ca. 1860s. Lew scratched letters along each string to indicate the tuning. Illustration by W. R. Goehring.

that was at the weslean [Wesleyan] meeting house are all pleased for your playing thare that night wall i hope you all have all got home safe and well i have ben wanting to hear from you ever since you have ben gone i shall feel very happy to hear that you have got home well and hearty Glory to the north if you have."[25] The Union shield and the white paper edged in red and blue date the letter to the Civil War.

Invitations to perform often came from the Snowdens' friends and acquaintances, who served as local producers for the event. Unlike the traveling popular entertainers who advertised in newspapers and surrounded their performances with all manner of publicity stunts, the Snowdens announced their shows by way of a simple handbill and word of mouth—the most expedient and inexpensive means for community artists. Arthur Kirby of Knox County wrote his friend "Bennie" Snowden in 1876 to invite the Snowden Family Band to play at Culp's schoolhouse. The school was a day's wagon ride across the county, but Ben and the rest of the family knew their way around the region; in Kirby's words, "I Supose you have been there before for i have Seen you There my Self." The invitation followed:

> As we are going to have a Suinging party the 12th off August on Saturday The neighborhood requested me to drop you a few Line to inform you that They want you to come and give us a Concert on that Same evening. The Suinging party is in The grove is rite by the School House now i want you to be sure and come if you possiblely can and if you can come Send me three or four bill if you have got them and i will put Them up for you
>
> I am Shure off a Big crowd if you will Come if you can come Send me the Bills by next Saturday if you can if you have no bills Struck wright any how if you will come on that Evening and i will put The word out my Self and the rest of the boys.[26]

A site like the one at Culp's schoolhouse or the Wesleyan meetinghouse in Harrison might hold as many as forty people, and on warm summer evenings the public could gather in even greater numbers to attend an outdoor concert on the grounds of the adjacent playground or graveyard. Nearing the concert site, the band attracted additional attention by playing a tune from the wagon as they passed. For this privilege the community would pay twenty-five cents for each adult, fifteen cents apiece for children. Fifty people—a good crowd—would bring the Snowdens eleven or twelve dollars. Sometimes they just passed the hat.

Opportunities to travel widely and earn money as musicians beckoned occasionally: "Ben if you And Lue would come Out here you could
make A fortune holding concerts," wrote their friends Alta and Alven
Scott from Missouri in 1883.[27] The Snowdens' decision to remain as local
performers likely was motivated in part by the politics of race. African
American traveling entertainers faced an array of degradations. They
were routinely denied food, lodging, and medical care. Until the Civil War,
all people of color in free states were suspected to be runaway slaves, and
the burden of proof was on the accused. In the decades that followed,
traveling artists were regularly subject to verbal abuse and physical violence at the hands of whites; in at least one case, a black minstrel was
lynched.[28] Blacks were safest where they were known by the white community, who might vouch for them in a moment of trouble.

> *When Wee Start out in the morning*
> *unto another town*
> *We Sing to yo a pay ing Song*
> *to all that StanDS aronD*
>
> *fare Well knox conty*
> *fare Well fore a Whyle*
> *fare Well knox conty Dear*
> *an frenDS that on ous Smile*

A "grand concert" enjoyed by audiences included "songs from the whole
company" in addition to their instrumental selections; the Snowdens knew
how to please a community quick to appreciate good singing. Knox
County historian A. Banning Norton cited Mount Vernon pioneer John
Mefford as "possessed of some poetical talent, and it is said, by some was
the author of a noted song about 'Hull's surrender.' He was a good singer,
which in early times, in a country, is considered a great accomplishment."
Singing assemblies had been a regular amusement since the early 1800s:

> On the 8th of April [1815] a "Singing Assembly" of ladies and gentlemen,
> comprising different singing societies in the county, gave a grand concert
> at the court-house in Mount Vernon, at 1 o'clock P.M. All persons feeling
> willing to unite and participate in the exercises came. It was one of the
> olden kind of gatherings, like the "Old Folks' Concert" given in Mount Ver-
> non this spring of 1862, as we have been assured by one of the vocalists
> who participated in both "singing assemblies."[29]

As residents of the area, the Snowdens knew their neighbors' activities and tastes, and their popularity as entertainers depended in part on satisfying audience expectations. George Booker, a respected singer in Mount Vernon's black community, attended family reunions and church socials at the Snowden farm when he was a boy. Recalling the band's repertoire, Booker especially noted religious music:

> They sang all the church hymns, and they sang all the spirituals. . . .
> When all a group of people were there, that's what they knew, so that's
> what they would sing, too, at a camp meeting that they used to have . . .
> down about Millwood, typically song of "Blessed Assurance" and then
> "Steal Away" and all that sort of thing. I'd say that maybe they'd close a
> program with something like that to be of a more or less spiritual heritage,
> and then to go on with others.[30]

Public singing found its most powerful expression in the camp meeting. Originating on the Kentucky frontier in 1798, the camp meeting combined intense emotional preaching, fervent singing, and the individual's experience of salvation before the community. This widespread religious phenomenon, subsequently christened the Great Awakening, permanently transformed the character of American religious practice. The format suited the Methodist church's missionary purposes nicely in central Ohio:

> The camp meeting was the great institution of the time. It was always held
> in some shady grove, with good springs, near some public road and easy of
> access. Log huts would be built in a hollow square, with a large platform
> for a pulpit at one side with rude seats in front to accommodate the congre-
> gation. The shanties would be filled by members and their families coming
> from many miles around. The meetings would usually last a week with
> preaching day and night. Large crowds of people always attended. The
> preaching was of a high order, and the best and most eloquent ministers of
> the church would generally be in attendance.
>
> The meetings at night, with lamp and torch lights in the grand old
> woods, the singing of the immense congregation, the weired [sic] appear-
> ance of the great trees, and dense foliage, with the blue canopy above, pre-
> sented a scene of grandeur, and sublimity of worship not likely to be
> forgotten.[31]

The church was an important source of musical style as well as repertoire. As a youth Ellen Cooper Snowden attended the Greer family's Methodist Episcopal Church in Danville, which encouraged singing as a regular part of religious expression.[32] Methodist taste in music, like the denomination's outlook generally, lay between the extremes of unbridled emotion and overly formalistic expression. On the matter of singing, *The Doctrines and Discipline* was explicit:

Quest.
How shall we guard against formality in singing?

Answ.
1. By choosing such hymns as are proper for the congregation.
2. By not singing too much at once; seldom more than five or six verses.
3. By suiting the tune to the words.
4. By often stopping short, and asking the people, "Now! do you know what you said last? Did you speak no more than you felt?"
5. Do not suffer the people to sing too slow. This naturally tends to formality, and is brought in by those who have either very strong or very weak voices.
6. In every large society let them learn to sing; and let them always learn our tunes first.
7. Let the women constantly sing their parts alone. Let no man sing with them unless he understands the notes, and sings the bass as it is composed in the tune book.
8. Introduce no new tune till they are perfect in the old.
9. Recommend our tune book. And if you cannot sing yourself, choose a person or two at each place to pitch the tune for you.
10. Exhort every person in the congregation to sing; not one in ten only.
11. Sing no hymns of your own composing.
12. If a preacher be present, let him alone give out the words.
13. When the singers would teach a tune to the congregation, they must sing only the tenor.
14. Let it be recommended to our people, not to attend the singing-schools which are not under our direction.
15. The preachers are desired not to encourage the singing of fuge tunes in our congregations.
16. We do not think that fuge-tunes are sinful, or improper to be used in private companies: but we do not approve of their being used in our public congregations, because public singing is part of divine worship, in which all the congregation ought to join.[33]

Given these precepts, it is not surprising that itinerant preacher William O'Bryan, who ministered to Ellen in her youth, was disappointed with the Danville congregation in January 1833:

Lords-day 20th. I went to Danville to prayer-meeting in the forenoon as usual. But soon after I got into the chapel, a form was placed in front of the pulpit, forming a square with the movable seats, on which some strangers sat. A man stood in the midst, and those on the said seats sounded the *Gamut*, Sol, la, me fa &c. The centre man said "Sound again"—they did. He then called out, *"Merrifield!"* which I took to mean, the tune. A strange man was in the pulpit, who I understood was a presbyterian preacher, and the singers, some of his society; and that he intended to preach there at certain times. When I saw so much will worship and formality, feeling unpleasant, I withdrew, believing I could profit more at home reading the Bible, or other religious book.[34]

Many people learned to sing from the singing schools, which spread Christian fervor among the unlearned but eager folk in small towns north and south. Traveling teachers taught the rudiments of music literacy by means of a shape-note system that used different shapes for each of the solmization syllables: *fa, sol, la, mi* for the four-shape system; *do, re, mi, fa, sol, la, si* (or *ti*) for the seven-shape systems (after 1846). Shape-note singers would first learn the tune by singing the solmization syllables ("fa, sol, sol, sol, fa, sol, sol, sol . . .") and then substitute the actual words. Martin Welker, who grew up only five miles from Ellen, recalled the early singing schools as sources of amusement and sociability:

The Singing School was a great event in the neighborhood, and was held every winter and attended by the young and old of both sexes. Often the big sled filled with straw and young people made a gay and lively sleighing party. A teacher was usually employed for so many nights or lessons. The singing was done by what was called the "buckwheat notes." These schools greatly improved the music of the congregation and also in families. The old people of today will no doubt remember the great pleasure they experienced in singing "Old Hundred," "America," "Green fields," "Coronation" and other tunes of "ye olden times."[35]

Singing in the African Methodist Episcopal (A.M.E.) Church, to which the Snowden family belonged, was far more exuberant and closer to African roots. The ring shout, a spiritually charged form of religious song and movement, continued in A.M.E. churches through the decades following the Civil War. Rooted in African ancestral religious practices, the ring shout was a powerful presence in African American services despite the appeals by some religious leaders for more staid forms of spiritual expression.[36] Fredrika Bremer, a Swedish traveler who visited an A.M.E. congregation in Cincinnati in 1850, "found in the African Church African ardor and African life. The church was full to overflowing, and the congregation sang their own hymns. The singing ascended and poured forth like a melodious torrent, and the heads, feet and elbows of the congregation moved all in unison with it, amid evident enchantment and delight in the singing."[37]

Rooted in European musical traditions, whites often encountered black singing with a mixture of admiration and incomprehension. "The voices of the colored people have a peculiar quality that nothing can imitate," wrote William Francis Allen in his pioneering collection of slave music, *Slave Songs of the United States*, "and the intonations and delicate variations of even one singer cannot be reproduced on paper."[38] Other, more casual observers confirmed Allen's description in the antebellum period.[39] Singing was typically observed in groups; a leader called out short melodic lines, and the chorus responded with overlapping rhythms in a musical language quite foreign to whites:

> There is no singing in *parts*, as we understand it, and yet no two appear to be singing the same thing—the leading singer starts the words of each verse, often improvising, and the others, who "base" him, as it is called, strike in with the refrain, or even join in the solo, when the words are familiar. When the "base" begins, the leader often stops, leaving the rest of the words to be guessed at, or it may be they are taken up by one of the other singers. And the "basers" themselves seem to follow their own whims, beginning when they please and leaving off when they please, striking an octave above or below . . . or hitting some other note that chords, so as to produce the effect of a marvellous complication and variety, and yet with the most perfect time, and rarely with any discord.[40]

Included in *Slave Songs of the United States* is a spiritual the Snowdens sang, "Good-Bye," used "at the breaking up of a meeting, with a general shaking of hands, and the name of him or her pronounced, whose hand is shaken":

> Good-bye, my brudder, good-bye,
> > Hallelujah!
> Good-bye, sister Sally, good-bye,
> > Hallelujah!

Going home,

            Hallelujah!

Jesus call me,

            Hallelujah!

Linger no longer,

            Hallelujah!

Tarry no longer,

            Hallelujah![41]

A British journalist traveling in the South in 1856 provided a detailed account of a slave spiritual sung at gatherings, "There's a Meeting Here Tonight," another song in the Snowden repertoire:

"Oh, I takes my text in Matthew,
And some in Revelation;
Oh, I know you by your garment—
There's a meeting here tonight,"

This is the entire effusion, and is constantly repeated, the last line being the chorus; some, however, are more elaborate:—

"In that morning, true believers,

            In that morning,

We will sit aside of Jesus

            In that morning,

If you should go fore I go,

            In that morning,

You will sit aside of Jesus

            In that morning,

True believers, where your tickets

            In that morning,

Master Jesus got your tickets

            In that morning."

And so on, with a number of variations, often extempore, but with the same refrain ever recurring, and joined in by all. Sometimes the metre is less regular, as—

"I want to sing as the angels sing,

            Daniel;

> I want to pray as the angels pray,
> > Daniel;
> I want to shout as the angels shout,
> > Daniel.
> O Lord, give me the eagle's wing.
> What time of the day,   Daniel?
> In the lion's den,   Daniel?
> I want to pray,   Daniel.
> O Lord, give me the eagle's wing."[42]

African Methodists accompanied their demonstrative singing style with instruments, a practice distinguishing the A.M.E. Church from other congregations of the period, black or white.[43] Consequently, the Snowdens could play and perform publicly on all manner of instruments and yet maintain their commitment to the A.M.E. Church without any sense of contradiction. But other churches viewed instrumental music as sinful, particularly when associated with dancing. In a "Sermon on Dancing" delivered at the Mount Zion Church in Green County, Ohio, on December 15, 1867, the Reverend J. F. Shaffer raised his voice "by the help of God, to show that the teachings of the Scriptures are directly to the contrary, in regard to this *amusement* of our day."[44] After describing a dance to such midwestern tunes as "Money Musk" and "Devil's Dream," one writer observed that "for such derelictions, people sometimes got 'fiddled out of church' or 'churched,' unless, of course, they could prove that they had not crossed their feet while walking to and fro with the music."[45] Friends of the Snowdens received this harsh rebuke for their merrymaking, as Ben discovered in a letter from his friend Nan Simpson: "your mother asked me when I was there what they done with Rogers in the church I will now tell you and you can tell your mother and sis [Sophia] and Lu [Lew] but please don't tell anyone else they have throwed them out of the church they will read them out for good next Sunday week they was put out for selling drinks and letting their boys go to dances and for haveing a dance in their house."[46]

George Booker, himself an elder in the A.M.E. Church, describes the Snowdens as solidly religious folk who made upbeat, lively music: "I imagine they were pretty lively entertainers; I can't see them in slow stuff. I think they had mostly upbeat tunes, really. . . . They had to have a lot of toe-tapping stuff. If they played the violin and so forth like that, they couldn't drag a whole lot of stuff along, could they, and entertain people 'cause they would soon get tired of that really."[47]

The Snowdens pasted published lyrics in a scrapbook, collected sheet music, exchanged lyrics with friends through the mail, and copied popular songs from songbooks available in the local library.[48] By the 1840s America had eclipsed Britain in the production of popular ballads. Touring artists introduced new songs and singing styles to the public across the West, promoting sheet music and instrument sales in the small towns and rural communities.[49] Sheet music was readily available in stores and by mail, and newspapers routinely published verse set to familiar traditional airs.

Popular music was designed to facilitate its appropriation by amateurs. Composers crafted new tunes to be simple and easily remembered, often building melodies from variations on the initial phrase of a tune. If you could whistle the first line, you could reconstruct some facsimile of the remainder. Amateurs playing the piano or other instruments could easily master a simple melody with few chord changes or sharps and flats.

Among the compositions included in the Snowden family scrapbook is a song, untitled, with the headline "New Words to an Old Tune." The melody was "Old Uncle Ned," a popular composition by songster Stephen Foster. First published in 1848, "Old Uncle Ned" quickly became a nationwide favorite among professional and amateur singers alike. When Henry Mayhew conducted interviews in the 1850s for his pioneer study of the English laboring class, he found "Old Uncle Ned" a favorite among London's blackface street singers. One traveler heard the song among Arabs in North Africa in 1853, and in 1857 Cincinnati sheet music publisher William C. Peters proclaimed that his edition of "Old Uncle Ned" had sold even more copies than Foster's "Susanna." The new anonymous rendition replaced a melancholy view of the plantation slave with that of a genteel lover:

> There was a little archer, and his name was Love,
>   And he died long, long ago;
> He had a little palace in the bright clouds above,
>   And he had a little quiver and a bow.
>
> Then lay down the sonnet and the rose,
>   Pick up the arrows and the bow;
> He'll shoot no more, the sweet boy Love—
>   He's gone where true lovers go.[50]

Once a song proved popular, composers consciously imitated its form when creating new works in hopes of duplicating its success, since nobody knew which songs would achieve widespread public acceptance until after publication. This conservative business practice of repeating the successful nonetheless afforded people like those at Culp's schoolhouse the comforting experience of following a familiar tune amid the pleasant outdoor distractions on a warm summer evening.[51]

The Snowdens sang the most current selections of the day. Renfind Withrew's 1855 letter to the Snowden family, for example, included a request for the words to Stephen Foster's "My Old Kentucky Home," first published by Firth & Pond in 1853. The Snowdens' repertoire also featured sequels to and parodies of currently popular songs. "Father's Come Home," sequel to the song "Come Home, Father" from the immensely popular melodrama *Ten Nights in a Bar Room*, shared the protemperance sensibilities of the original:

Yes, Mary, tell mother that father has left
  The drink that made her so sad;
You can say he has taken the temperance pledge,
  I know it will make her heart glad;

And tell her he wishes to clasp mother and child,
  And vow on his knees, to be true;
For father's come home, to reason, at length,
  Dear Mary, to mother and you![52]

Like American popular song generally, the Snowdens' repertoire ranged from the sentimental to the comic. Sentimental songs like "Bell Brandon" conveyed the emotions of love and bereavement:

On the trunk of an aged tree I carved them,
  And our names on the sturdy oak remain,
But I now repair in sorrow to its shelter,
  And murmer [*sic*] to the wild winds my pain.

After I sat there in solitude repining,
  For the beauty dream night brought me,
Death has wed the little beauty, Belle Brandon,
And she sleeps 'neath the old arbour tree.[53]

Sentimentality's emphasis on heartfelt emotion dictated aesthetics as well as repertoire. Listeners judged performances less on musical virtuosity than on the ability to convey what seemed to be genuine emotion. Sheet music included few directions regarding performance so as not to inhibit the singer's personal expression.

Many midcentury songs bespoke nostalgia for an idealized past, a theme reflecting Americans' feelings of rootlessness. The population had doubled in the two decades before the Civil War, and millions had left their homes for opportunities in the city or the expanding West.[54] Yearning for the past infused the Snowdens' repertoire in such songs as John Howard Payne's and Henry Rowley Bishop's "Home, Sweet Home"; Stephen Foster's "My Old Kentucky Home"; and John C. Baker's "Forty Years Ago":

> I've wandered to the village, Tom;
> I've sat beneath the tree,
> Up on the school-house play-ground,
> Which sheltered you and me;
> But none were there to greet me, Tom,
> And few were left to know,
> That played with us upon the green,
> Some forty years ago.[55]

The Civil War gave new expression to the era's fascination with mortality, as soldiers were separated from loved ones to join a conflict in which over 600,000 Americans died.[56] Songs like "Home, Sweet Home" took on particular poignancy, and new songs were composed to instill patriotism and commemorate valor. "Ben tell your sisters if they will please send me the words to too songs i will tell what two I wish to have the words to Curnell Ellsworth and Sister Mary i will send them one dollar that is fifty cents a peace," implored their friend George Root, naming a famous song about a Civil War hero.[57] "Colonel Ellsworth" commemorated the first battlefield death to shock the Union in May 1861. A gallant young officer, Ellsworth had directed his troop of exotically garbed Zouaves as part of a campaign to seize control of Alexandria, Virginia. Having hauled down the "Secession flag" from a lodging house, Ellsworth was shot "by a concealed foe" while walking downstairs. Details of the event quickly reached the nation by newspaper. Mrs. Sam Cowell, wife of the "king of comic songs in the 1850s," devoted several pages to the incident in a diary she kept while accompanying her husband on a concert tour: "The news of the assassination of Col. Ellsworth creates the greatest excitement in the city [of Baltimore], and threats of vengeance are heard on every hand.— The firemen, especially, are fearfully excited. Nothing else is discussed on the street, and every one declares that the cowardly deed will call down a bloody retribution."[58]

Popular music carried a strongly moralistic tone toward the vices of alcohol and tobacco; these issues, along with abolitionism, were strongly connected with the Republican party. At the height of the temperance era, the band performed Stephen Foster's "Comrades, Fill No Glass for Me":

Then by a mother's sacred tear,
By all that memory should revere,
Though boon companions ye may be,
Oh! comrades, fill no glass for me![59]

Morality and emotionalism were, at the same time, the subjects of frequent lampoon in comic songs. A Harvard University student penned "My Last Cigar," with its irreverent view of the human struggle in life and death:

When off the blue Canaries one glorious summer day,
I leaned upon the quarter deck and puffed my cares away;
The volume smoke arose like incense from afar,
I heaved a sigh to think forsooth it was my last cigar.[60]

Comedy, of course, was central to the minstrel stage, whose songs also found their way into Snowden concerts. Minstrel songs varied in the inhumanity with which they treated blacks, and the Snowdens avoided those employing demeaning stereotypes. Genteel minstrel songs predominated; no songs with created "Negro" dialect appeared in the family's repertoire. In later years the Snowdens sang the compositions of black composer James Bland, including "Oh, Dem Golden Slippers" and "In the Morning by the Bright Light."

Popular songs, spirituals, dance tunes—all were favorites of the Snowdens and their audience of rural Ohioans in the middle decades of the nineteenth century. All musicians exert selectivity in choosing a repertoire that reflects their own sensibilities as well as public demand, but for the Snowdens the constraints were particularly acute: they were free people of color performing in a white community divided on the issue of slavery and often hostile to blacks. Working as community artists, therefore, involved the Snowdens in a continual push-pull of resistance to and accommodation of whites' expectations. In a society marred by racial prejudice and discrimination, the Snowdens avoided overtly abolitionist songs. Members of a morally conservative community, the Snowdens offered religious and temperance songs; participants in a culture that emphasized respectability, the band chose the relatively benign, parody-tinged sorts of minstrel songs over those with phony slave dialect or grotesque imagery. And in selecting music free of demeaning racial stereotypes and including spirituals and instrumental music of African American origin, the Snowdens resisted oppression and asserted a distinct cultural identity. In these ways the family managed to win popularity as entertainers, garner respect within their community, and preserve their identity as African Americans.

> *Without your Silks an Satin*
> *Wee can perform yo See*
> *an that Will Save the penny*
> *an Soon Will connto beaS*
>
> *fare Well knox conty*
> *fare Well fore a Whyle*
> *fare Well knox conty Dear*
> *an frenDS that on ous Smile*

The Snowdens' musical performances took on the burden of economic necessity following Thomas's death at age fifty-three in July 1856.[61] Suddenly at risk to Ellen, at thirty-nine a widow with seven children to support, was the family homestead.[62] Hosmer Curtis, an attorney and one of Mount Vernon's pioneer settlers, held the mortgage on their home. A single payment on the Snowden house of $120 plus interest was due Curtis each year on the first of October. The arrangement would have typically suited the Snowdens, since it fell after the busy summer season of performances.[63] Ellen missed the payment in 1856, and Curtis petitioned the county Court of Common Pleas against the Snowden family for payment of debt the following spring. By April 1859 the family's indebtedness on the mortgage with interest had grown to $257.89. In December of that year, the court determined that if payment in full were not forthcoming within ten days, the Snowden property would be sold at public auction to recover the money due Curtis.[64]

$90.00

One year after date for value received I promise to pay to Potter & Richards or Order Ninety Dollars with interest for value received this 2d day of July 1859.

Attest Jle Devin

Eleanor her + mark Snowden

$90.

Two Years from date for value received I promise to pay Potter & Richards or Order Ninety Dollars with interest paid annually from this 2d day of July 1859.

Attest Jle Devin

Eleanor her + mark Snowden

$46.75

Two years from date for value received I promise to pay Potter & Richards or Order Ninety Dollars with interest to be paid annually from this 2d day of July 1859.

Attest J. C. Devin

Eleanor her + mark Snowden

Promissory notes from Ellen Snowden, 1859. Ellen secured the loan to meet her mortgage payments; unable to read or write, she signed her notes with an X.

Perhaps significantly, 1859 was a year of conflicting prospects for Knox County musicians: Dan Emmett introduced "Dixie" on the New York stage, while the Snowdens assumed a large indebtedness—loans totaling $226.75—in order to hold onto their farm.[65] Ben and Lew hired themselves out as laborers on nearby farms, doing jobs Lew carefully recorded in a ledger of debt payment titled "To Creditor—1859–1860": "double team $1.75 per day three days in the field farming John Grahams orchard amounting to $5.25 . . . shovling in wheat by mike lions house three quarters of a day amounting to 50 cents . . . one day loading corn that you loaded alowed me $1 for . . . payed to you in money $5.00 by the girls when you was thrashing at johnsons . . . paid $3.00 by bennie the first time he rode old rone . . . paid to you by mother at our gate $9.00."[66] And the Snowdens gave concerts, as their handbill noted, "to secure means to pay the back indebtedness upon their homestead." "We are young but yet courageous," sang the Snowden children in a verse fragment about "sav[ing] the pence an penney" until they "come to ten times ten is a hundred."[67]

For a time the Snowdens managed to forestall foreclosure on their property, but when in 1864 the remainder owed on the mortgage was still unpaid, the county sheriff put a portion of the property—two acres of their eight-acre homestead—up for sale.[68] Still, the Snowden family survived; in that same year Hosmer Curtis signed over to Ellen Snowden the deed to a homestead that remains part of the black community to this day.[69]

> *When wee git out in the morning*
> *an walk arounD the room*
> *Wee think of ohlD Knox Conty*
> *an off our good olD home*
>
> *fare Well knox conty*
> *fare Well for a Whyle*
> *fare Well knox conty Dear*
> *an frenDS that on ous Smile*

The Snowden Family Band traveled to perform out of economic necessity, but their plain clothes distinguished them from the more lavish popular entertainments that traveled to towns across Ohio and the West. Professional entertainers were performing for the growing populations of northeastern cities early in the nineteenth century, New York becoming the entertainment capital for the new nation in the years following the War of 1812. As more Americans migrated westward in the middle decades of the century, entertainers followed closely behind.[70] Mount Vernon's location made it a logical stop for America's first popular entertainers in the Old Northwest. Situated along a sixty-mile, north-south road from Mansfield to Newark, Mount Vernon became an accessible stop for even the largest touring companies after the railroad entered the community in 1856.

Theatrical troupes touring Mount Vernon performed in Woodward Hall, the town's venue for entertainments. Erected in 1852, the theater symbolized Mount Vernon's evolution from a frontier settlement to a stable community with some measure of expendable wealth.[71] At street level the hall was given over to commercial establishments, enhancing the facility's profitability. Theatergoers entered the second level by a stairway from the street and walked the long hallway, passing the offices of doctors and attorneys, to the ticket box. Beyond the ticket box, another stairway led to the spacious hall itself, at the far end of which was a raised stage. In addition to hosting professional touring companies, the large, open hall with movable seats was well suited for lectures, meetings, political rallies, local amateur shows, and athletic events.[72] Touring was unpredictable in these early years of professional popular entertainment. Even if producers had traveled to New York to book acts, they could not be certain of the troupe's timely arrival. Some shows never actually formed, and others went bankrupt midtour. Unscrupulous show managers might agree to a performance in one town and subsequently ignore the arrangement if a better offer materialized elsewhere.[73] Still, Woodward Hall offered a varied if intermittent program of professional entertainment throughout the winter months.

Numerous singing groups appeared, accompanied typically on violin, guitar, melodeon, or by small brass ensembles. The popularity of these singing groups began in 1839 with the tour of the Tyrolese Ranier Family, who offered simple Austrian songs featuring close harmony and clear enunciation. American troupes soon formed as imitators of the Austrians, presenting concerts of sentimental ballads and comic songs.[74] Ossian's Bards, among the best-known troupes, provided a "chaste and fashionable Chamber Concert" at the Woodward in February 1853 that was sufficiently well received to warrant a return engagement in 1859. The *Democratic Banner* reviewed this later performance favorably, noting that the

BLIND TOM CONCERTS

AT

WOODWARD'S HALL!

Saturday Eve'ng, December 4.

N. B.—Tickets for Reserved Seats may be had in advance at WHITCOMP & CHASE'S Book Store.

THE GREAT

MUSICAL

PRODIGY

OF

THE AGE

THE MOST

MARVELOUS

MUSICAL

GENIUS

LIVING

THE WONDERFUL NEGRO BOY PIANIST,

BLIND TOM

THE GREAT

MUSICAL MYSTERY

OF THE

NINETEENTH CENTURY!!

POSITIVELY ONE NIGHT ONLY.

Advertising program for the performance of pianist Blind Tom in Mount Vernon's Woodward Hall, December 4, 1868. One of the few black traveling entertainers of the time, Thomas Bethune was promoted as an idiot savant. Courtesy Knox County Historical Society, Knox County, Ohio.

"intelligent and appreciative audience" received the "humorous pieces, most especially . . . with the greatest applause."[75] The Alleghanians, among the earliest groups traveling in the West, appeared in Mount Vernon in February 1856, having just returned from a tour in California. Their program, featuring a quartet of vocalists accompanied by a brass band, promised "to meet the approbation of their former friends and patrons, and the public generally," for an admission of twenty-five cents.[76]

Ballad singer Ellen Ningham offered "a variety of new and beautiful Fancy Dances, in Costume, Including Highland Flings, Sailor's Hornpipe, Irish, Scotch, Chinese, Greek, Tyrolean, German, and African Dances, Polkas, Waltzes, Comic Dances, & c." Complementing Ningham's performance that evening was comic vocalist Johnny Booker, introducing "a great variety of New and Original Comic Songs, Ballads, Recitations, Comicalitios, & c." Despite the extremely disagreeable weather, Ningham and Booker drew fine houses and were warmly received.[77]

Of all the shows that came to town, the grandest was the circus. Circuses arrived in Mount Vernon as surely as warm weather, and two or more troupes often performed locally in a single season.[78] The circus came to town on the backs of elephants parading down Main Street, a visual symbol of the giant scale of the extravaganza. It came led by a brass band or by a calliope that could be heard all the way in Gambier, five miles east.[79] It came in huge tents that could hold fifteen thousand spectators, rising up to grand heights in the morning only to be gone the next day. And the whole town came out to see it.

On Wednesday, April 28, 1852, Raymond and Company and Van Amburgh and Company's Menageries United arrived in Mount Vernon, claiming the largest collection of living wild animals under one roof (a tent the size of a modern football field). In addition to its menagerie of 150 beasts, the company featured one of the first and best-known circus stars. "Mr. Van Amburgh, The most renowned of all Lion Conquerors, will at a certain period of the exhibition, enter the dens of his Terrific Group of Lions, Tigers, Leopards, Cougars, Panthers, &c., the same as performed by him in all the principal Cities of Europe and America."[80] Johnson and Company's Empire Circus arrived two months later, on Thursday, June 24. As with all classic circuses of the period, equestrians were at the heart of the Empire. These exhibitions of acrobatics on horseback presented feats of incredible physical energy and timing between rider and horse, enthusiastically appreciated in an era in which the horse remained the common mode of travel.[81] But to distinguish themselves from the competition, shows including the Empire Circus offered a variety of other acts that gradually became part of the circus roster: "Producing upon each representation a succession of Equestrian, Acrobatic, Dramatic, and Pantomimic 'chef d'oeuvres,' interlarded with diverting Comedettas and Grand National Spectacles, with an entire change of programme at each performance, and in which the whole strength of the various departments will be brought into requisition."[82]

P. T. Barnum brought his Grand Colossal Museum and Menagerie—"the largest traveling exhibition in the World"—to Mount Vernon on Thursday, September 16, 1852. Barnum the showman, more than anyone else, articulated the formula for successful American popular entertainment. Barnum institutionalized the star attraction, matching an artist's talent with his own artful promotion to ensure massive public consumption. Only the year before, in 1851, Barnum had transformed into a national sensation a Swedish soprano, Jenny Lind; he had orchestrated her touring performances with an array of public events to emphasize her beauty and philanthropy as much as her abilities as a songstress.[83] Barnum also recognized and capitalized on the commercial power of the exotic; his first coup was promoting a black woman whom he claimed to be the 160-year-old nanny of George Washington. Barnum knew that people whose lives were governed by routine and whose social experiences were bounded by the immediate community—elements that characterized all but a few sophisticated families—were just the audience for the exotic, even the preposterous.[84]

Already gone from the circus were the "Ethiopian delineators," blackfaced entertainers who had offered songs, dance, and humor in the sawdust ring from the 1820s through the 1840s. Dan Emmett's first professional experience as a blackface entertainer came in the circus in the late 1830s. It was while working with one Cincinnati circus that Emmett composed his first minstrel song, "Bill Crowder," for equestrian and blackface singer Frank Whitaker. By 1841 Emmett was performing with the Cincinnati Circus Company as a banjo player in the orchestra and as a blackface entertainer in the ring with Frank Brower.[85] When Emmett and Brower joined Billy Whitlock and Dick Pelham to form the Virginia Minstrels in 1843, they established a distinctive new venue for blackface performers.

Within a decade of minstrelsy's introduction on the New York stage, traveling troupes had begun to venture west; like the circus, the minstrel show evolved quickly into a standard format that could be imitated by new groups. Minstrel shows before the Civil War were fast-paced varieties of music, dance, and humor performed by those who claimed to have learned from the "exotic" Southern slave. The Thirteen Stars, "right from Broadway, New York," performed in Mount Vernon on December 22, 1858. An editorial description of these metropolitan minstrels in the *Democratic Banner* addressed a readership already familiar with minstrelsy:

> Their singing is sweet and beautiful, their instrumental music is better than that of any other minstrel organization now before the public, and the living statues of southern plantation life, burlesques, afterpieces, etc., etc., are new and irresistibly funny. C. H. Mortimer is the most accomplished tenor we know of in "the profession," and he is only equaled by Cool White as a director of ceremonies and genteel comedian. Douglass has a fine bass voice which he knows exactly how to use, and Melville plays the violin splendidly. Rice and Weaver are the funny men, and they are genuine comedians in their line as much as Burton and Placide in theirs. Plethoric individuals will do well to lay in an extra stock of vest buttons before hearing Weaver's "Shule Agra" or Rice's Lecture on Women's Rights. . . . Master Barney (a protege of Weaver's), is not only a fine singer but he dances a jig with all the skill, ease and grace of all the grown professors of jigology.[86]

Minstrelsy made a parody of African American life a popular sensation, while black performers themselves were excluded from professional theatrical venues until well after the Civil War, when they began performing as minstrels or composing popular songs for the minstrel stage. Although a few black artists—most notably James Bland and Billy Kersands—did attain a measure of popular success, they were subject to all manner of racial prejudice and discrimination.

> *And when we travel rounD and rounD*
> *an to our home return*
> *Wee Will meat a harty Welcome*
> *saying I am yo com*
>
> *fare Well knox conty*
> *fare Well fore a Whyle*
> *fare Well knox conty Dear*
> *an frenDS that on ous Smile*

The Snowdens certainly benefited from the popular musical culture emerging in America in the decades before the Civil War. It contributed to

Detail of the rim of one of Lew Snowden's banjos, engraved "L. D. Snowden," ca. 1870. Mail order catalogs and local music stores carried commercially manufactured instruments like this fretless banjo, probably made by the Buckbee company. Photo by Michael Matros.

their repertoire and developed an audience generally accustomed to viewing musical entertainment. Their instruments were largely store-bought, purchased from music stores that by the 1850s were meeting the growing demand for pianos for the parlor, horns for brass bands, and stringed instruments.[87] The Snowden Family Band offered some of the hyperbole and variety of the traveling shows, but their connection to a homeplace distinguished them from their counterparts in the theater or sawdust ring. No matter how direct the exchange between entertainer and audience on opposing sides of the footlights, touring artists had little contact with the communities in which they played. The rigors of nearly constant travel and the tight scheduling demanded for a series of one-night stands made virtual gypsies of these troupes. Their unique stage experiences and social network of agents, producers, and advance men constituted a separate world, one reinforced by their distinctive dress and language.[88] Professional camaraderie replaced the ties of family and home and in time assumed its own institutional character. For example, the fraternal organization known as the Benevolent and Protective Order of Elks (more commonly known as the Elks), founded in New York City in 1867, began as a social club of thirteen minstrels and variety performers calling themselves the Jolly Corks.[89]

The Snowdens played in venues common to the community— schools, township buildings, grange halls, and graveyards. Many people knew the Snowdens from their regular performances at their home. Located in the old village of Clinton, at the northern edge of Mount Vernon, the family's house was situated directly across from the fine brick tavern built by Samuel Smith in 1808. Refreshments in hand, men and women would leave Smith's Tavern and cross the narrow road to seat themselves on the grass beneath the open, second-story gable that served as the Snowdens' stage.

Only Ben and Lew Snowden survived into the twentieth century. They are the Snowdens elderly black residents remember seeing or hearing about. Andrew Lewis, for example, came to town in 1929 and recalled many older people mentioning them in the 1930s: "There was a lot of talk about the Snowden brothers . . . they were musical, everybody knew them." Andrew's daughter Gabriela knew that the Snowden brothers played in "a minstrel show": "I've been hearing about them by word of mouth, talk." Stella Lee, born in Mount Vernon in 1905, recalled: "My mother and dad took me out there [to the Snowden home] when I was a child. . . . They were minstrel men." John Payne heard from his father, John, Sr., about the Snowdens "playing the banjo and singing," and that they "sorta had a stage and gave a show"; the musicians were mostly talked about by the older people, he remembered. James Payne learned about the Snowden family as a child from his piano teacher, Clyde Turner, whose father had been Ben and Lew Snowden's guardian; Clyde "often spoke about them. . . . I was thinking they had a balcony." James's mother, Vera Payne, who moved to Mount Vernon in 1915, remembered that "they used a banjo. They had the first outdoor, open-air concerts. I think it was on the second floor." George Booker, born in 1915, heard about the family from his parents and grandparents when he was about five years old. Particularly interesting was "that they had a stage they let down. . . . When we used to go out to reunions you could still see the part where the stage had been framed in at that particular time, and they just let it down and closed it back up again after they'd have the show."[90]

Smith's Tavern, located across from the Snowdens' home in Clinton, ca. 1920.
Built in 1808, the tavern served travelers along the old stagecoach route from
Zanesville to Mansfield; it was demolished in 1947.

As musicians the Snowdens participated in family reunions and birthday parties and were invited into the homes of their neighbors, both black and white. "[Misters] Snowden & Mrs Snowden Are Respectfully Invited to attend a Birthday Party At Mr. Samuel Alberts of their daughter on Monday Evening," the Alberts—a white farming family—wrote to Ben, Lew, and Ellen in 1879. "Please bring your music."[91]

This intertwining of music and community life fostered a sort of intimacy inaccessible to the traveling artists who merely dropped in and moved on. As a performing band, Snowden family members were in regular contact with their neighbors, and music figured naturally into their friendships. Themselves farmers, Ben and Lew wrote to white farm boys, and the black schoolgirls Sophia, Annie, Elsie, Martha, and Phebe exchanged songs with their white girlfriends. In 1858, for example, twenty-one-year-old Sophia Snowden received a letter from her friends Sarah and Bell Blair of Mount Vernon. The girls wrote affectionately and casually to Sophia, addressing the letter to "My Dear Friend" and "Well, Miss Suffy." Sarah and Bell, who were white, were responding to Sophia's last letter to them following her recent visit to the Blair home. Sarah Blair wanted to come down to the county fair and hoped to see the Snowdens then, too: "I want you to have your band in good tune when I come down for I intend to bring my man along with me." E. D. Root, who lived some fifty miles southwest of Mount Vernon, offered friendly encouragement upon hearing from Sophia of her family's new musical ventures: "you say Elsy and Lu-iee has learned to play the violin i am glad to hear that because you are all trying to improve."[92]

The Snowdens maintained a close relationship with the Simpsons of Newville, a white family who lived some twenty miles away just north of the county line in Richland County. Nan Simpson was particularly fond of Ben, and her letters included frequent invitations to visit:

> Ben
> as it is drawing towards night and raining mother and myself was in the cellar churning She Said She wished you and Lew would come in and stay till morning this is one of my lonesome nights I feel more like crying than anything else I can tell you the truth we have all thought more of you folks this day than we have for a month now Ben if you folks has any friends on this earth it is our family and when you give this letter to your mother try and coax her to come up this Summer we dont want you to give a concert unless you want to just think how pleasant it would be for us all to be together another night. . . .
>
> write Soon as ever you can
> from Nan[93]

Although she asserted a real interest in and affection for the family, Nan nevertheless voiced whites' typical expectations of black performers. Under slavery masters regularly demanded that their chattel entertain them, whether summoning a fiddler to the big house or visiting the slave quarters to take in the music and dance; African Americans often had no choice about when, where, what, and for whom they would perform.[94] In free Ohio the Snowdens performed for and associated with whites relatively like themselves in terms of age, occupation, wealth, and social status, but they still faced expectations about racial relations affecting how they might exercise their talent.

The Snowdens' role in the musical life of the region extended beyond giving concerts; correspondence to family members regularly included requests for songs. Lonely for the Snowdens' company, Nan Simpson wrote Ben to inquire, "what are you doing to night singing laughing crying I am half crying. . . . [T]here is a woman in town here that wants you to send her that song gathering up the shells." In 1860 Ben received a letter from his white friend Reuben Oliver of Cardington, some fifteen miles northwest of Mount Vernon. Reuben, a young farmer supporting a family, wanted to hear from Ben and pressed him for some songs: "you must write me the best song you can think of and send it to me in a letter. . . . send the tobacco song if you please."[95]

A song could maintain its integrity even in exchange by mail, because people had heard these songs performed by the Snowden Family Band: "I wish you would write me that song called goodby," Bell Blair wrote to Sophia, "and an other you sang I cannot tell the name of but it has a trol lol to it."[96] Almeda Lewis began a letter to Sophia, whom she affectionately called Sis, with the words to the song "O How I Wish I Was Singgle [sic] Again." Almeda also mentioned a song she evidently had learned from Lew: "sis i want you to rite me that song about forty years ago i would give all i am wort if i new that. . . . sis be sure and rite me that song if you please i will look for a letter the next mail. . . . tell lu I hant forgot hupde duden do. . . . tell benny i want him to rite me the greshen [Grecian] bend song tell him i will speak a good word to some girl out here for him. . . . remember me when this you see your true friend Almeda. Sis don't forget forty years ago."[97] "Hop de Dood'n Doo" was a minstrel song popular in the mid-1850s, and "The Grecian Bend" lampooned the new neoclassical fashion in women's clothing, prompted by the archaeological discoveries of Troy and other early Western classical civilizations.[98]

The exchange of song lyrics continued throughout the Snowdens' lives, maintained even when friends moved away. Alta and Alven Scott wrote to their "Dear Friends" in 1883 from Gallatin, Davis County, Missouri. Alta recounted the death of their young son and the family's purchase of a farm:

> i sit down To write you a few lines To day we are in Missourie we like the county the Best kind well we have bad Luck since we came here we Lost our little Boy he died With Typhoid Pneumonia he Was sick just 15 dayes

it Was hard to give him up We have bought us a nice Place 75 acres with
good Improvements on it a nice Big whit house on it With green window
shutters it is beautiful country through Davis County Ben i am going to
send you That Piece there is Danger in the Town i Would have sent it to
Day but i forgot to bring it i am in Gallatin Writing this letter Ben Will you
send us some Of your pieces send us the Golden slippers and There is meeting here to Night and In the Morning By the bright light and I will send
you as manny of my pieces as you want Ben if you And Lue would come
Out here you could make A fortune holding concerts Now Ben you and lue
send me those Pieces will you and i will send that right away.

> your Friend
> Alta Scott[99]

A few days later Alta sent a follow-up reminder: "I will send you that
Piece to day Alven is a going to town will you Please send us some of yours
give my best Respects to your mother."[100]

George Root awaited the Snowdens' return home from the Wesleyan
meetinghouse concert with the anxiousness of someone newly inspired to
learn music. In his earnest plea for lessons, Root named Sophia and Annie
as fiddlers. With their sister Elsie, the Snowden girls are possibly the only
black female fiddlers documented in this era:

> wall Ben tel your too Sisters Sophiah and Ann to practice playing there vio-
> lins and learn all the new tunes they can and play and i will learn all i can
> to i wish i could come and live with you a bout one month i should like to
> come and learn to play the violin and Sing wall Ben i tell you i will give
> you and Sophiah and An one hundred dolars to let me come and live with
> you one munth that is twenty five dollars a peace and Some over if you
> three will teach me to play the violin and learn me all the Songs you can
> and tunes i have got my violin Strung up now all fore Strings on now.[101]

George Root's request to the Snowdens was not made for want of
formal musical training. By the 1850s music teachers offered a wide range
of courses in response to the growing popular interest in music.[102] Root
instead followed the standard practice of old-time fiddle players by seeking out the local master.[103] Sharing tunes between fiddlers may have been
commonplace, but Root's letter is truly remarkable: As Southern slave
masters waged war to protect their black property, in the West a man of
European descent fervently asked to apprentice himself to three African
American musicians, two of them women. In a traditional society in which

Wee Will Save the pene oan
penney untill they com
to be oas oan ten timd tenis al
un Dress oar that a su...
oa chours fare will

Without yaur silks and satin
Will confes for me no See
an that Will Save the penne
y and Soon Will counter heard
chours fare will

When wee git oup in the mao
ing an walk aroun the co
m. Wee think off old D hu
xcoun ty anoff our good old D
oame
Chous fairll
When wee oar SoDon De
Wee will mak good mus
play to min Doud off kno
county an frien D s that far o way

Page from "We Are Goin to Leave Knox County," the only Snowden composition known to have survived, ca. 1860s. Participants in an oral tradition, the family barely documented their songs in writing yet were well known as composers.

men were expected to occupy all public roles, it was exceptional for *any* woman to play country fiddle music in concerts, and even more so that black women fiddlers would perform. The Snowdens recognized this attraction and featured it prominently in their promotional handbill: "THEY HAVE TWO FEMALE VIOLINISTS. . . . COME AND SEE THE VIOLIN MASTERED BY FEMALES." We cannot know if the Snowdens accepted Root's proposal, but at a time when the family was in desperate financial straits and in danger of losing their homestead, the prospect of earning a hundred dollars would have been welcome indeed. Furthermore, the apprenticeship between George Root and the Snowdens had already begun; the Snowdens resided in the Root home when they played in Harrison: "i wish you would have Stade to hour house a bout fore weeks longer i can play Gay and happy and Sing it to."[104]

Scholars have long speculated about the contact between blacks and whites on the frontier that may have inspired the minstrel show, but a piece of minstrel sheet music cannot reveal what went on between musicians sitting in the kitchen of George Root or Ellen Snowden. In the correspondence of the farmers and schoolgirls who wrote the Snowdens— letters sufficiently important to these musicians that they have passed carefully to the present day—we can imagine more clearly the personal exchanges that contributed to the texture of American music.

> *an iff Wee are return agan*
> *un to your happy lanD*
> *Wee hope yo Will all com out*
> *to hear the SnowDean BanD*
>
> *fare Well knox conty*
> *fare Well fore a Whyle*
> *fare Well knox conty Dear*
> *an frenDs that on ous Smile*

3. I Am Sitting Sad and Lonely

I am sitting sad and lonely
Where oft I've sat before,
And thinking of the bright, bright days
That will return no more;
Oh! days of childhood, days of youth!
In mercy were ye given,
To shadow forth that better life,
That knows no change in Heaven.
—Anonymous poem
in the Snowden scrapbook, ca. 1858

B orn in the free North, schooled in reading and writing, the children of Thomas and Ellen Snowden realized the dreams of many blacks in midcentury America. Literacy marked their lives as extraordinarily different from that of their parents. Historians Bert James Loewenberg and Ruth Bogin note with regard to black literacy: "The written word was a means of practical liberation. . . . In freedom it was the primary step to holding a job that was not mere drudgery; to reading the terms of a contract; to knowing the law; to following the news; to learning what others had written in books. Beyond all else, it opened the way to grasp the complex culture built on alphabet and printing press."[1] Since antebellum times, blacks had grasped at opportunities for education as a means of gaining independence and respectability. Denied in slavery, education remained elusive even in freedom.

By law African Americans in Ohio were barred from public schools

Portrait in the Snowden collection, probably Sophia Snowden, ca. early 1870s.

until 1848, often attending so-called colored schools woefully inadequate in resources. Barely a tenth of Ohio's African American population attended school in 1850, while nearly a fifth of the state's black adults were illiterate.[2] For those fortunate enough to receive some schooling, education often held a high moral purpose beyond personal advancement: Education meant the uplift of the African American people as a whole. In 1855 a black schoolgirl wrote to her white friend: "We need [education] more than you people do, & ought to strive harder, because the greater part of our people, are yet in bondage. We that are free, are expected to be the means of bringing them out of Slavery, & how can we do it, unless we have proper educational advantages? We must get the knowledge, & use it well."[3]

Thomas and Ellen Snowden could not take advantage of the educational opportunities that did exist, but their children could. In 1850, shortly after the law opened public education to blacks, the family's two school-aged children, Sophia and Ben (ages thirteen and ten, respectively) joined their white neighbors at the Morris Township schoolhouse. A decade later all seven Snowden children were in school.[4]

Much of the Snowden children's creative and social life depended upon the written word. The girls, especially, wrote letters, composed songs and poetry, and kept a family scrapbook, largely clippings from the popular press. The very act of making a scrapbook, of cutting and saving and pasting information from newspapers and books, symbolized an engagement with the world at large for the Snowden girls. Among the family's effects is a certificate "entitl[ing] the holder to free admission to the White Hall Library and Reading Rooms" for one year beginning July 1, 1855.[5] Beyond the home and the family, a new force—popular culture—now reached into the lives of the Snowdens to offer models and prescriptions for proper living.

Born in 1855, Annie Snowden corresponded regularly with her closest friends. Lizzie and Mary Hicks lived in nearby Fredericktown, and the girls visited one another frequently. Lizzie wrote often to Annie, even on days she planned to see her friend in person. Lizzie told about her success raising birds, her problems in caring for her aged mother, and the local news she thought Annie would appreciate: "Eb Adams died day before yesterday and he was buried yesterday he died with the consumption"; "Frank   brought his wife home from the crazy asylum And she is sound and well now"; "There was a fire last night in town I will tell you all about it to night."[6]

THER'S COME HOME.

A SEQUEL TO "COME HOME FATHER."

Yes, Mary, my Mary, your father's come home;
You waited through all the long night;
He was deaf to your pleadings, —— reason was
drowned,
But, oh! it came back with the ligh'
It seems like a dream, oh! a terrible dream,
But alas! now I know it was true:
Poor Benny is dead, but your father's come home,
Dear Mary, to mother and you.

CHORUS.

Oh! no more through the dark weary hours,
Little Mary in sadness shall roam;
Ah! how glad to her ears are the words which she
hears;
Dear Mary, your father's come home.

Please, Mary, tell mother, that father's come home,
And kneels by our little boy's bed;
And he prays for God's help that the husband may
fill
The place of the boy that is dead;
And say, though he left her forsaken to weep,
All alone to bear sorrow and pain,
He'll never more cause her a pang or a tear,
If once she will trust him again.

CHORUS.

Oh! no more shall the wife watch and weep,
All in vain for the loved one to come;
And all gone are the cares, as the message she hears,
Tell mother that father's come home.

Yes, Mary, tell mother that father has left
The drink that made her so sad;
You can say he has taken the temperance pledge,
I know it will make her heart glad;
And tell her he wishes to clasp mother and child,
And vow on his knees, to be true;
For father's come home, to reason, at length,
Dear Mary, to mother and you!

CHORUS.

Oh! no more, to the mother and child,
Shall the night bleak and desolate come,
For, the fire shall be bright, and their hearts shall be
light,
While saying dear father's come home!

ures the bird itself.
or young. Several
n the frequent escape
hole its pursuers can-
e observer. Its flesh
regarded as disagree-
d occasionally sold in

The Sword of Bunker Hill.

He lay upon his dying bed,
His eye was growing dim,
When with a feeble voice he called
His weeping son to him:
Weep not, my boy the veteran said,
I bow to Heaven's high will;
But quickly from yon antlers bring,
The Sword of Bunker Hill.

The sword was brought, the soldier's eye
Lit with a sudden flame,
And as he grasped the ancient blade,
He murmured Warren's name;
Then said, my son, I leave you gold,
But what is richer still,
I leave you, mark me, mark me now,
The Sword of Bunker Hill.

'Twas on that dread immortal day,
I dared the Britons band,
A captain raised that sword on me,
I tore it from his hand,
And while the glorious battle raged,
It lightened Freedom's will;
For boy, the God of Freedom, blessed
The Sword of Bunker Hill.

Mr.
the whole ur'
each of   d ti
                   when
o   ar

A page from the Snowden scrapbook of the mid-1850s, with sentimental verse and an unidentified photograph. The scrapbook largely consists of clippings from the popular press. Courtesy Knox County Historical Society, Knox County, Ohio.

One letter detailed a romance of much "sitting room talk," owing to the couple's vast disparity in age and the persuasive element of "dollars and cents":

> Its reported that Caroline White or I expect you would know her better as Kit White her Mother was a Lambert before she was Married the folks say she was married the other night in vernon she is just entering her 15 year and the fellow they say she married is about 36 or 40 well his own aunt says he is 40 I Know he goes to see her and that's all I do Know him and her went to vernon the other day and she got her a $10 bonnet and then they went tuesday to vernon and it is rumored about that they are married she had on her new bonnet all trimed in white and a great long veil at the side and more white ribbon on her neck & head than you would want to pile up and everything was as fine and dashy as a butterfly. . . . the mans name is Billy (Meriam) his fathers name is Jake Meriam perhaps her mother Knows his father Billy gives music lessons
>
> Its a perfect table and sitting room talk about the difference of ages. I think if she has married him her and her mother was a looking out for the dollars & cents of the thing in stead of happiness for Whites isnt worth much and Meriams are very wealthy farmers I guess this is enough about young girls marrying men old enough for their daddy or great-grand daddy.[7]

Lizzie also wrote about school and church life in Fredericktown: "there is a colored boy that goes to school here he is 16 or 17 and he goes in the primary and he was so scared to day that he could not recite he stays down to George Turners Annie he is the ugliest-nigger man you bout ever laid your eyes on they have young converts prayer meeting Charly Edwards Egg Gibson Saireh Neviors Mr ___ prayed the other night I guess they are in earnest they are all young converts."[8]

Knox County public schools emphasized the basic skills of reading, writing, and arithmetic. Mary Hicks, apologizing for her poor handwriting because "my pen and ink is at school and I had to write this letter in such a hurry," described her pleasure in entering high school: "Mr ___ teaches our school and is superintendent of the primary secondary and grammar school and he is the pastor of the presbyterian church. we have nice times in the highschool we have so much fun."[9] Sometimes, students stayed out of school because they did not like the teacher, as Lizzie Hicks explained in a letter to Annie:

I don't go to school any more now I intend to go next term for I expect Ike Cassell will teach & he is an excellent teacher but the teacher we have now isnt fit to teach a dog, I would just about as leave be in purgatory as to go to school to such an Idiot as he is his name is Alf McIntyre. . . . His hair is almost white they call him flat head and toe head here is a rhyme they got upon McIntyre. An eagle flew north and south with toe headed McIntyre in his mouth and when it found he was a fool they dropped him here in this union School.[10]

The "idiot" McIntyre also showed a zest for corporal punishment:

He whiped a young lady yesterday her name was Jennie Tish he told her she wasn't virtuous and she was a nuisance to the school. And she told him he had better be careful how he slandered her character for her father could sue him for such talk and make him prove She wasn't virtuous and he just took her and gave her a complete thrashing now you know he wasn't a gentleman to whip a young girl she is in fact a young lady for she is some 16 or 17 and she wears long clothes.[11]

Beyond its traditional duty to educate in basic skills, schooling aimed to develop the moral virtues of the new industrial society.[12] Elsie Snowden, eleven years old in 1865, reminded her classmates of the importance of industriousness in "The Birds," a poem she composed for her recitation in school:

The little birds are singing
Amid the flowers of may
When on the little leaflets
The tiny breezes play

The flowers they are blooming
Every day their best
The little birds are busy
Building up their nests

The little bee is humming
Among the flowers once more
For it is always busy
Laying up it winter store

And now to all my schoolmates
Far better it would be
If we in all our lessons
Be as busy as the bee[13]

Schools inculcated the virtues of industry, self-reliance, and propriety, themes promulgated in the developing popular culture. By 1850 the
majority of the population was American born, with no direct experience
of English rule. A broad middle stratum of American society now popu-
lated the nation's burgeoning coastal cities in the North and settled the
vast territory to the west; the national population had nearly doubled between the censuses of 1830 and 1860. America faced the difficult task
of establishing a way of life—economic, political, religious, expressive—
identifiably "American." The presidency of Andrew Jackson, a man of
modest origins who had proved his worth through deeds of dedication
to the nation, symbolized the importance of a democracy attuned to a
broad citizenry.[14]

The new economy, based on capital, also stimulated the emergence
of mass culture. By 1830 the British factory system, which enabled the
cheap mass production of cloth, had taken hold in New England. In the
next three decades, a wide variety of products became available, designed
to attract a growing middle class with increasing wealth. Initially mar-
keted in the population centers of the East Coast, the products of a growing consumer culture quickly spread to the West.[15]

By 1850, forty years since its designation as county seat, Mount Vernon had swelled to a population of 4,202, in a county of 27,735 people.
Log houses had given way to frame and brick buildings designed in archi-
tectural styles imported from the East. Handsome federal-style and Greek
revival houses lined the streets near the downtown shopping district. The
county courthouse, erected in the 1830s, was a striking brick Greek revival structure.[16]

Vital industry and commerce had taken hold by midcentury. In 1833
brothers Charles and Elias Cooper established an iron foundry, producing
stoves, plows, and other implements for farms in the surrounding countryside of central Ohio. A few years later the C. & E. Cooper Company ven-
tured into the manufacture of steam engines and tractors, soon becoming
the industry standards. Mount Vernon's business establishments numbered nearly fifty, including druggists, chair makers, photographers, por-

trait painters, clothiers, wagon makers, tinners, shoemakers, bakers, and blind manufacturers. The railroad came to town in 1856, ensuring that the latest styles and fashions reached the growing proportion of rural Ohioans possessing a measure of leisure time and expendable wealth.[17]

The messages of popular culture resounded most powerfully through the print media. For the first time a large segment of the population could read and write, and books and magazines soon developed to serve this readership. With men increasingly removed from home as work shifted to factories and businesses, women became the primary consumers of popular literature. Magazines, including *Godey's Lady's Book*, specifically addressed women's domestic concerns; by the Civil War, *Godey's* readers numbered 150,000.[18] Knox County's weekly newspapers featured poetry, articles on childrearing, serialized romantic stories, and columns on housekeeping and gardening along with national and international news.

Like many young women, Sophia Snowden, born in 1837, listened closely to the messages of sentimental culture, which offered explicit prescriptions for the world of womanhood. In the 1850s through the Civil War, Sophia searched song lyrics, poetry, short stories, and illustrations from newspapers and books for their reflection of her own experiences and beliefs. Cutting and pasting these bits in an old family ledger, Sophia made a scrapbook of her ideas, dreams, and fears.[19]

Sophia both absorbed and modified materials from the popular press. She clipped and saved the obituaries of people significant to her, and she inked in the names of family and friends at the top of printed songs and poems. On a lament to one whose pet bird had died, Sophia wrote the name of a friend; other pages revealed a mysterious "Willie," whose name Sophia inserted into stories about a boy who left home to the sorrow of those who remained behind.

Every page of Sophia's scrapbook recorded her interest in womanhood. She kept poetry lauding woman's special virtues, essays discussing woman's position in the home, and illustrations proclaiming the tenderness of feeling among girlfriends and between mother and daughter. Her scrapbook was scattered with odes to love and romance, clearly a concern for an unmarried young woman of marriageable age, and she collected verses expressing hopes for the future. And, in the speeches of Frederick Douglass, articles on Africa, and news accounts of John Brown's hanging, the scrapbook also reflected the distinctive interest of a person of color.

The scrapbook was a document both public and private. Sophia undoubtedly chose song lyrics and humorous anecdotes for use in the family band's performances. Poetry provided material for recitations in school: Sophia had marked up much of the verse with underlines and brackets, and in the margin of one page, someone wrote, "I think she underlines for emphasis." Less apparent to outsiders, however, were the private meanings Sophia attached to the items she collected.

A major theme of sentimental culture that resonated with the Snowdens was propriety. As communities in the West absorbed vast numbers of farmers, bankers, and merchants hoping to capitalize on land cultivation and speculation, neighbors no longer knew one another from having lived together for generations. With so many "outsiders," background and reputation unknown, a new social dilemma arose: How could you tell the decent and trustworthy from the deceptive and larcenous?[20] Appearances alone could deceive, as the Snowden children read in the local newspaper: "Thousands are coming to ruin these days, by placing far too high an estimate on mere outward show. . . . 'A man without learning, and wearing fine clothes / Is like a gold ring on a dirty pig's nose.'"[21]

Sophia's own family continually faced scrutiny for their respectability. The family band played dance music featuring three fiddlers, and, although many rural Ohioans loved fiddle music, the more conservative churches rejected it as the devil's work. Their very status as performers invited suspicions of moral impropriety. Traveling entertainers had gained a reputation for trickery, largely stemming from the grand, ridiculous solicitations of P. T. Barnum and other show producers; instead of being astounded and amazed, the public often felt simply misled. Newspaper editorials routinely offered assurances about traveling entertainers to allay suspicions about their character. Of Van Amburgh's circus, for example, the *Democratic Banner* declared, "This Company has a world-wide reputation, and always performs everything they promise." An editorial in the *Wooster Democrat*, from a town north of Knox County, testified on behalf of the Foster Brothers' "dramatic gaieties": "We bespeak for them the patronage and commendation of the citizens of our neighboring city, and assure them that they will not only find the company at the head of their profession, and able to fulfill all they promise, but will find them affable, high minded, and honorable men." In defense of a minstrel band, the *Banner* responded: "Some evil minded person in Newark, in a spirit of diabolical meanness, circulated false and malicious rumors in this place. . . . But Mr. Cornelius at once, by his prompt and honorable behavior, put the seal of falsehood upon these contemptible slanders."[22]

Aware that, particularly as black performers, they might receive cool (if not hostile) treatment outside their home community, the Snowdens included prominent assurances about propriety in their advertising handbill.[23] Audiences who had not seen the band before could read this supporting commentary: "The citizens of Mt. Vernon, recemmend [sic] to you the Snowden Family. We have known them from their youth up, and they are worthy of all the patronage that can be afforded them. They are highly respected by the citizens of this place and wherever they have performed." To underscore their propriety, the band offered "hundreds of certificates of recommendation, establishing the character of their performances."[24] In its earnest solicitation of the most respectable citizens, inviting "Christians, Preachers, Lawyers, Doctors" to come to the show, the handbill documented both the family's problematic status and the ascendancy of the professional class as keepers of community morality.[25]

In the midst of widespread concerns about propriety, sincerity became a prevailing virtue. One could judge personal integrity, the newspapers suggested, by measuring the sincerity of a person's expression of emotions. Life at its most genuine was guided by the heart, and those places and events evoking heartfelt emotion achieved sacred status: the home, nature, the past, womanhood, and the most feared and respected of all events, death. It was fashionable, suddenly, to voice longings, hopes, moods, and affections. In a letter to his Snowden friends in 1855, Renfind Withrew lamented, "O how I should love to hear you p[l]ay to night As I fell [sic] Somewhat lonely and sad."[26]

Another preoccupation of the emerging sentimental culture was the definition of the position of women. Massive changes in the nature of work, a significant effect of the growth of industrial capitalism, precipitated a redefinition of family life. In the agrarian economy, family members shared in productive roles centered on the homeplace. Although the tasks often were differentiated by age and sex, family members worked together, each contributing to the economic well-being of the group. The factory system, however, removed production of many goods from the home, and many services—from birthing to burial—were increasingly delivered by professionals. As men went off to work, women searched for a new role divorced from the productive labor that had provided them status and meaning.[27]

Sentimental culture offered women a domain of nearly complete authority: the home. Through their roles as the moral and practical core of the family, keepers of values and sweepers of hearths, women were encouraged to create a congenial family environment. Feminine arts frequently were defined in terms of domestic accomplishments: cooking, cleaning, decorating the house, and attending to personal appearance. Temperamentally, the ideal woman was tender and selfless. Women's contributions, in sum, were emotional supportiveness and moral virtue.[28]

For roughest path, in darkest glooms,
    There is a star with bright, clear ray;
There is a flower that ever blooms,
And like a rose tree 'mid the tombs
    With beauty glads our way.

        . . . .

'Tis woman sheds so fair a light
    Upon this weary pilgrimage,
She is the flower whose beauty bright
Fills youth with visions of delight,
    And gladdens sinking age.

In the sentimental ideal, virtue meant unrelenting optimism despite hardship. The very charge of managing the family's emotional and physical well-being was virtuous. Invoking puritanical concepts of trial and reward, ditties such as "Women's Lot" proffered a heavenly reward for life's burdens:

Oh! say not woman's lot is hard,
    Her path a path of sorrow;
To-day, perchance, some joy debarr
    May yield more joy tomorrow.

It is not hard—it cannot be—
    To speak in tones of gladness,
To hush the sight of misery,
    And soothe the brow of sadness.

        . . . .

It is not hard, when storms arise,
    'Mid darkness and dejection,
To look to Heaven with trusting eyes,
    And ask its kind protection.

Then say not woman's lot is hard,
   Her path the path of sorrow;
To-day, perchance, some joy debarr'd
   May yield sweet peace to-morrow.

But Sophia learned that men could not be expected to share the feminine attributes of tenderness and gentility, engaged as they were in the
cold world of commerce. The different temperament of the sexes was the
subject of the essay "Women and Men," included in her scrapbook:

Women, especially young women either believe falsely or judge harshly of
men in one thing. You, young loving creatures who dream of your men,
lover by night and by day—you fancy that he does the same of you. He
does not: he cannot; nor is it right he should. One hour, perhaps, your presence has captivated him, seduced him even into weakness; the next, he
will be worldly working his way as a man among men forgetting, for the
time being, your very existence. Possibly, if you saw him, his outer-self,
hard and stern, so different to the self you know, would strike you with
pain. . . . Yet this must all be: you have no right to murmur. You cannot
rule a man's soul—no woman ever did—except by holding unworthy sway
over unworthy passions. Be content if you lie in his heart, as that heart lies
in his bosom—deep and calm—its beatings unseen, uncounted—often-
times unfelt—but still giving life to his whole being.

For both men and women, the home took on a new meaning in midcentury. No longer a source of economic production, the home, and the
women who "made" the home, incorporated all of the positive attributes
now divorced from the world of work: beauty, refinement, civility, intimacy, trust. Home was a haven providing respite for the weary breadwin-
ner and protecting the young from danger:

Fragrant of flowers, adorned with gems of art,
   My sanctum is the sweetest of all bowers,
Where, sometimes with a dear and cherished friend,
   I pass so happily the golden hours;—
Nor wealth, ambition, nor a love of fame,
   Shall ever tempt me from this place to roam,
Sacred to friendship, loyalty and truth,
   Surrounded by the blest delights of home!

Detail from the Snowden scrapbook, showing an idealized image of family life, ca. 1850s. Courtesy Knox County Historical Society, Knox County, Ohio.

Where burns the fireside brightest,
   Cheering the social breast?
Where beats the fond heart lightest?
   Its humble hopes possessed?
Where is the hour of sadness
   With meek-eyed patience borne?
Worth more than those of gladness,
   Which mirth's gay cheeks adorn?
Pleasure is marked with fleetness
   To those who ever roam,
While grief itself has sweetness,
   At home—sweet home!

The idealized family gathering around the Victorian hearth was decidedly nuclear. Many verses, like those in "The Home Circle," identified the home's inhabitants from a child's eye:[29]

A mother dear around us moves,
   With still and quiet pace;
A father's pleasant countenance
   Is full of love and grace:
A brother's kindness next we view,
   A brother's not alone,
For loving sisters hasten 'round,
   To cheer us in our home.

Women's abilities as housekeepers became a matter of intensive public preoccupation. Sophia included a variety of articles designed to improve her skills as a homemaker: "To destroy red ants. . . . Place a piece of fat bacon, or a pan of grease or butter, near the place where they enter the kitchen or pantry. This will soon attract them together, when they can easily be removed, or destroyed by a little hot water." "Recipe [for] Washington Cake.—1½ pound of flour, 1 pound sugar, 10 ounces butter, 4 eggs, ½ pint milk, 1 teaspoon salaeratus, 1 teaspoonful cinnamon, 1 nutmeg." "The Garden.—November is a good time to clean out and manure strawberry beds—." "The Healthfulness of Lemons. When people feel the need of an acid, if they would let vinegar alone, and use lemons or apples, they would feel just as well satisfied and receive no injury."[30]

As portrayed in sentimental songs and literature, the expression of love guided all human association, uniting lovers, friends, and family. The ideal loving relationship was one of gentleness of spirit, purity of intention, and unswerving commitment. In the poem "Come to Me in Dreams," Sophia could enter a world where lovers existed as spirits divorced from bodily existence:

> Come in beautiful dreams, love,
> Oh! come and we'll fly
> Like two winged spirits
> Of love through the sky;
> With hand clasped in hand
> On our dream wings we'll go
> Where the starlight and moonlight
> Are blending their glow;
> And on bright clouds we'll linger
> Of purple and gold,
> Till love angels envy
> The bliss they behold.

In the sentimental view, love afforded meaning, revealed nature's beauty, and united all spirits in Christian harmony:

> But there's a beauty richer far
> Than glows at morning's dawn,
> Outvieing earth's most lustrous star,
> Or flowers that deck the lawn:
> It is the beauty of the mind,
> Cultur'd and trained to love—
> The heart's affections all inclin'd,
> And fixed on God above!

Often, love's most intense expression came in grief and mourning. Described by one contemporary historian as "exercises in necrophilia,"[31] the sentimental preoccupation with mortality reflected death's particular closeness in the years before the Civil War.[32] The routine tasks and rituals of caring for the dead still took place within the home, since hospitals and funeral parlors were scarce. Adults often died young, although many lived long enough to see their young children die before them. Death lay in

tuberculosis and in accident, striking often with little warning or chance
for reprieve:

> In Spring's bright, gay, and balmy hours,
> When verdant wreaths bedeck the bowers;
> When violets blue, with modest heads,
> Peep meekly from their grassy beds;
> When dimpled silvery brooks are seen:
> Winding through the meadows green;
>   Death comes.

In the sentimental era the details of a person's last moments on earth
were a matter of great interest. Sophia saved many published accounts of
the deaths of noted clergy, and family friends sent news of deaths. In
death's details people searched for signs of greater meaning in life and of
immortality, comforting the living.[33] "There has been a good many deaths
here this winter," wrote friend Eliza Campbell from Smyrna, Ohio, an
eastern Ohio community where Ben and Lew Snowden competed as racehorse drivers. "Mrs. Whitington died in February Maggie cousin She was
as well prepared to go as any lady I ever saw I was with her for three days
before She died I miss her a great deal and Mrs. Hibbs was confined to
her bed nine months and She went home Shouting glory to god."[34]

Sophia and her family were all too well acquainted with death, and
the entries in her scrapbook attest to every tragedy. At age seven Sophia
lost her younger sister Mary, laid to rest at age two. Years later Sophia
entered in her scrapbook a poem that articulated the burden of loss:

> Thy little hands so oft caressed
>   Our mother's pallid cheek,
> And yet thy young and infant form
>   Was first in death to sleep.
>
>   . . . .
>
> I dream of thee oft, though long, long years
>   Have passed since first in glee
> We played in cherub infancy
>   Upon our mother's knee.

Thomas and Ellen Snowden had lost their firstborn son, Oliver, at age eleven in 1846, when Sophia was nine:

> Oh call my brother back to me,
>   I cannot play alone;
> The summer comes with flower and bee,
>   Where is my brother gone?
>
> The butterfly is glancing bright
>   Across the sun beam's track;
> I care not now to chase its flight—
>   Oh! Call my brother back.

The death that changed the family most profoundly was Thomas's, in 1856. With Thomas gone the household was the responsibility of Ellen, age thirty-nine, and her children. Ellen could turn to Sophia, her oldest child, then nineteen, for both practical and emotional support. Sophia was old enough to empathize with her widowed mother:

> Oh! Father, then, for her and thee,
>   Gushed madly forth the scorching tears,
> And oft, and long, and bitterly,
>   Those tears have gushed in latter years;
> For, as the world grows cold around,
>   And things take on their real hue,
> 'Tis sad to learn that love is found
>   Alone above the stars with you.

As a confidante to Ellen, Sophia would have shared her memories of youth and her sorrows. Sophia recorded her impressions of Ellen by saving a number of poems with the printed title of "Ellen" or "To Ella." Next to one poignant poem about the passing of youthful happiness, Sophia simply wrote the name "Ellá":

> I am sitting sad and lonely
>   Where oft I've sat before,
> And thinking of the bright, bright days
>   That will return no more;
> Oh! days of childhood, days of youth!

In mercy were ye given
To shadow forth that better life,
 That knows no change in Heaven.

Long years have pass'd since those bright days,
 And still I love to trace
E'en though it be in memory's glass,
 Each well remember'd face;
And though the world seems chang'd to me,
 And gloom is o'er me cast,
I still can catch some ray of light
 In thinking of the past.

'Tis true my step is not so light,
 My face is not as fair,
And silver threads are mingled with
 What once was dark brown hair;
But yet, the change of face or form
 Could not such grief impart:
The worm lies hid among the leaves;
 The canker at the heart.

I'm sitting sad and lonely
 Where oft I've sat before,
And thinking of the bright, bright days
 That will return no more;
A mist is gath'ring o'er my eye,
 A shadow o'er my heart,
For the fairy visions of my youth
 Like twilight dews depart.

The image of a golden past comforted Americans as society experienced all sorts of transformations:

I would not escape from Memory's band
 For all that the eye can view:
For there's dearer dust in Memory's land
 Than the ore of rich Peru—
I clasped the fetter by memory twined,
The wanderer's heart and soul to bind.

References to the family's own past dotted the scrapbook. Years after Thomas's death, the Burgesses—the white people who brought Thomas north—still were meaningful to the Snowdens: Sophia kept an 1865 letter to the editor from one pastor John Burgess of Keokuk, Illinois, thanking the townspeople for donations to his church; on the same page was a tiny clipping that read simply, "Mrs L. C. Burgess 453 Mount Vernon, Ohio." *New Market*, first home of Thomas Snowden, also appeared in handwriting aside the pasted entries.

Youth was sentimentalized as a period free of cares and responsibilities:

> It is the "star of other days,"
> I watched it long ago;
> When hope was young, and sang sweet lays,
> To charm each fancied woe.
> Ah! I was gay and happy then,
> And free I roamed each hill and glen.

But youth too often intertwined with grieving. In May 1870 Annie died at the age of twenty-five, joined two springs later by her sister Elsie, age eighteen. Eliza Campbell wrote from Smyrna, upon hearing the news of Elsie's passing: "you have our prayrs and Sympathy in your bareavement and I hope that your loss is her Eternal gain I hope her prospects were brightened near the close of her life and that god took her in mercy please inform us as soon as convenient and give us all the particulars I feel anxious to know if She was Sensable to the last Mother wants to know if it was consumption She wrote that She had lung Fever."[35]

Sentimental culture pieced together a collage of images more than a document of the realities and contradictions of American life. It obscured the inhumane conditions in the factories and the growing divisions between rich and poor that undermined the democratic ideal. It ignored the prejudices toward newly arrived immigrants and the tensions between black and white Americans that would erupt into civil war. Sentimental culture assigned a standard of behavior and temperament ill suited to the economic situations of many women, like the widowed Ellen Snowden, who had to provide for their families.

African American women met persistent racial discrimination, modifying their experience of sentimental culture.[36] Sophia, a young black woman in rural Ohio, thus had a complex relationship with sentimental

Postmortem photograph, reprinted from a tintype or ambrotype, of a Snowden daughter, probably Martha or Phebe, ca. 1865. Her fingers were positioned as if she were plucking the guitar's strings, illustrating how significant music was in the girl's life.

culture, accepting some elements while resisting others. To understand her expressions and impressions, it is helpful to read the narratives of African American women written in the last century. Particularly useful is Harriet Jacobs's 1861 narrative, *Incidents in the Life of a Slave Girl*, in which the author detailed the dynamic relationship between the dominant popular culture and the distinctive experiences of African American women. In conveying her desire to maintain virtue in the face of sexual advances by white men, and in her devotion to her children, Jacobs evoked themes likely to enlist the sympathy of white women who shared those same commitments. But, according to literary historian Valerie Smith, "The sentimental fiction genre seems inappropriate for Jacobs's purposes."[37] In its emphasis on propriety, its rejection of explicit realism, and its casting of women as acquiescent, the sentimental novel could not fully convey Jacobs's life in slavery and her assertive response to that condition. Black women did not feel free to express their anger, too, because whites often were their transcribers.[38]

Jacobs attempted to overcome these limits by manipulating the conventional literary styles and formulaic plot lines of this popular format. She succeeded in establishing deeper levels of meaning even as she deployed the language of sentimentality: "However much her story may resemble superficially the story of the sentimental heroine, as a black woman she plays for different stakes."[39]

Sentimental expression similarly was socially useful for the Snowdens. When the children recited popular poetry in school and sang well-known ballads in their concerts, they satisfied their community's standards of taste and respectability—standards derived, in part, from the popular culture reaching all Americans. Sentimental expression also offered a measure of emotional privacy from the intrusions of whites who imposed themselves, physically and psychologically, on black women in slavery and freedom. The key to interpreting Sophia's collected images from popular culture, as a scholar noted with respect to black women's narratives, "lies in seeing through the screens . . . and in accepting the will of these women to possess their own lives."[40]

Sophia and her sisters, like their white girlfriends, were aware of these contradictions even as they embraced the sentimental mode. By the 1850s some women recognized that, barred from contributing directly to the family's economic welfare, they had little power to significantly control their own destinies or contribute to those around them. Sophia and her friends may have been swayed by romantic images, but they also anticipated rather more sober realities. Her friend Almeda Lewis sent along the words to a song conveying the downside of family life, "O How I Wish I Was Singgle [*sic*] Again":

When i was young and singgle
I lived at my ease
But now i am married
A husband to please
Four small Children to maintain
O how i wish i was singgle again
Singgle O singgle O singgle again
O how i wish i was singgle

Washing and irening
I daily haft to do
Carding and spinning i do remember to
house for to sweep spring to go to
Children are crying O dear wat will i do

one Comes mama i want to go to bed
an other Comes mama i want a piece of bread
wash those Children and send them to bed
before thy father curses and wishes they were ded

se those young men are strolling over town
as though they were worth 10,000 pound
searching of their pockets not a penny you will find
so falce and fickle a young mans mind

so with the young men they first
begin to love its nothing but my
honey dear and little turtle dove
but after they are married it is no
sutch a thing its get up and get
my breakfast you darty lasy thin[41]

Wistful images of romance carried a cruel irony for Sophia. In 1850, when she was thirteen, only sixty-one blacks or mulattoes lived in all of Knox County; of these, only two were men between the ages of ten and thirty-six, and one of these was Sophia's brother Ben.[42] Sophia's chances of finding a romantic partner acceptable to the community were slim, a fact of life she recognized. "The Old Maid's Soliloquy," a poem Sophia underlined frequently (represented here in italics), debated with some humor the possibility of remaining unmarried:

Here all alone, *from night to night,*
    I sit and gaze into the fire,
Wondering what more than I have got
    Any sane woman can desire.

No children here disturb my peace,
    Or husband cross, does grieve me,
I've everything that heart can wish,
    And joys complete surround me.

No little brats disturb my rest,
    I rise each morn at pleasure;
The old maid's one that truly best
    Her joys too great to measure.

A pretty cot in some quiet spot,
    With nature's beauties round me,
To me would be the happiest lot
    That fell to woman ever.

Still a voice seems to me saying;
    Something's wanting; yet I swan—
O! *now I think cold weather's coming,*
    And I should really like a man.

Keenly interested in the current debates about relations between men and women, Sophia found essays critical of the idealized role of women. An essay, "Which Is the Weaker Sex," pointed out that women were expected to wear fashions ill suited to the weather, withstand "the stink of rum and tobacco smoke" in men, and accept "abuse of all sorts from drunken husbands." "Call not woman the weaker vessel," the essay concluded, "for had she not been stronger than man, the race would long since have been extinct. Hers is a state of endurance which man could not bear." Sophia also saved the announcement for an upcoming lecture on the plight of women by Miss Anna E. Dickenson, "the greatest living female orator," whose presentation was billed as "political in character, and replete with facts, arguments, and appeals suited to the times."

A sentimental image of girls at play, from the Snowden scrapbook, ca. 1850s. Pasted next to the engraving are two poems about the loss of a loved one, "Memories of a Sister" and "Memory's Casket." Courtesy Knox County Historical Society, Knox County, Ohio.

The Snowden girls experienced friendship not only as an emotional bond, in sentimental culture's terms, but also as an economic engagement. A poem in Sophia's scrapbook, taken from the newspaper, described friendship in its emotional and psychological qualities as "the charm of life! To meet / Where mind its kindred mind can greet." But Phebe Snowden, born in 1845, praised the more concrete benefits of friendship in a poem:

True friendship is a cord that binds
Each hart and mind together
And links the soul and links
That never can be parted

How sweet it is to have a friend
 That you can rely upon
When out of money or of food
When turned from house or home

    . . . .

And when we see our neighbor in Want
Of what we could easy lend
We must not stop one moment to think
But remember it is an act of a friend[43]

Economic realities severely limited the aspirations of many young black women. The sentimental ideal was meaningful to Sophia's cousin Helen, who wrote in 1869 about her life in Warsaw, New York. Helen expressed interest in attending an institution for domestic training: "is there a college out ther for to work or learn how to keep house and other work I should like to go to one." Helen's chance of realizing her dream, however, was slim, owing to the circumstances at home: "I have not been well for a long time our school began the 30th of august but I don't go now pa has not got any body to keep house yet and it is to hard work for me to keep house and go to school to. . . . pa is well now he was verry sick last winter we did not expect him to live New years. . . . pa says he is going away to get some one to keep house so that i can go to school tuition is 4 dollars a term." Twenty-three years later Helen was still at home, keeping house for her aged father.[44]

Ellen's situation as a widow also cautioned the Snowden girls against embracing the sentimental ideal too firmly. Most black women could not afford to stay at home exclusively; they supported their families through domestic work in the homes of whites, earning low wages and little dignity. Ellen's own efforts to maintain her family strained the era's consensus that a woman's place was in the home with her children. The band's handbill addressed this concern by offering an economic justification: "Providence having taken him [Thomas] away, they are now traveling under the guidance of their mother, who has accompanied them only since his death." Analyzing the historical position of black women, Elizabeth Higginbotham notes that "Black women who have taken on economic and social roles to aid the survival of their families are viewed as having given up some of their womanhood."[45]

Motivated, perhaps, by the contradictions between the sentimental vision of life and her own experiences, Sophia felt a strong need to affirm the cause of change for women and blacks in America. Her political concern for the plight of women related naturally to the cause of abolition. The early women's movement drew much of its inspiration from abolitionist efforts; leading black abolitionists such as Sojourner Truth and Frederick Douglass—both former slaves—were among the first to speak out for the economic and political rights of women. White women were active in the abolitionist movement as well, often comparing the oppressive conditions of marriage with those of slavery. The most influential publication in the cause of abolition, Harriet Beecher Stowe's *Uncle Tom's Cabin*, garnered support for the antislavery cause by evoking the sympathies toward blacks that sentimental novels typically directed toward women.[46]

Sophia's concern over slavery was not an abstraction, as it was for many white women abolitionists. Slavery had been the lot of her mother and father, and others in her extended family suffered in bondage still. Her Uncle Benjamin—brother of Thomas Snowden, cousin Helen's father—was himself a runaway slave living under the constant threat of capture and return to his former master.[47]

When in 1859 John Brown led a raid on Harpers Ferry, Virginia, in an abortive effort to liberate those in bondage and incite a general rebellion against slavery, Sophia was stirred to honor Brown in her scrapbook with his portrait and a rendering of the scene of his execution. Black women seemed particularly inspired by Brown's sacrifice, as indicated by letters to antislavery activists. "From a Woman of the Race He Died For" from Kendalville, Indiana, expressed the pain of family separation that lay at the heart of slavery's inhumanity:

From the Snowden scrapbook, an 1859 engraving of abolitionist John Brown, executed for leading an unsuccessful raid into Virginia to free those in slavery. The scrapbook revealed the family's concerns with politics and race relations as well as sentimental culture. Courtesy Knox County Historical Society, Knox County, Ohio.

In the name of the young girl sold from the warm clasp of a mother's arms to the clutches of a libertine or a profligate,—in the name of the slave mother, her heart rocked to and fro by the agony of her mournful separations,—I thank you, that you have been brave enough to reach out your hands to the crushed and blighted of my race. You have rocked the bloody Bastile; and I hope that from your sad fate great good may arise to the cause of freedom.[48]

Another letter written "in behalf of the colored women of Brooklyn" expressed gratitude for Brown's deeds that the Snowden women undoubtedly shared:

We truly appreciate your most noble and humane effort, and recognize in you a Saviour commissioned to redeem us, the American people, from the great National Sin of Slavery; and though you have apparently failed in the object of your desires, yet the influence that we believe it will eventually exert, will accomplish all your intentions. We consider you a model of true patriotism, and one whom our common country will yet regard as the greatest it has produced, because you have sacrificed all for its sake. We rejoice in the consciousness of your perfect resignation. We shall ever hold you dear in our remembrance, and shall infuse the same feelings in our posterity. We have always entertained a love for the country which gave us birth, despite the wrongs inflicted upon us, and have always been hopeful that the future would augur better things. We feel now that your glorious act for the cause of humanity has afforded us an unexpected realization of some of our seemingly vain hopes. And now, in view of the coming crisis which is to terminate all your labors of love for this life, our mortal natures fail to sustain us under the trying affliction; but when we view it from our religious standpoint, we feel that earth is not worthy of you, and that your spirit yearneth for a higher and holier existence. Therefore we willingly give you up, and submit to His will "who doeth all things well."[49]

Articles and poetry praised Henry Clay, whose moderate views regarding slavery in the years preceding the rise of Lincoln showed sympathy for the plight of black Americans:

He stands erect! the brave, the free,
The Champion blest of Liberty.
Should threatening clouds our sky o'ercast,
Still will the brave one stem the blast;
Still onward press without delay,
And win the goal shall HENRY CLAY.

Religion appeared on nearly every page, a reflection of the Snowdens' deep religious convictions. Literacy opened the pages of the family Bible for the Snowden children, providing a firm moral basis for their lives.[50] Sentimental odes to family and death continually evoked religious imagery, and many clippings included comments of clergy known to the Snowdens; Sophia also kept several death notices of preachers. Three published articles documented the death of Rev. J. H. Power, for many years a member of the North Ohio Conference of the Methodist Episcopal Church. A vigorous preacher and writer, Rev. Powers was most noted for his intellectually stimulating treatises, whose "subject matter was suggested largely by the wants of the people, made known to him by practical acquaintance with them." Next to a speech by Abraham Lincoln, Sophia pasted one by Frederick Douglass, given at Boston's Faneuil Hall near the close of the Civil War "to rejoice over the great victory"—in distinctly biblical terms:

> I tell you, the negro is coming up—he is rising—rising. [Laughter and applause.] Why, only a little while ago we were the Lazaruses of the South; the Dives of the South was the slaveholder; and how singular it is that we have here another illustration of that Scripture! Once there was a certain rich man who fared sumptuously every day, and was arrayed in purple and fine linen. He came North, clothed in silk and in satin, and shining with gold, and his breast sparkling with diamonds—his table loaded with the good things of the world. And a certain Lazarus sat at his gate, desiring the crumbs that fell from his table. Such was the record. But now a change has taken place. That rich man is lifting up his eyes in torment down there [tremendous applause.] and seeing Lazarus afar off, in Abraham's bosom [tumultuous laughter and applause] is all the time calling on Father Abraham to send Lazarus back. But Father Abraham says, "If they fear not Grant or Sherman, neither will they be persuaded though I send Lazarus unto them." [Prolonged and vociferous applause] I say we are way up yonder now, no mistake. [This was said with an expressive gesture that called forth another outburst of applause.]

Sophia witnessed the end of the war, and in the decade that followed she saw an increasing migration of blacks into the county that promised a more vital African American community. But when Sophia died at age forty-one in 1878, her own contribution to that community was stilled. Unmarried, childless, denied the opportunity to establish her own home, Sophia appeared to have achieved little of the sentimental ideal of womanhood that so clearly informed her life. Yet in her music Sophia gave life to an important part of her cultural and familial heritage. The oldest Snowden child surviving to adulthood, Sophia was a second mother to her younger siblings and a sister to her mother, amplifying Ellen's happiness and supporting her through her many sorrows. Sophia found personal and spiritual significance in her devotion to family, mutually informed by the popular culture of mid-nineteenth-century America and by long-standing black tradition.[51] Sophia faced obstacles and disappointments, but she also gained love and friendship from many. A keen sense of loss struck those who knew her, as Nan Simpson wrote to Ben shortly after Sophia's death: "I supose you all feel very lonesome about one of your Best friends that you have lost I am writing this on behalf of Mother and aunt . . . I tell you they are that bad troubled at this time about your mother being left so desolate that they both cry half the time. . . . I have not told one in this town about sis being dead but is sympathiseing with you in your trouble."[52]

4. Ohio's Not the Place for Me

Ohio's not the place for me;
For I am much surprised
So many of her sons to see
In garments of disguise.
Her name has gone throughout the world,
Free labor—soil—and men—
But slaves had better far be hurled
Into the lion's den.

Farewell, Ohio!
I cannot stop in thee;
I'll travel on to Canada,
Where colored men are free
          —*unknown black composer, 1850*

"Free labor—soil—and men" powerfully expressed the hopes of thousands of midcentury Americans.[1] The West beckoned to many as a place of fresh starts, of success based on individual merit, not on the odious social categories of the slaving South or the elite East. Historian Frederick Jackson Turner captured this vision in his famous work *Rise of the New West:* "The ideal of the west was its emphasis upon the worth and possibilities of the common man, its belief in the right of every man to rise to the full measure of his own nature, under conditions of social mobility."[2] But the West provided social and political opportunity only for whites. Blacks faced continuing discrimination, as historian Leon Litwack observed in his now-classic study of the politics of race before the Civil War: "Although slavery eventually confined itself to the region below the Mason-Dixon Line, discrimination against the Negro and a firmly held belief in the superiority of the white

Ben Snowden as a man of about thirty, ca. 1870.

race were not restricted to one section but were shared by an overwhelming majority of white Americans in both the North and the South." Litwack echoed Frank Quillin's 1913 study, *The Color Line in Ohio:*

> We are forced to conclude that the negroes of Ohio, during the first half of the nineteenth century, were in a miserable condition, economically, morally, and mentally. This naturally fixed to a great extent their status in the life of the State, but everywhere we see the one other element, race prejudice, constantly entering in to color the view that the white man took of the black man. To him "hope yielded not to the future" for the color line was everywhere and everlasting, forming an impassible barrier between the two races, which the black man could never hope to surmount.[3]

Something even more powerful than custom and opinion hardened the color line in Ohio: the legal system itself. For blacks "free labor" could not equal "free men" until they could claim the rights and responsibilities of full citizenship, foremost among those the right to vote. And nothing short of an alteration of the Constitution could bring that to pass.

The Civil War made a national drama of the rights of African Americans, but debate continued on the status of blacks long after the last cannon had fired. Reconstruction—a movement to assimilate the huge numbers of freed blacks within a social and economic fabric much weakened by war—was the program of the Republican party, the party of Lincoln. On the other side was the "Democracy," the party supporting the continued repression of blacks, entrenched on both sides of the Mason-Dixon line. Mount Vernon's two weekly newspapers, the *Democratic Banner* and the *Republican,* had enacted their own civil war over the issue of slavery; in the war years the *Republican*'s masthead claimed it the paper of "free labor, soil and men." In late 1869 and early 1870, the papers took on with equal enthusiasm the issue of voting rights for blacks. Reporting the news from the *Congressional Record* and from the Ohio state legislature, the papers represented the Fifteenth Amendment to the Constitution as the redemption or the bane of the Republic.

Knox Countians followed discussion of the amendment for months. The *Banner*'s editor, Lecky Harper, insisted that the "Radicals" degraded the white man by supporting the Fifteenth, and it was bad politics besides: "respectable" Republicans, he said, would join the opposition rather than stand with blacks as equals. Every week the *Republican*'s editor, William Bascom, reported progress on the amendment in each state, occasionally including articles on the movement for women's suffrage.[4] Having built its name as the party of abolitionism during the Civil War, the Republican party now looked to black voters as a potential constituency. Beyond its moral urgency, ratification had the added attraction of finally laying to rest the national absorption in the fate of blacks, as Bascom noted: "It will be a happy day for the country when the negro is entirely removed from politics, and left to fight his own way like other folks."[5]

A reader's letter to the *Republican*, published February 1, 1870, asked: "Will you please give us the exact language of the Fifteenth Amendment, about which the copperheads are howling so dismally. There is no end to their moans. They think their last chance for restoration of power and patronage is about gone. Give us the amendment and oblige." The editor obliged, commenting, "How anyone who has a respect for Democratic principles and regard for the great doctrine of equal rights, can object to it we cannot see." Knox County's readers saw the following simple text: "Article 15. The right of citizens of the United States to vote shall not be denied or abridged by the United States or by any State on account of race, color, or previous condition of servitude. Section 2. The Congress shall have power to enforce this article by appropriate legislation." The Democratic press, in turn, positioned itself as the "White Man's Party" and assured readers that the amendment would fail in Congress.[6] On March 30, 1870, Congress finally ratified the Fifteenth Amendment, and a dream became law for African American men.

Rural black Ohioans took to the streets in celebration. The *Republican* of April 19 reported a black celebration in a small coal-mining town sixty miles to the east of Mount Vernon: "The colored men of Washington and vicinity will on the 13th inst., hold a grand jubilee over the ratification of the 15th Amendment." Mount Vernon and Newark also hosted black companies in military-style regalia (perhaps homemade), parading through town in drill formations. On May 10 an observer of a Newark parade complimented the Mount Vernon Zouaves for their "scientific military evolutions"; he also found noteworthy the paraders' banner inscriptions:

The colored citizens of Newark celebrated the fifteenth amendment in conjunction with their fellow citizens from Columbus, Fredericktown, Mt. Vernon, Zanesville and other points in the following manner. On the arrival of the train from Zanesville the procession formed at the depot, the Mt. Vernon Zouaves under the command of Capt. George P. Wilson in front pre-

ceded by the Delaware Colored Brass Band. . . . Next came a company of
infantry from Zanesville . . . ; then the Grant and Colfax Guards from
Zanesville commanded by Capt. Jones and each of the last were under
command of Col. C. H. Adams of Zanesville, whose dignified and impos-
ing appearance in military uniform elicited the admiration of the bystand-
ers. The procession . . . marched thence to the church, and reformed on
Locust in the following order. First, the Mt. Vernon Zouaves, Capt. Wilson,
preceded by the Delaware Brass Band. Next, company of infantry from
Zanesville, Capt. Hargrave; next a company of infantry from Columbus,
commanded by Capt. Edward Brown; next, the Grant and Colfax Guards,
Zanesville, commanded by Capt. Jones; next a handsomely decorated open
top vehicle, with 20 handsomely dressed girls, with flags in hand representing all the states that adopted the 15th amendment; next civilians in carriages and on foot. The procession was interspersed with numerous
banners bearing appropriate inscriptions, among which were the following: Martyrs of Liberty, John Brown and A. Lincoln; We are coming Gen.
Grant, 900,000 strong; H. R. Revels [black Congressman] De Profundis
41st Congress; 15th Amendment; train Circleville Democratic Jackass in
front of it, kicking at it; When shall these three meet again, traitors, rebellion, slavery; New Jersey like a mule stands still; New York like a Craw-
fish goes backward; Ohio like wisdom goes forward; Shoo Fly. . . . Great
praise is due to Capt. Wilson for the manner in which his company of Zouaves performed some of the most scientific military evolutions.[7]

The *Republican* commented: "The Newark *American* gives a glowing account of the ratification meeting at that place, by the 15 [*sic*] Amendment
boys, last week. It was the universal remark that every thing was well
done, decently and in order. Our colored people are making friends by
their excellent conduct." Bascom also noted the fine drill display in Mount
Vernon: "There was a general turnout on the streets, on Wednesday eve,
to see the 15th amendment boys in their new uniform. They have formed
a military company, with about 40 members, and they go into the positions as if they mean business. Success to them." Forty participants significantly represented the black and mulatto male population, which
numbered ninety-seven individuals (of all ages) out of a county population of 25,601 in 1870.[8]

Blacks celebrated ratification most forcefully, however, by streaming
to the polls statewide. The *Banner* published an elections report from
southwestern Ohio that indicted Republicans as manipulators of black
voters and emphasized the Democratic wins, but the story also confirmed
"an avalanche" of black voters at the polls:

Batavia, Ohio April 5, 1870
Clermont. Four hundred negroes voted the Radical ticket in this county on
Monday last, yet the county has given an increased Democratic majority.
At New Richmond 167 negroes voted the Radical ticket. The Germans
joined the Democrats en masse, and with their assistance the Radicals
were completely routed. At Felicity ninety-five blacks voted the Radical
ticket, while respectable Republicans voted with the Democrats, which
gave us a majority of 108. At Batavia the blacks came out to the polls like
an avalanche, but all for naught. The whole Democratic ticket elected. The
negroes were drilled during Saturday and Sunday how to conduct themselves at the election, and everything showed preconcerted action upon
their part. The election indicates to a certainty that the county will give
1000 majority next fall. . . . Cuffy and his black allies can't rule in Clermont [County].[9]

Monday, April 4, was an important voting day in Knox County. The
Republican's article on the ratification decision appeared on April 5, but
by then Ben and Lew Snowden had already left their home to exercise
their right to vote.[10] Several positions were up for election in Morris Township, and the local officials held considerable power; they maintained the
roads and the graveyard, made zoning decisions, and assessed taxes.[11] It
was only a short distance to the polling place at the township schoolhouse,
a location the brothers knew well. They and their sisters had attended
school with their white neighbors there; they had played fiddle and banjo
there, too, in the Snowden Family Band.

Residents and property owners in Morris Township for the past fifteen
years, Ben and Lew knew whom they wanted to vote for. They also knew
there might be some trouble if they tried to vote. Only two nights before,
on Saturday night, some people from Zanesville had plastered Mount Vernon with a strident broadside announcing that blacks who attempted to
vote would do so fraudulently because laws had not been passed to enforce
the ratified amendment.

The brothers had come prepared: If any question should arise, they
could hand over a copy of President Ulysses S. Grant's speech affirming
the passage of the Fifteenth Amendment. Surely the words of the president
would carry some weight, if Ben and Lew's own word was not enough.
They had clipped Grant's text from the newspaper:

A measure which makes at once four millions of people voters, who were
before declared by the highest tribunal in the land not citizens of the

Lew Snowden in his early twenties, ca. 1870. He held a riding crop, suggesting his lifelong enthusiasm for horse racing.

United States, not eligible to become so with an assertion at the time of declaration of independence the opinion was fixed and universal in the civilized portion of the white race, and regarded as an axiom in morals as well as in politics, that black men had no rights which white men were bound to respect, is indeed a measure of grander importance than any other one act of this kind from the foundation of our Government to the present time.[12]

But Knox County's politicians held fast to their habits, regardless of changes in the law. On Monday, April 4, the township officials denied Ben and Lew their right to vote. Two days later Ben Snowden filed a petition protesting the action in the Knox County Court of Common Pleas, undoubtedly one of the nation's first suits of voter discrimination under the Fifteenth Amendment:

The said Benjamin Snowden plaintiff complains of the said defendants Hezekiah Young, John Parrott and Christian Knox and says that the said defendants were the judges of a certain election held in and for the township of Morris in the county of Knox and in the state of Ohio and on the fourth day of April A.D. 1870 for the purpose of electing three township trustees one township clerk one township treasurer one constable and one township assessor within and for said township of Morris and that the said defendants as such judges did open the polls for said election at the school house which is the usual place of holding the election in said township at eight o clock AM on said fourth day of April A.D. 1870 as aforesaid. and that the plaintiff was then and there a citizen of said state of Ohio and a resident and legal voter of the said election in said township of Morris and . . . the said plaintiff did on the same fourth day of April A.D. 1870 and whilst said polls were still kept open by the said defendants for the exercising of the votes of the electors of said township at said election offer his vote or ballot for the election of three trustees one treasurer, one clerk, one constable, and one assessor within and for said township as aforesaid and requested the same defendants to exercise the same yet the said defendants not regarding their duty in that behalf then and there refused to receive the vote or ballot of said plaintiff whereby said plaintiff was deprived of his right to vote at said election to the damage of plaintiff in the sum of five hundred dollars Wherefore plaintiff asks judgement against the said defendants for the said sum of five hundred dollars his charge so as aforesaid sustained.[13]

If the Snowdens had intended to act privately, quietly, they failed conspicuously: the Republican newspaper, in its next edition, broadcast

both their attempt to vote and the subsequent complaint. Scanning the
Republican's political news page for election results, local and statewide,
readers would have seen a column titled "Blind Prejudiced Judges," sum-
marizing the events in Morris Township. The plaintiffs were well known
enough so that the columnist could simply refer to "the Snowdens," without describing them by race, place of residence, or occupation:

> At the election last Monday the trustees of Morris Tp. refused the votes of
> the Snowdens. They [trustees] will be prosecuted for their stupid obsti-
> nacy. They attempted to justify their action on the ground, 1st that they
> had no legal evidence that the 15th Amendment was adopted. When a
> copy of the paper containing the message of the President, and the procla-
> mation of the Secretary of State was shown them they refused to receive
> the votes, and then said that the measure was incomplete, inasmuch as the
> section provided that Congress had the authority to pass all laws necessary
> to enforce it, and that Congress not having passed any law to enforce it,
> the provision was not yet in force.
>
> This is a very transparent fallacy. The amendment has force and ef-
> fect from the time the Secretary of State certifies to its ratification. This
> was on the 30th of March. It was so published to the world, and all Ameri-
> can citizens were bound to take notice of it as the law of the land, and to
> respect it accordingly. By it the blacks were made *voters*, the same as
> whites, all over the United States. In Ohio, in Knox Co. in Morris Tp, they
> were citizens, and voters, the same as others. They had a right to vote, and
> the judges of elections had no more right to refuse the votes of the Snow-
> dens than they had that of Mr. Bonar, or Mr. Swan [prominent whites].
> The laws of Ohio that would punish them, if they had refused the votes of
> these gentlemen, will also punish the judges for refusing the votes of the
> Snowdens. . . .
>
> There is no legal excuse for the conduct of the Morris Trustees. They
> are liable to the penalties of the law for their action in refusing these votes,
> simply and only because they were black men. They permitted their demo-
> cratic prejudices to carry them quite too far. We know these men do not
> like to submit, but they must come to it, and the sooner the better for their
> own well being.[14]

The laws of Ohio did not, however, protect with an undiscriminating
reach. The Snowdens' case dragged on for six years, with the judge order-
ing continuances nineteen times. No explanation was given for any of the
delays. Finally, on December 4, 1876, the court handed down its judgment against the plaintiff. Ben Snowden was instructed to reimburse the

defendants for their costs in conjunction with the case and to pay court costs as well. Ben's liability totaled $21.75, nearly a month's wages.

Ben and Lew's actions took tremendous courage. White men controlled virtually all aspects of public life, and individuals who attempted to exercise their newfound rights risked harsh reprisals. Only two days after Ben filed his suit, the *Banner*, ever vitriolic against blacks, reported a story sure to chill those who hoped to exercise their legal rights in opposition to local custom: "A negro, in attempting to vote, was killed at Greenville, Darke county [Ohio]. Particulars not learned."[15] Ben and Lew did not suffer so extremely, perhaps because the local Republicans had embraced them, but they had faced a well-entrenched hostility to the rights of African Americans.[16]

Ohio's first state constitution, in 1802, reserved voting privileges exclusively for white men. A half century later, black suffrage failed again; delegates at the Ohio Constitutional Convention of 1850–51 ratified a motion to deny black suffrage, by a vote of seventy-five to thirteen. Both of Knox County's delegates voted with the majority. As the Civil War came to a close, black voting rights again became a pressing issue. The state Democratic convention in 1865 declared, "The effort now being made to confer the right of suffrage upon negroes was an invidious attempt to overthrow popular institutions by bringing the right to vote into disgrace."[17] The Democratic view prevailed two years later in a referendum to amend Ohio's constitution to permit voting by "all male citizens" in the state. Knox County's voters, divided on the issue, rejected black suffrage by a margin of 395 among the 5,455 votes cast. Informed by this referendum, the state legislature failed to ratify the Fifteenth Amendment two years later, reversing its decision only when it seemed that the amendment would soon become law.[18]

Undaunted by the social and economic costs of resisting discrimination, members of the Snowden family frequently entered the courts to protect their interests. For seven years following the death of Thomas Snowden in 1856, the family had fought in court to keep their homestead from foreclosure. They were successful in part: Ellen Snowden was permitted to keep the home, but she was required to forfeit one-fourth of the farm property.

A new struggle emerged in 1864, when Ellen attempted to plant a summer crop of tobacco.[19] Ellen leased two acres of land near her home for cultivation. When the owners subsequently sold the plot, they promised to provide Ellen with land elsewhere. Relying upon this arrangement,

Ellen raised seedlings for planting, only to be denied access to the land. Ellen petitioned the Knox County Court of Common Pleas to recover ninety dollars in damages for her time and expense in preparing to plant.

Tobacco was a crop Ellen knew well, having grown up in the tobacco country of southern Maryland. As a child she had watched her kin plant tobacco seedlings and tend to the fragile leaves through repeated growing seasons. Now, as a widowed farmer in Ohio, she needed to use that experience to keep her family solvent. Her petition carried a cruel irony: in slavery Ellen's people were forced to plant tobacco, but the rewards of the harvest were the master's; in freedom Ellen could take the profits, but she had to fight for the opportunity to plant.[20]

Ellen won the case, and when the defendants appealed, the court again ruled in her favor. The court awarded Ellen only twenty-five dollars of the ninety dollars she had requested in damages, perhaps because tobacco prices had fallen dramatically in 1864.[21] But Ellen might have measured her victory in more than economic terms. Writing about black working women in slavery and freedom, historian Jacqueline Jones remarks that "for most black women . . . freedom had meaning primarily in a family context. The institution of slavery had posed a constant threat to the stability of family relationships. . . . Only at home could they exercise considerable control over their own lives and those of their husbands and children and impose a semblance of order on the physical world."[22] Ellen, who could sign her court petitions only with an X, had successfully used the legal system to hold onto her farm and support her children.

Economic issues had long influenced race relations in the state. Ohio had not allowed slavery for many reasons, including genuine aversion on moral and ethical grounds, but also because white settlers feared that forced labor would greatly devalue their own labor.[23] During the Civil War years, many white Ohioans—even those who supported abolition—feared the influx of free blacks who might become competitors for scarce jobs, a fear the vehemently proslavery *Banner* eagerly summoned in such articles as "Hordes of Negroes Coming!" published in February 1861. The "hordes" turned out to be eighteen free blacks from the South who had arrived in Columbus and Zanesville, but the bigger picture was far more serious, according to editor Harper: "The legitimate effect of this immigration will be to degrade and prostrate white labor at the North, reduce the wages of our mechanics and all kinds of operatives to the standard of the 'pauper labor' of Europe." The article closed with the taunt, "Laboring men who voted for Lincoln how do you like these 'first fruits' of the great Republican Victory?"[24]

Through relative good fortune and their choice of occupations, the Snowdens managed to avoid some of this economically based prejudice. Whites had no reason to view Thomas Snowden, one of the few African American independent farmers in Knox County, as a competitor in a tight job market. The family similarly posed no economic threat to whites in their musical careers. Indeed, as entertainers to largely white audiences, the Snowdens conformed to the dominant expectation that blacks, if they must be present at all, work in the service of whites.[25]

The state legislature, in its early years, not only turned down black suffrage but also passed a series of statutes restricting black civil rights. First instituted in 1804 and expanded in 1807, Ohio's black codes were infamous as among the most severe in the nation. Their main purpose was to discourage black migration into the state. Touring the state to stir support for the abolitionist movement, Frederick Douglass declared that Ohio had devised the black codes because it was tainted by proximity to slavery states:

> The moral pestilence that walketh in darkness along her southern border, has spread blight and mildew over her legislation. Her statute-book is polluted,—she is disgraced by her villainous black laws. Let her repeal those infernal laws—blot them forever from her statute-book, and thus cease to afford impunity to every white ruffian who may desire to insult, or plunder, who may desire to rob, or commit other outrages on her coloured population.[26]

By an act ratified in 1807, all blacks were required within twenty days of taking up residence to post five hundred dollars bond to guarantee their good behavior and future maintenance. African Americans were denied the right to vote, to petition the state government, to participate in the administration of justice, to serve in the military, and to attend public schools. The last of the restrictions barring integrated education was not repealed until 1887.

The black laws also were designed to discourage interaction between blacks and whites within the state. It was a penal offense to employ a black for one hour unless that person could present a certificate of freedom, and any violator of this law was to be fined not less than ten dollars nor more than fifty dollars. Penalties for aiding a fugitive's escape or hindering the capture of a fugitive slave were as high as one thousand dollars, with those informing upon such illegal activities receiving half of the fine.[27] In practice, however, enforcement varied across jurisdictions. In only a few instances were blacks actually required to post bond with the county clerk [28]

By the late 1840s liberal political factions across the state had gained sufficient force to bring about a partial revision of the black codes. One such change directly affected the lives of the Snowden children: new legislation providing for the education of black youth. Previously, common schools permitted whites only, and an 1829 act had expressly excluded blacks and mulattoes from the public schools. Few black children received more than a few weeks' instruction in a year, offered by local black residents or sympathetic whites willing to brave public ill will for their efforts. The new law of 1848 enabled black children to attend white schools in districts with fewer than twenty African American children, provided no white parent or taxpayer filed an objection with school officials.[29]

A decade later all of the Snowden children had received some education in the local school. The Snowdens may have fared better, academically, than many black children who lived in areas with larger African American populations. The schooling law of 1848 also gave birth to so-called colored schools in towns or city districts with twenty or more children desiring an education; funding for these schools came from taxes levied against black property owners. Reverdy C. Ransom, of nearby Guernsey County, Ohio, attended a colored school, held a few months a year in the African Methodist Episcopal Church building. He found this school deficient in contrast to those attended by whites: "The school was noisy, undisciplined, ungraded. We had but one teacher for all the classes and subjects that might be taught. . . . I remained in the colored school, covering the same ground year after year."[30]

Despite the state's restrictive laws, Ohio's black population grew steadily throughout the first half of the nineteenth century. The Ohio territory included 337 African Americans in 1800, a number that grew to 25,279 by 1850. But the black presence statewide remained small throughout the antebellum period, never reaching 3 percent of the total population. Most African Americans resided in Ohio's southern section, close to the slaveholding states of Kentucky and Virginia. Although black population density was greatest in the state's urban areas, especially Cincinnati, at midcentury nearly two thirds of the state's African Americans resided in rural areas such as Knox County.[31]

Blacks in Knox County constituted a tiny fraction of the population. Like Ellen Cooper and Thomas Snowden, blacks frequently came as single young adults accompanying white families migrating from the middle-Atlantic states and the Upper South.[32] Over time these individuals married and established families of their own, and new black families continued to settle the area. Whereas only two independent black households resided in the county in 1830, that number had increased to ten by the close of the decade. These two- and sometimes three-generation families included individuals of all ages. By 1840 the number of blacks within Knox County had grown to fifty-one; of these, twenty-six resided in Mount Vernon, and only ten blacks still lived in white households.

In 1850, when the population reached a prewar high of 28,082, the Snowdens were among the county's sixty-one blacks. Fifty-seven of these individuals lived in eleven families; the other four resided in the homes of whites. Black families were dispersed across six townships, so that only a single family unit resided in a given locale. Like the county's white population, most blacks resided in Mount Vernon, which offered the greatest economic opportunities for those without property. But the town's forty-one black residents were widely separated; a cluster of three families with a total of fifteen people resided in the town's fourth ward, constituting the county's densest concentration of blacks.[33]

Knox County blacks made their livelihoods chiefly as laborers and in the service of whites. Of the seventeen adult males for whom the 1850 census listed an occupation, eleven were laborers. Most of these worked at the C. & E. Cooper Company, a steam engine factory. Along with the women who doubtless provided domestic service to whites, these laborers constituted the black working class. Two barbers, a soapmaker, and a cook made up the slightly higher-status tier of skilled labor. As one of two independent farmers, Thomas Snowden occupied a position—however modest—at the top of the county's black social hierarchy.[34]

At the center of this rising community stood the African Methodist Episcopal (A.M.E.) Church.[35] When James A. Ralls, a preacher who migrated to Mount Vernon from Virginia in 1865, suggested forming a local A.M.E. congregation, members of the three prominent black families formerly associated with the A.M.E. Church in Captina, to the east—the Turner, Simmons, and Wooten families—founded the Wayman Chapel.

The Wayman Chapel of the African Methodist Episcopal Church, Mount Vernon, ca. 1900. The individuals posing were probably church officials meeting in Mount Vernon from throughout central Ohio. The church was a center for sociability in the black community. Courtesy George Booker.

The group organized a formal congregation in 1870, and in 1876 they completed the brick church that ministered to a congregation of some forty individuals, including the Snowdens.[36]

Viewed as an institution committed to middle-class notions of respectability, the A.M.E. Church enjoyed congenial relations with several white churches in Mount Vernon. In its first years of existence, the Christian and United Presbyterian churches offered basement rooms as a meeting place for the fledgling congregation. When funds to erect a permanent building ran out, local churches raised additional money to help complete the project. White churches provided the A.M.E. Church with its older hymnals and sometimes opened their programs to blacks. Mount Vernon's white First Congregational Church hosted the Fisk Jubilee Singers, who gained international acclaim for their renditions of black spirituals, in their first tour in the fall of 1871.[37]

A center of sociability, culture, and solidarity for the African American community, the A.M.E. Church provided opportunities for the Snowdens and other local black residents to make contacts with blacks throughout central Ohio. After moving to Mount Vernon, former members of the Captina church, primarily from the Simmons family, held family reunions each summer, alternating meetings between Captina and Wayman Chapel. Wayman Chapel became well known for its sponsorship of camp meetings, held at the local fairgrounds.[38] A handbill in the Snowden collection announced the 1887 meeting.

Supported and respected in the county's small black community, the Snowdens nevertheless faced a white population often hostile to blacks. The Democratic newspaper treated blacks as curiosities, explaining "What Makes the Negro Black" or "the rare phenomena of a negro turning white . . . the change produced by the absorption of the pigomentum nigram, or coloring matter of the skin." Even the antislavery *Republican* managed to combine Barnum and Greeley in a report on black Siamese twin sisters, "freaks of nature" managed professionally by their mother Monimo, "who has been lately freed from the bondage of slavery." On tour in Edinburgh, Scotland, Christiana and Lilley Makol "are gaily dressed, and frankly converse with their visitors, and sing to them little songs in duet sweetly enough. On the occasion of our visit to them, the stouter one, in reply to a question, announced that she is considered the prettier one, but her sister very quickly put up the claim of being the gooder one." Readers were informed that "the proceeds of exhibition, after paying expenses, are to be applied in rescuing also from the galling yoke, the father and the other sisters and brothers of whom there are eight." How suggestive that metaphor "galling yoke" seems, as a shorthand for slavery, in the context of an anecdote about two disparate parts forming a mysterious and freakish whole.[39]

Readers encountered the persistent theme of blacks' inferiority. The *Banner* carried a report of a black man who fell asleep in an intoxicated stupor with his head across a railroad track, as well as this diatribe excerpted from the *London Times:* "The negro is a lazy animal, without any foresight, and therefore requiring to be led and compelled—he is decidedly inferior, very little raised above a mere animal. . . . [He is] void of self reliance, and is the creature of circumstances—scarcely fitted to take

OHIO STATE

CAMP-MEETING

—AT—

MT. VERNON, O.,

AUG. 24 to SEPT. 1, 1887.

TICKET ARRANGEMENT:

A Season Ticket, costing 50 cents, is not transferable, but will admit the holder thereof into the Camp Grounds as often as desired during the meeting, and will have to be surrendered to the gate-keeper at the close of the Camp-meeting. Show the ticket as you pass through the gate. Season ticket for Horse will cost 50 cents.

EACH TENT-HOLDER

Is entitled to a FAMILY TICKET, for $1.00, admitting all the members of the family proper to the number of six, during the meeting. This ticket DOES NOT include the horse ticket.

Single Admission, for each Individual, over 12 years of age, is 10 cents; single admission for horse, 10 cents. 10 cents for privilege of feeding horse at stall; 25 cents for feed of horse, hay and oats.

The gates will be open every day of the meeting. Children under 12 years of age come in free at all times. Children's meeting every day at 1 p. m. to which all children are invited. Young people's meeting every day at 6 p. m.

Provision at Dining Hall and Lunch Stand to supply the wants of all who may attend.

RATES OF BOARDING:

For the Term,	$6.00
For the Term, Boarding and Lodging,	8.00
Single Meal, Dinner,	40c
Breakfast or Supper,	25c
Boarding per day,	80c
Boarding and Lodging per day,	$1.00

IMPERTUS MARTIN, Supt.

Camp meeting notice in the Snowden collection, 1887. Camp meet-ings were an important institution in Knox County from its first settle-ment; the A.M.E. Church regularly sponsored camp meetings in the 1870s and 1880s.

care of himself—has no care for to-morrow—has no desire for property strong enough to induce him to labor—lives from hand to mouth."[40]

Blacks were nuisances and economic liabilities, such tales instructed, but more significant, they were murderous criminals. The Democratic paper routinely printed accounts of brutality by blacks against whites throughout the country. Knox County readers regularly saw columns about revenge murders by slaves, with headlines such as "Horrible Murder—A Master Killed and Burned by His Slaves" and "A Horrible Murder in Tennessee—A Planter Killed by His Slave." Slave children, too, were reported to host "diabolical designs" against whites, as in the *Banner*'s report of a black girl who fed her master's family ground glass mixed in with the flour as vengeance for being corrected.[41] But Mount Vernon's Democratic paper offered a solution to alleged atrocities against whites: execution. Repeatedly, the *Banner* published news reports drawn from across the country justifying the shooting, burning, and lynching of African Americans, exemplified by the 1858 article "A Negro Slave Shot by His Clergyman."[42]

Saturated with stories of racial violence, Knox Countians sometimes caused havoc in their own towns. On January 23, 1857, three young white Mount Vernon men entered the barbershop in the basement of Woodward Hall run by Jacob Jackson, a black man. One of the men, Columbus Johnston, "got shaved, but was about walking off without paying, when Jackson reminded him of the fact; thereupon he commenced abusing Jackson in the most violent manner, and from abuse soon proceeded to blows. A most disgraceful row ensued, and Johnston being assisted by his cronies, they well nigh beat Jackson to death." On the following day Jacob Jackson made a formal complaint about the matter; Johnston attacked him again, "but through the timely interference of Sheriff Underwood, he was prevented from committing any violence." The *Banner* labeled the incident a "disgraceful row"—principally because young Johnston was soused— but the paper's pervasive racial stereotypes had in fact legitimated racial discord.[43]

Of all the forms of interracial contact, none alarmed whites more than the prospect of miscegenation, banned by law until 1887. The *Banner* reported the case of "an intelligent-appearing female" from Wayne County who ran off with a black man who had worked on the family farm for some time, "having been induced to return the tender passion[!] which he professed for her." Such relationships were perceived as soiling the white family's social standing, whatever the consequences for the couple.

An unidentified friend of the Snowdens photographed in a Mount Vernon studio playing Lew Snowden's banjo, ca. early 1870s, documenting the Snowdens' musical relationships with other area blacks. The tintype shows the banjo "upside down," with the short string toward the floor, an effort to correct for the reversal of the image in the photographic process.

In "A White Heiress Elopes with a Negro," the *Banner* extended sympathy to the bride's Michigan family by noting that it was "said to have occupied a position in society which was first class, and the blow is consequently a terrible one."[44]

Interracial liaison was so contrary to local standards that a rare political cartoon took up the subject. In the June 15, 1858, *Banner,* a drawing captioned "Black Republicanism Illustrated!" depicted a black man, hand prominently resting on the rump of a white woman, being read to by a white man. The editor asserted, "The above cut is a life-like representation of a scene which took place the other day in the editorial office of the Mt. Vernon *Republican.*—It represents WM. H. COCHRAN, Esq., the editor of that paper, as Justice of the Peace, marrying a black man to a white woman." Readers then were guided to the larger implications: "To elevate the negro and to degrade and disfranchise white men is the great object of the party now arrayed against the Democracy."[45]

Despite recurrent representations of horrible relations between blacks and whites, central Ohioans were far from monolithic on issues of race in the years before the Civil War. Their neighbors to the south and north were a more consistent bunch: in southern Ohio, settled by Virginians and Kentuckians, antiblack sentiment predominated; northern Ohio, particularly the Western Reserve area, was settled by New Englanders from whose ranks emerged numerous prominent abolitionists. White Knox Countians—emigrants from Pennsylvania, Delaware, Maryland, and Virginia—expressed racial attitudes that reflected their regional origins. A few, such as the Quakers emigrating from Frederick, Maryland, to settle the community of Fredericktown, recognized slavery as an evil and came to Ohio from slaveholding states of the Upper South to be rid of its sinfulness. To these individuals, and to the Yankees who settled in small numbers in the central part of the state, the nation's African Americans were to be treated with the respect due to all.[46]

Knox Countians expressed this division of opinion in the presidential election of 1856, by which time slavery had become a central national issue. In an article entitled "Africa for Fremont," the *Banner* highlighted the significance of racial politics in the upcoming election:

A "cullud gemman," we understand, visited Mt. Liberty [a nearby town], a few days ago, and expressed a wish to obtain one of the churches to deliver a "discose." The citizens up there being good natured and obliging acceded to his wishes, and a considerable number turned out to hear what

BLACK REPUBLICANISM ILLUSTRATED!

The Editor of the Republican Carrying out his Principles,
BY MARRYING A NEGRO TO A WHITE WOMAN!

The above cut is a life-like representation of a scene which took place the other day in the editorial office of the Mt. Vernon *Republican.*— It represents WM. H. COCHRAN, Esq., the editor of that paper, as Justice of the Peace, marrying a black man to a white woman. The reader will please understand that the individual on the right hand is intended for Mr. Cochran, who, although he supports a white face, has a very black heart. The *pictur* is a magnificent illustration of Black Republicanism, and shows where the abominable doctrines advocated by Greeley, Seward, Garrison, Wendall Phillips, Wade, Chase, Wm. H. Cochran, Abby Kelley, and other opposition leaders, naturally lead to. To elevate the negro and to degrade and disfranchise white men is the great object of the party now arrayed against the Democracy. These beautiful philanthropists not only claim that the African race are entitled to the same political and social rights with white men; but whenever opportunity offers, they openly carry their accursed doctrines into practice, and advocate an amalgamation of the races!— Wonder if this kind of *fusion* is to constitute one of the planks in the next Black Republican platform?

There are hosts of good men who act with the Republican party, who, from their souls, abominate the vile doctrines of Negro Equality and Amalgamation, as practiced by W. H. Cochran; but we tell these men that unless they cut loose from the Abolitionists they will be very apt to have their morals corrupted.

Political cartoon in the June 15, 1858, Mount Vernon Democratic Banner dubbing the Republican's editor "William Cochran," the name of an Oberlin-based abolitionist. Mount Vernon's antiabolitionist press often invoked "amalgamation" as one of the terrible consequences of the Republicans' program. Ohio Historical Society, Columbus.

he had to say. He took a text from the Bible but soon launched out into a regular "Fremont, Freedom, and Fiddlesticks" harangue, which utterly disgusted nearly every person present. When he got through he invited some of "de friends of de cause" to hand round a hat and raise money for "bleeding Kansas," but not one red cent was raised! "Freedom shriekers" appear to meet with poor encouragement in Mt. Liberty! Vermont and Africa will doubtless go for Fremont, but the balance of the Union will go for Buchanan and Breckenridge.[47]

In fact, the vote in Knox County was evenly divided between the Republican Fremont and the Democrat Buchanan, with Fremont the winner by only 298 votes out of over 5,000 cast. Cincinnati's Hamilton County, by contrast, favored Buchanan over Fremont by a margin of some 40 percent, while in Cleveland's Eastern-influenced Cuyahoga County, Fremont garnered over 60 percent of the popular vote.[48]

Activists in Knox County stirred support for both sides of the slavery dilemma in the decades preceding the Civil War.[49] The *Banner* supported the colonization of African Americans in Africa as a solution to racial problems, and an agent of the American Colonization Society visited Mount Vernon in 1854.[50] Ohioans had taken interest in the relocation of blacks as early as 1815; the Ohio Colonization Society formally organized in Columbus in 1827. Although the African colony of Liberia was promoted as a black utopia, the majority of African Americans repudiated these emigration initiatives. When Ohio blacks met at a state convention in Cincinnati in 1852, they rejected a proposal for emigration by a margin of four to one.[51]

Abolitionists regularly toured a circuit that stopped in Mount Vernon, bringing together guest speakers, black and white, with local citizens in support of the cause.[52] But abolitionists sometimes met a hostile public. Two incidents at Mount Vernon's First Congregational Church, an early center for antislavery activity, involved violence so great that newlyweds Thomas and Ellen Snowden likely heard the row from their home just north of town:

In March, 1836, while Rev. W. T. Allen, a son of an Alabama slave-holder was lecturing in the basement of the church, the first mob in Mt. Vernon attacked it and the meeting was broken up, but while the crowd was being collected by the strains of martial music under a banner bearing the inscription "No Discussion," Allen escaped. While the eggs and clubs were flying and the mob was trying to put a rope around his neck with which to

drag him out and hang him, the women crowded around him and kept
the mob off, acting as a bodyguard until he got into the street. . . . The
second attack by a mob occurred in January, 1837. Prof. Wm. Cochran of
Oberlin, while addressing an anti-slavery meeting in the church was inter-
rupted by what was known as the Mt. Vernon Meat Axe Club, who by hurl-
ing stones and missiles of various sorts, smashed windows, put out lights
and succeeded in breaking up the meeting. Prof. Cochran escaped, but the
ugly crowd of marauders were so incensed at their failure to capture him
that they hastened to the home of Dr. Baxter in Miller township where he
had an appointment, assailed the house and shamefully maltreated Dr.
Baxter. The next night Prof. Cochran had an appointment at the house of
David Bixby in Pike township. Here the raiders again made an attack,
broke in the doors, struck Mr. Bixby to the floor twice and so frightened
and clubbed his wife that her life for a time was despaired of.[53]

Abolitionism appealed to some residents because they were involved
in assisting fugitive slaves. Those who escaped slavery in Virginia and
Kentucky often passed through central Ohio en route to Canada. Knox
County served as a stop on the Underground Railroad, a loosely connected
series of "stations" where fugitives might obtain safe haven, clothing, and
food before continuing their journey.[54] The Underground Railroad held
personal significance for the Snowden family: Thomas's brother Benjamin
escaped from slavery in Maryland with the aid of abolitionists. Benjamin
Snowden settled in Warsaw, New York, where he worked for the railroad
and raised a family. The New York Snowdens kept in touch with their
Ohio kin throughout their lives.[55]

In 1850 the specter of bounty-hungry slave catchers increased dramatically. Congress passed the Fugitive Slave Act that year, legally val-
idating the capture and return of runaway slaves, wherever they might be
apprehended. The act effectively placed all blacks, free or slave, in jeopardy of incriminating attack or outright seizure.[56] Blacks in Knox County
were at new peril, as they could read in the *Republican:* a black man
named Rice, living in adjacent Morrow County, "was recently induced by
false pretenses of kidnappers, to go to Columbus, where he was seized,
and forced on board the cars for Cincinnati." Rice pleaded with a U.S.
commissioner in Cincinnati to permit witnesses from Mount Gilead to cor-
roborate his free status, but he was ignored. The case was decided less
than twenty minutes after Rice appeared before the commissioner, and
U.S. marshals hurried the unfortunate man down the stairs and across the
Ohio River into Kentucky.[57]

Benjamin Snowden (right), brother of Thomas, with family members, ca. 1885. Benjamin had escaped slavery in Maryland and relocated to upstate New York by the Underground Railroad.

Particularly at risk were individuals like the Snowdens. African Americans in Ohio were safest close to home, where local whites might vouch for their identity, but as musicians the Snowdens left home frequently for days at a time, often traveling great distances before finding relative safety in the homes of friends and acquaintances. Riding by wagon along winding, isolated rural roads from morning until night, the Snowdens could never know if tragedy awaited them in their next encounter with a white person. Their friend E. D. Root wrote of his family's concern for the Snowdens' safety in light of their "account and situation," possibly a reference to their race: "We are all glad to hear from you and we are glad to hear you are all well and have got back home safe and well i hope you have done well by travelling on your account and situation i was wondering what had become of you all a few days a go and we did not know but you ware all dead."[58]

Laws governing black-white relations eventually changed, but local custom was more resistant.[59] In an episode that sealed her family's fate, Ellen Snowden held fast to the family's hard-won and still precarious social stability at the expense of her son's happiness and the continuation of the Snowden name. Ben Snowden, thirty-eight years old in 1878, courted twenty-three-year-old Nan Simpson for two years, but the affair was to have a sad ending. Nan, the white daughter of the widowed Rebecca Simpson, resided in Newville, a town virtually in the wilderness just north of the Knox County border, in Richland County.[60] Nan lived quietly, isolatedly, quilting and tending to house chores with her aged mother and aunt. Her brother Tom was a farmer, usually away during harvesting and other farm work. The bright spot in Nan's life seemed to be the infrequent but welcomed visits of Ellen Snowden and her children—her eldest daughter, Sophia, and her two sons, Ben and Lew—and the Simpsons' reciprocal journeys to the Snowden home. Ben and Lew hunted in the Newville area, and they had relationships with white farmers their own age, as Nan's brother likely was, but the actual circumstances of how the families got together are unknown.

Nan told of the news in and around her home in Newville—murders, camp meetings, get-togethers—and pressed Ben to write and visit frequently, revealing a growing affection: "oh Bennie do write to me soon I hant happy to night nor I wont be till I hear from you." Nan's wishes regarding Ben were suggested in the postscript to one letter: "May Peace and Piety you attend May you never loose nor want afriend May you have all that you Desire May you have the girl that you admire."[61]

Enticing the Snowdens to visit Newville, Nan attempted to pair Lew up with her neighbor Nancy, reporting that "this girl across the street is as good looking as ever." Nan's matchmaking efforts became rather elaborate at one point:

> Now Ben I told that girl across the street what you told me to about writing to Lew she says she will write this week I expect he will get her letter the Same day that you get this she is going to direct her letter the Same way that I do mine send it to the same box tell him to be sure and answer it just till I see how bad struck she will get for she thinks there is nobody in this world like Lew it will be fun for me to See her rejoice over his letter when She gets the answer make him write.[62]

As Ben's letters became less frequent, Nan wrote with increasing urgency about their relationship: "this is two letters I have sent to you without any answer I was afraid I had said something in my last letter that had offended you if I have I want you to tell me of it I will certainly take it back if I did say anything I did not mean to so you must forgive me for it and I will try and not do so again." The letter closed with another plea for forgiveness: "I must bring my scribbling to aclose for this time hoping you will forgive me for the past if I have done anything that is rong."[63] Nan's worries over their relationship plagued her even in the night: "I dreamed I saw you flying through the air at me and when you came to me you would not speak to me I wakened then in misery."[64]

But if the barriers between Ben and Nan were the usual interpersonal ones, they were also those of custom. For blacks, social acceptance depended on treading carefully within the well-defined limits of propriety. Ellen Snowden had much to fear from Ben's romantic breach of the social order, and she acted accordingly.[65]

Increasingly Nan's letters alluded to family conflict: "you asked me if I cared if you came up did you think that I would say anything against you or any of your family coming I would be glad to have you and Lu and mother and Sis all to come and stay aweek with us." Ellen, however, evidently objected to both Nan and her mother:

> Ben the first thing I speak about is that note you sent me about your mother talking about me calling my mother aliar I dont mind anything about it but one thing I do know I never called my mother aliar in earnest in my life. . . . I don't think I have harmed your mother that makes her so bitter against me but then I think I know what is the matter with her and

as for mother smoking she goes out of the house at home so drop that and
say no more about it.

Nan did not drop the subject, adding as a postscript, "afew words more
about that smoking business mother told me to tell you she is very sorry
about it that she offended you about it she says if she had known it she
would not have smoked at all for she likes you all."[66]

Ellen objected to the Simpsons' values and behavior. Respectable
folk, as Ellen believed her family to be, did not countenance insincerity,
infidelity to family members, and acts of public impropriety. Particularly
unseemly, especially among women, was the use of tobacco.[67] Ellen also
knew that even if she did approve of the Simpsons, the social costs of
crossing the color line were too great.

Under pressure Nan started sending her letters to Ben secretly by addressing them to "Sis," Sophia. Eventually, the strain of a clandestine relationship became too great, and Nan pleaded with Ben to burn her letters:

> Ben
> I dont know hardly how to express my thoughts to you this week: I am
> afraid your mother will find this out that I am writing to you some times I
> think if I was to go into your family she would be awfully out about it for I
> am sure she dont like me and I thought so when I was there does she rage
> so about Lew going to see that girl
>   I want you to gather up all the notes that I ever sent you and burn
> them for fear she gets aholt of them when you answer this note send it on
> paper alone for my folks never sees any of the notes that you send to me
>   so I will close again
>
>   write soon from
>   Nan
>
> Still try and make your folks come out if you can
> when you write again tell me if Lew knows if we are writeing[68]

The situation worsened for Ben and Nan. On one occasion Ben and
Lew rode through Newville without stopping for a visit: "we was told by
one of the neighbor woman here that She seen you and him go through
town and one of you looked back at the house after you had got past if
you and him go through without stopping I will know what to do if I am
ever in Vernon just do as you did go past and not stop I will try to think
of Something else."[69]

*Lew Snowden prominently displaying his African ivory-bead watch fob, ca.
1870. He posed in the distinctive garb of the Zouaves, next to his instruments:
two banjos, two tambourines, and a triangle.*

Remarkably, the Snowdens and the Simpsons did maintain their friendship. Writing to her "kind friend," Nan inquired of Ben, "now when you write tell me all the news about your girl and if you and her is married yet and if Lew is married yet."[70] More than forty years later, the elderly Ben and Lew Snowden would die as men who had never married.

At times resisting and accommodating whites' expectations, the Snowdens also asserted their African American identity in ways small and large. Most subtle of these was Lew Snowden's wearing of ivory beads from Africa. Documented in photographs from the 1860s through 1920, Lew regularly wore a beautiful string of ivory beads—the luxury goods, perhaps, of some distant African noble—quite visibly, as a broad arc of watch fob. No more regal a pose can be imagined than that of the young Lew wearing his ivory beads, surrounded by his instruments.[71] He faced the camera squarely—a man at ease, but a man certain of himself. Perhaps the beads held a source of talismanic power.[72]

Today, generations removed from the pocket of Lew Snowden, these ivory treasures bespeak a rare material connection of African Americans to African roots. They have been well tended by Marie Moorehead, whose aged eyes and hands appraise them with special affection. The beads invoke a remarkable moment in American history, when a proud black man played the banjo before whites, wearing Africa right below his heart.

5. I Wish I Was in Dixie

Now if you want to drive 'way sorrow,
Come an hear dis song to-morrow;
Look away—look 'way, away Dixie Land.
Den hoe it down an scratch yer grabble,
To Dixies land I'm bound to trabble.
Look away—look 'way, away Dixie Land.
　　　　　—"Dixie's Land" (1859)

In the 1990 public-broadcast television series "The Civil War," a sprightly flute version of the tune "Dixie" wove in and out, offset occasionally by a more rhythmic, syncopated fiddle (and occasionally mandolin) version.[1] This fiercely nonpartisan telling—or so it seemed, to our Northern ears—used "Dixie" to construct Southernness, but not the whole of Southernness. We were to focus on the manicured and stately lawn; on the quiet room in the large house where one might write poetically in a diary; on the brave rebel soldier, no older than a boy, on a doomed mission to preserve a way of life. We were not supposed to think about the South of cold irons rubbing raw the ankle of the recaptured runaway; or of the faded ink of the estate inventory listing the dollar value of Sarah and Henry, no better than cow and pig; or of the fire hose aimed against citizens with enough force to peel the bark off a tree, just a generation ago.

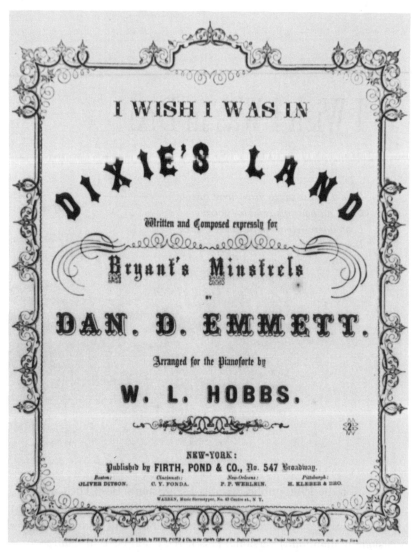

Cover of first issue of "Dixie," 1860, published by Firth, Pond & Co. Private collection.

It is not by chance that "The Civil War" rendered "Dixie" only as an instrumental number, with no vocal interpretation. The show did include "The Battle Hymn of the Republic" as a solo for voice, but in the late twentieth century, "Dixie" cannot be heard without racial overtones. Most African Americans, whose ancestors suffered under the Confederate social arrangement, hear "Dixie" as a grim reminder of hatred and acts of oppression that pierce our social fabric to the present. At least since the 1960s, an era informed by the civil rights and black identity movements, blacks have actively protested the public display of symbols of the Confederacy, "Dixie" notorious among them. In a 1966 article in *Mademoiselle* about the first group of black students at the University of Mississippi (fourteen blacks among six thousand whites), two of the subjects, Earnest Watson and Irvin Walker, discussed the insult of suffering "Dixie" at sports events:

> The most traumatic moment on these occasions is when the band blares out "Dixie." "Can you imagine what it's like," asks Irvin, "to have all these white people stand up around you for the song, and you stay sitting there, a Negro?" There have been repeated debates among them . . . about whether they should stand up for the anthem of the Old Confederacy. "It's like the alma mater here," Irvin would insist, "it's really the school song. I feel like standing up for the school song if I'm a student." Replied Earnest, "But you got to realize what it means to most of them. Sure, I wish they'd have some fight song I could stand up and cheer for. But not 'Dixie,' man. Not that one. That's the worst thing about going to the games. If they wouldn't play 'Dixie' so much, it'd be O.K." And Irvin jibed, "Next year, you watch. I'm gonna have me a rebel flag to wave and I'm gonna stand up for 'Dixie.'"[2]

Under the headline "'Dixie' Anthem, Confederate Flags Demean Citadel's Black Cadets," the *Christian Science Monitor* reported a student protest in 1967 of the playing of "Dixie" at The Citadel, the military college of South Carolina in Charleston. Black cadets attending their school's football games "had refused to play, sing, or stand for Dixie." Similar protests were made at the University of Virginia, Georgia Tech, Tulane University, and other institutions.[3] As recently as 1989, with matters not improved, students at The Citadel renewed their objections to the song.[4]

The current identification of "Dixie" exclusively with the South belies its earlier connection to Americans on both sides of the Mason-Dixon line. Dan Emmett was a confirmed Union partisan, like most minstrel perform-

ers.[5] He supposedly approved a revision of the song as a Union piece before the fall of Fort Sumter, with new words by blind hymn writer Frances
J. Crosby:

On! ye patriots to the battle,
Hear Fort Moultrie's cannon rattle!
Then away, then away, then away to the fight!
Go meet those Southern traitors,
With iron will.
And should your courage falter, boys,
Remember Bunker Hill.
  Hurrah! Hurrah! The Stars and Stripes forever!
  Hurrah! Hurrah! Our Union shall not sever![6]

In 1895, when the Confederate Veterans' Association proposed to host a
celebration in Washington to honor Emmett and his famous song, the
event was expected to warm the hearts of all Americans: "In this era of
peace between the sections . . . thousands of people from every portion of
the United States will be only too glad to unite with the ex-confederates
in the proposed demonstration, and already some of the leading men who
fought on the Union side are enthusiastically in favor of carrying out the
programme. Dixie is as lively and popular an air today as it ever was, and
its reputation is not confined to the American continent. . . . [W]herever
it is played by a big, strong band the auditors cannot help keeping time
to the music." In 1908 a columnist for the New York *Tribune* discussing
the song's transformation into "the war song of the South" noted that
"though 'Dixie' came to be looked upon as characteristically a song of the
South, the hearts of the Northern people never grew cold to it. President
Lincoln loved it, and to-day it is the most popular song in the country,
irrespective of section."[7] The *Tribune* writer, like many Americans, knew
the famous story of Lincoln's request after the surrender at Appomattox
that the band play "Dixie," "for . . . we have captured the Confederacy,
and Dixie now belongs to the Union."[8]

In 1934 a writer in the music magazine *Etude* could announce without absurdity that "the sectional sentiment attached to *Dixie* has been
long forgotten; and today it is heard everywhere—North, East, South,
West."[9] Even Emmett's gravestone, erected in 1925, freed "Dixie" from
the South by asserting that the song "inspired the courage of the Southern
people and now thrills the hearts of a reunited nation." If Americans in-

deed abandoned a regional conception of the song more than a half century ago, they have reclaimed it with a vengeance.

Dixie gained currency as a general term for the South because of the song, and the word similarly carries conflicting meanings. To some the word evokes all the problematic, race-involved associations as the song itself. For others it just means things Southern, although African Americans are not often the creators or intended receivers of this usage. For example, when the Metropolitan Council of New York City hosted a black-tie benefit for the American Craft Museum in December 1990, the publicity for the event, "A Dixie Moondance," promised (for $75 a person) "Southern-inspired music, food and decor along with a raffle of luxury items, vacation and craft objects." Neither the planners nor the participants, most of whom were whites, considered *Dixie* a word encoding racism.[10]

In his frequent interviews about the song, Emmett described *Dixie* as the showmen's term for the black South. Sheet music of Emmett's subsequent songs offered an etymology of *Dixie* as a reference to a Manhattan Island slaveowner, Dixey, who sold his charges down South. Elsewhere the word has been defined as a corruption of either the "Dixon" of the Mason-Dixon line or *dix*, Louisiana's ten-dollar note. White minstrels considered "Dixie" only a general locale, "the negro's paradise on earth."[11]

Almost immediately, "Dixie" achieved the status of a classic, at home and worldwide. In the Civil War era, "whistling 'Dixie'" sometimes meant putting your sectional sentiment where your mouth was:

Henry Hale, one of the best scouts in the country, left Leavenworth . . . with despatches. . . . He saw one old secessionist with a little shot-gun, and thought it would be a nice thing to drive off the fellow, and take his horse into Lexington. So he engaged the man in conversation, and getting an opportunity, put his revolver to the secessionist's head, ordered him to tie his gun to the saddle, to dismount, and finally to skedaddle. The old man made tracks rapidly, glad to escape with his life. Hale took the horse by the bridle, and rode on whistling "Yankee Doodle." He had ridden a mile or two, when at a turn of the road, he was suddenly ordered to halt. The old secessionist had procured another gun, and got ahead of him. The gun was squarely aimed at Hale's head. "Get off that horse," cried the secessionist. Hale got down. "Tie that revolver to the saddle." He obeyed. "Pull off your pants." Hale did it. "Skedaddle!" an order which Hale at once carried into effect, merely saying, "Well, Captain, I thought my shirt would come next—good-bye." The secessionist went off with the two horses, whistling "Dixie;" while Hale marched seven miles into Lexington, with only his coat and shirt on. His coat contained his despatches. He will never be permitted to forget that seven miles' march.[12]

One hundred years later, the place of "Dixie" in the American musical firmament was no less secure. Hans Nathan, Dan Emmett's biographer, oddly defined what makes the song quintessentially American, but he rightly conveyed its rootedness in the stratum of common folk:

> The longevity of "Dixie" is due chiefly to its inherent qualities as a work of art, modest and unpretentious though it may be. . . . The tune is characterized by a heavy, nonchalant, inelegant strut. . . . If music, lyrics, and dance style are taken as an entity, there emerges a special kind of humor that mixes grotesqueness with lustiness and down-to-earth contentment—comparable, to overstate the case, to a blend of Brueghel and Mickey Mouse. These specific qualities could have been developed nowhere but in the United States. And for this reason, "Dixie" may be called one of the most American musical products of the nineteenth century.[13]

Perhaps unconsciously, Nathan drew a suggestive link between Disney's mouse and minstrel music, but it isn't hard to see their affinities. Of the many examples of minstrelsy's enduring legacy in popular culture, "Dixie" can confidently be assigned top spot on the music charts, and surely Mickey Mouse is the most graphic offspring of blackface minstrels' portrayals of the plantation slave. Black, wide-eyed, childlike, falsetto-voiced, and ever the clown, Mickey Mouse even takes his costuming from the burnt-cork brotherhood: see the oversized white gloves, suspender buttons (minus suspenders), big feet, coy stance. The mouse first minced across a screen in 1928 in the classic *Steamboat Willie*, roughly one hundred years after blacks were first cartooned by white "Ethiopian delineators" in the circus ring. Those isolated, occasional performances were radically and forevermore transformed in 1843, when Dan Emmett created an entire evening of performance by his Virginia Minstrels (all Northerners).

"Dixie," star of the minstrel stage if not the silver screen, carries a history more complex and emotionally charged than its celluloid rodent cousin. This wonderful tune and its frequently amended text occupy a battleground of contested meanings, as surely as it once held forth in those terrible blood-soaked fields of our national discord. At various times it has rallied Union soldiers against the secessionists, and vice versa; cheered the presidencies of both Abraham Lincoln and Jefferson Davis; elicited standing ovations from both the abolitionist Republicans and proslavery Democrats in Congress. Generations of African Americans have been enraged and offended by "Dixie"; others, in a small community in central Ohio, have claimed the song as an authentic product of black tradition.

And, for an untold number of Americans, "Dixie" is no more than the aural version of Mickey Mouse. Like "Turkey in the Straw" and "Arkansas Traveler," "Dixie" is Foghorn Leghorn music, evoking nothing more than the sound track for Saturday morning cartoons on television. To see "Dixie" as chicken music is, of course, to appreciate not its anthemlike appeal but its connection to an inelegant, parodic, dialect-ridden medium, the minstrel show.

The first audience for blackface minstrelsy, working-class city folk only a shade better off than their stage caricatures, came not just to laugh and enjoy the music but to gather something about their position in the new social landscape of America.[14] Minstrels offered songs, dances, jokes, and oratory targeted, at first, at the plantation slave, but the enterprise of representing "the other" onstage bespoke concerns beyond the theatrical scrim: how subgroups in economic and social friction as never before might cohere into Americans, and what the new social hierarchy would and should look like. The solution of minstrelsy, as it would be for generations of popular entertainments, was to represent the "other" in stereotype. Before long, stage depictions of blacks resolved into stock characterizations, joined by the German, Irish, Chinese, and Jew as types, laughable and comfortingly inferior.

Blacks, too, entered the minstrel theater as spectators, eventually joining the burnt-cork fraternity as entertainers. That blacks could actually smear on blackface to participate in this confirmedly parodic medium tells much about the production and control of arts. It tells a story of limited opportunity for blacks as theater artists, with few other venues for their talents; it suggests that black artists might have wished to control and moderate the images of blacks onstage; it reminds us that a given song or dance or piece of oratory, even from the minstrel stage, carries not one meaning but a host of possible meanings, depending on who produces it, who receives it, and for whom it is intended.[15]

"Dixie" has always been understood as a minstrel parody and not an actual documentation of black experience, but the Snowden headstone invites us to read the song for its relevance to African Americans in the last century:

Ben   Lew
Snowden

Placed by the local black American Legion as a gesture of respect, perhaps of redress, during the bicentennial[16]—a time when Ohio's small towns were loading up on fireworks supplies and painting the fire hydrants to resemble Uncle Sam—the Snowden brothers' headstone, unlike "Dixie," is unambiguous. It forcefully contradicts the contemporary view, voiced by music historian Norm Cohen, that "of 'Dixie,' we need only note that it was composed by the white minstrel performer Daniel Decatur Emmett, and had little, if any, inspiration from ante-bellum black folksong."[17]

Complicating the issue of authorship of "Dixie" and other minstrel songs is the fluid process by which blackface minstrels found and created music, dance, and texts for use onstage. If "authenticity" was something to boast about in representing plantation blacks, so was originality. Emmett's own words about writing "Dixie," for example, are inconsistent and dramatic, the stuff of legend: sequestered in a room of his New York apartment, under pressure, Emmett came up with this glorious walk-around in one tortured night, or in a matter of minutes, or over a few days. The basic story is that Jerry Bryant, who had hired Emmett to write songs for his minstrel troupe, told Emmett on a Saturday night that he needed a new walk-around on Monday morning, and Emmett wrote the song on one rainy Sunday evening. Emmett elsewhere ornamented the account to emphasize how swiftly the song emerged once he had hit on the opening line: "Suddenly, . . . I jumped up and sat down at the table to work. In less than an hour I had the first verse and chorus. After that it was easy." A newspaper clipping from 1895 declared that "it was very hastily composed, and was gotten up within three days to be tried at a performance at which Emmett was to do one of his popular walk arounds." In another report Emmett looked out the window, thought "I wish I was in Dixie," and, "Like a flash the thought suggested the first line for a walk-around, and a little later the minstrel, fiddle in hand, was working out the melody." In 1903 Emmett gave this version to a reporter from his hometown newspaper, later printed in Emmett's front-page obituary in July 1904: "I was standing by the window, gazing out at the drizzly, raw day, and the old circus feeling came over me. I hummed the old refrain 'I wish I was in Dixie,' and the inspiration struck me. I took my pen and in ten minutes had written the first verses with music. The remaining verses were easy."[18]

Complicating the tale of how he wrote the song, Emmett late in his life told people in Minnesota, where he was visiting his brother Lafayette, that he had written the song years before he came to New York.[19]

Emmett's accounts described a breathtaking fit of original composition, yet minstrel performers routinely claimed that they derived their material from the authentic arts of black people. Emmett referred to "I wish I was in Dixie" as an "old refrain" from the circus; more suggestive, given the Snowden story, is his announcement that "I heard an old colored man down south say 'I Wish I Were in Dixie.'" Robert Toll aptly summarizes this fundamental contradiction about the creative processes of minstrelsy: "Although blackface performers rarely credited specific material to blacks because they wanted to be known as creative artists as well as entertainers, many early minstrels claimed that they did 'field work' among Southern Negroes while they were traveling."[20]

For generations some residents of Knox County have told a story that corroborates this process (in the North, not the South), with Emmett as the borrower and the Snowden family as the local sources. The significance of this linkage cannot be overstated; other than the minstrels' self-serving claims, scholars of the early decades of minstrelsy have found little to confirm their theories of how these white performers found, used, and modified black arts.

By asserting that the Snowden brothers *taught* the song "Dixie," not that they wrote it, Ben and Lew's headstone stresses the family's role as musical resources rather than composers. Letters and other requests asking for songs confirm this view: in writing to ask for "their" music, no one ever voiced a distinction between songs the Snowden family composed and songs they picked up elsewhere. When Alta Scott promised Ben and Lew that she would send a song and asked in turn for "some of yours"; and when she asked Ben for "some Of your pieces send us the Golden slippers and There is meeting here to Night and In the Morning By the bright light"; and when Bell Blair asked Sophia for "that song called goodby and an other you sang"; and when Nan Simpson asked Ben to send her neighbor "that song gathering up the shells"; and when Reuben Oliver asked Ben for "the best song you can think of," authorship was an irrelevant concept. What these correspondents wanted, clearly, was a song from the family's repertoire, no matter its provenance.

This informal, orally based exchange of music speaks of a context very different from the professional theatrical culture in which Dan Emmett was immersed. Mount Vernon's black residents continue to express a

vision of collaborative, not individualistic, composition when they reflect
on the relationship between Dan Emmett and the Snowdens. (Notably,
most residents who link them are unaware that a pile of letters confirms
precisely this sort of musical exchange.) In the words of George Booker:
"Musicians are all interrelated, and they do a lot of things. Maybe one guy
likes this real well and say, 'Well, I'll take that.' And then another one will
say, 'Let me have this one, and I'll do this for my show.' Maybe that's the
way a lot of things go back and forth." He imagines the exchange between
Dan Emmett and the Snowdens as informal, spontaneous, and creative,
relatively free of concern over ownership. For Booker, then, the very question of who wrote "Dixie" is a misunderstanding of the process in which
musicians create and share. He admits to having heard, over the past forty
years, that "maybe the musicians copied each others' ideas. . . . Say, 'let's
do it this way, do it that way, do it this way,' and then maybe one person
will finish a complete thing. But as far as only controversy and hearsay
that Dan Emmett was helped along the way by the Snowdens to write
'Dixie' . . . that's not confirmed fact—we don't know, do we?"[21]

Marie Moorehead, the senior local historian of the Mount Vernon
black community, now a resident of Columbus, also credits "Dixie" as
a collaboration between Emmett and the Snowdens: "He [Emmett] had
probably gotten a lot of it from the Snowdens." And Ethel Hammond,
pianist for the A.M.E. Church, now deceased, voiced this theme in the
Mount Vernon News in 1967: "I remember reading old music magazines
and seeing the song with his [Emmett's] name on it. I would imagine the
Snowden brothers had something to do with Emmett writing the song,
though." Marie had saved the Hammond article, referring to it when she
described which part of "Dixie" her black friends credited to the Snowdens: "Well, it's the words in particular that they feel the Snowdens, they
say, a lot of them believe; now that lady's picture there [Ethel Hammond],
she said that it was at the time, well, people said that Dan Emmett was
never in the South. Now, *why* would he write a song like that? And she
said they [local blacks] were *sure* that the words came from, they'd heard,
the Snowdens."[22]

Townspeople take this process as part of an ongoing friendship between Emmett and the Snowdens. Marie Moorehead ventures that the
Snowdens "probably felt that he [Emmett] was their friend." George
Booker says, "I dare say he [Emmett] was their friend. It was a good relationship between the two because they had music in common for one thing
and humanity . . . for another. You respond to people who treat you right;

News Photo

EMMETT MEMORIES — Mrs. Ethel J. Hammond, 79, of 110 E. Ohio Ave. plays a few tunes on her organ piled high with gospel sheet music that she plays on Sundays at a local church. She is one of the few remaining Mount Vernon citizens who remembers Dan Emmett during his last years in town.

Local Woman Recalls
Times of Dan Emmett

An August 2, 1967, Mount Vernon News *feature on Ethel Hammond, a black Mount Vernon resident who suggested that the Snowdens had helped in the writing of "Dixie." Ohio Historical Society, Columbus.*

had he not been a good friend of theirs, why no doubt [they] wouldn't have been playing and doing things together."[23]

Community members suppose the Snowdens were involved partly because they disbelieve Emmett's claim of writing "Dixie" virtually spontaneously. "Dixie" was the only song he made this claim about, and nothing in his career indicated a gift for extomporuniinus song making. In fact, Emmett's vast manuscript collection in the state library in Columbus offers exactly the opposite evidence: Emmett, a meticulous copyist, spent countless hours collecting and composing songs and sayings for the minstrel stage, complete with stage directions and costuming ideas; little evidently was left for the improvisational moment. Marie Moorehead is one who finds the sudden creation of "Dixie" unbelievable: "[A] young man, who used to go to school here, he told me that he read where Dan Emmett was supposed to write—what they call—at the end of a show—what did they call it? Yeah, the walk-around. And they wanted a song at the end of the show, and *Dan Emmett wrote that overnight* [vocal emphasis]. . . . *And they said that he wrote it overnight!*" [disbelief in voice].[24]

Black residents do say that the Snowdens were improvisational song makers, in contrast, linking them with long-standing African and African American artistic processes. George Booker recounted how the Snowden Family Band improvised its secular material, after describing their sacred pieces: "The other ones, I know no doubt they compose[d] as they went along to maybe fit an occasion that they wanted to do." Crediting the Snowdens with partial authorship of "Dixie," Ethel Hammond then explained how they might have composed it improvisationally: "Why, Negroes make up many songs by sitting around and humming a tune and tapping their feet. Pretty soon we end up singing, and a song is born."[25] Hammond's understanding of black music may sound stereotypical, but in fact she identified the well-documented tradition of improvisation among Africans and African Americans. One of the earliest popular representations of plantation life, the novel *The Valley of Shenandoah*, published in 1824, mentioned slaves' improvisational song making during a corn-shucking event: "Some one . . . strikes up, and singly gives a few rude stanzas, sometimes in rhyme, and sometimes in short expressive sentences, while the rest unite in chorus, and this he continues, until some other improvisatore relieves him." Thomas Wentworth Higginson, a song collector and the colonel of the 1st Regiment, South Carolina Volunteers—the first black regiment to serve in the Civil War—recorded a similar process in the Sea Islands of South Carolina in the early 1860s; a black oarsman told Higginson: "'Den I made a sing, just puttin' a word, and den annuder word.' Then he began singing, and the men, after listening a moment, joined in the chorus as if it were an old acquaintance, though they evidently had never heard it before. I saw how easily a new 'sing' took root among them." In his broad analysis of slavery, historian Eugene Genovese noted: "Visitors [to plantations] expressed wonder at the spontaneity and improvisation the slaves displayed. The songs, often made up on the spot, bristled with sharp wit, both malicious and gentle."[26]

Improvisation, guided by its close companion rhythm, is the heart of all great African and African-derived arts, from weaving to architecture, from music and dance to oratory. African American fiddling and banjo music, the Snowdens' music, is highly rhythmic and improvisatory in structure. Emmett, however, like his fellow minstrels, was a descendant of a strongly melodic, text-bound musical tradition. Anglo-Irish folksingers and fiddlers use ornamentation more than improvisation to modify lyric or melody. Emmett may have varied his fiddling on the minstrel stage from night to night, or digressed into the repartee with the audience that marked lowbrow theater from its high-toned sister, but he was not an improvisational artist. Even his status as a professional composer and performer limited improvisation: Emmett could obtain copyright on only one version of a song, no matter how it varied in actual performance, and onstage he was obliged to render his published songs reasonably like their sheet-music versions or else risk disappointment—even abuse—from the crowd.

Cultural preferences also guide how artists document and preserve their work, and here, too, the Snowdens differed greatly from Emmett. Emmett worked hard at his penmanship, as his subsequent admirers noted,[27] and his voluminous copying of material was in keeping with Western European theatrical traditions. In contrast, Thomas and Ellen Snowden's children, literate people from an oral tradition, evidently exchanged lyrics in writing (although they knew nothing of musical notation), yet only one handwritten composition by the Snowdens is extant. Such an omission stems not from carelessness but from their particular approach to their music, which we might characterize as guardianship rather than ownership. Indeed, the Snowdens were unusually careful keepers of the stuff of their heritage, from Lew's African ivory beads to their scrapbook to their wealth of correspondence; they even preserved the black dresses worn by Ellen, displaying them in the bedroom for nearly thirty years after her death.[28] We may regard it as a tragic loss that their compositions, save one, never made it materially to the present, but the family was simply not oriented toward royalties, repute in posterity, or promotion in the way popular artists of that time surely were. As church folk, perhaps the Snowdens also felt their gifts and their songs were the property not of mortals but of their Maker.

Mount Vernon's black residents believe that Dan Emmett had access to the music of the Snowden family by way of Ben and Lew. Of course, it was not hard to gather material from them, since they publicly performed a broad repertoire of songs and tunes and regularly sent lyrics to correspondents. To link Emmett to this network, however, requires placing him in time and space with the family. Here we reintroduce Thomas and Ellen Snowden, because if any music was shared between Emmett and the Snowdens before the 1859 debut of "Dixie" on Broadway, the Snowden parents are the likely participants. Oral historians have found that community memory often is off by a generation—actions may be ascribed to the individuals memorable within the informants' own lifetimes, even when the actual participants are one generation removed in time.[29] For example, a person might say that her great-grandfather was freed from slavery when it was actually the great-great-grandfather. A similar elision may obtain in the Snowden-Emmett story: Sophia, Ben, and Lew were youngsters when Emmett was a professional minstrel, but the Snowden parents were age peers to Emmett—Ellen was two years younger, and Thomas was thirteen years older.

Dan Emmett's maternal grandparents, Daniel and Sarah Zerrick, had settled in Clinton in 1806.[30] Their land was adjacent to the Snowden farm. Emmett's family had another long-standing connection to the African American community: Emmett's birthplace was a modest house on Ohio Avenue (then called Front Street), also the home address for generations of black people and of the A.M.E. Church. Emmett's father, Abraham, operated his blacksmith business on Front Street.[31] The Snowdens kept horses—Ben and Lew were to become competitive racehorse drivers—and, like many country people, they came to town for shoeing. Then, the blacksmith's shop was a place where men talked about horses, told lies, took a respite from the day's chores, and even played a little music. Was it in the dim light of a dirt-floor blacksmith shop that the musician-farmer Thomas Snowden whistled the tune Dan Emmett would make world famous? Abe Emmett's place already is legendary as the site that summoned minstrelsy into being—there, one story goes, a traveling

*The retirement home of Dan Emmett, ca. 1900. Emmett built the modest dwell-
ing on a part of the Zerrick family homestead, adjacent to the Snowden property. Ohio Historical Society, Columbus.*

troupe that needed a fill-in discovered and hired the young fiddler Dan
Emmett, an experience that inspired him to become a professional musician.[32]

    To construct a scenario of contact between Emmett and the Snow-
dens, we need to improve on the sparse details available concerning
Emmett's whereabouts between the 1830s and 1859. The standard biographical record notes his army stint and circus travels in the 1830s, his
arrival in New York City in the 1840s, and his eventual engagement with
Bryant's Minstrels in the late 1850s, but virtually nothing has been published documenting Emmett traveling back home to Knox County, where

his family and friends remained.[33] Except by way of the mail, Emmett could have learned "Dixie" from the Snowdens only by visiting Knox County.

Here we turn to a fascinating unpublished biography of Emmett, handwritten in 1935 by a distant relative and family friend, May McClane. May's maternal aunt was the sister-in-law of Martha Emmett Lewis, Dan Emmett's sister, a piano teacher and singer in Mount Vernon. The writer, herself from a musical family, described Emmett as a local dance fiddler after he left the army in 1835: "He then returned home and for a time secured occasional engagements to play the violin for Barn Dances in the country and villages all over Knox Co. O. and in adjoining counties enabling him to earn a little money." Elsewhere McClane recounted how her family members met Emmett and formed a bond because they all were musicians. Her uncle, John Newton Lewis, met the minstrel in the 1840s; her father, David Rittenhouse McClane, met Emmett in 1856 in Mount Vernon and took drumming lessons from him in 1857. McClane noted that this tutorial "was actually pursued for the reason that my father knew Mr. Emmett would not be home long, and that he must make every moment count. . . . He and Dan Emmett were in the same drum corps many times to play for military affairs." She also cited visits to Mount Vernon by Emmett and his first wife, Catherine, from 1852 through the 1860s. McClane's most dramatic story of Emmett as an active musician in the county involved his role as the foremost fiddler at the *infare*, a postnuptial party featuring a supper and square dance. Throughout the 1850s, McClane wrote, Knox County couples set the dates of their infares expressly to secure Emmett as the fiddler, as her own parents had in 1862:

> In the 1850s and 1860s it had become fashionable to set the time of the infare some distant day following the wedding. . . . Immediate preparations were begun for their [her parents'] infare. The first of all was to write to Dan Emmett in New York City, telling him of their marriage as he was a friend of my mother's from her childhood and of my father from 1856, and asking him to name a date when he could come to Mount Vernon, to play for the dancing at their party. In 1861, it took almost a week for a letter to go to New York and receive an answer in return. . . . It would have been a keen disappointment if he had not been able to come for this wonderful event, for he and he alone had played for the dances at the infares of many of my relatives, no less than six couples that I am positively sure of. And not in my relationship alone, but for dozens of people here and in

the county. If you could not get Dan Emmett to play for your wedding, you simply were "out of luck." And it was not always easy to get him, because of his increasing engagements thruout the years when he was more often away from home than at home. Tho he came often as he could, his visits were not long ones, only in his vacations and many a couple set their wedding date in those times when he was sure to be here.[34]

If he was in town when the Snowdens were active performers—by the mid-1850s—Emmett no doubt would have found out about them, had he not known the family from earlier times. He was, after all, in the business of representing blacks onstage and an avid collector. Why would he *not* have helped himself to the music of talented black acquaintances? As Robert Toll notes, early blackface performers "had ample opportunity to learn about black music, dance, and lore while traveling widely in the South and West before minstrelsy became a sedentary, urban form. They were constantly on the lookout for material to construct unique stage acts with a strong folk appeal." Perhaps Emmett confirmed his own "fieldwork" in this statement about how minstrel companies might have discovered "Dixie" and added it to their repertoires: "Show people generally, if not always, have a chance to hear every local song as they pass through the different sections of [the] country, and particularly so with minstrel companies, who are always on the look out for songs and sayings that will answer their business."[35] Certainly, Emmett would have known that the Snowden repertoire—like the Snowdens themselves—was likely to remain in obscurity, confined to rural towns far from the East Coast minstrel theaters.

Admittedly, the flow of music in the minstrel era was bidirectional. If minstrel songs sprang from sources in black folk culture, they also flowed quickly back into the repertoires of amateur musicians nationwide, black and white. A Swedish visitor to South Carolina in 1850, for example, heard slaves singing songs she supposed to be "peculiarly improvisations" and then proceeded to name them, unaware that they were chestnuts from minstrel composers Stephen Foster and James Bland: "Susanna," "Old Uncle Ned," "Carry Me Back to Old Virginny," and so on.[36] Yet we wonder whether the overlap in the repertoires of Dan Emmett and the Snowdens is merely coincidental. Several songs in the Emmett manuscript collection were also in the Snowden repertoire, according to the family's correspondents: "Hupde Duden Do," "We Are Coming Sister Mary," "Captain Jinks," and "20 Years Ago" (for the Snowdens, "Forty Years Ago").[37]

Might Emmett have learned such songs from the Snowdens, just as they might have built their repertoire partly from the popular phenomenon of minstrelsy?

Emmett did compose songs based on the people and places he knew in Knox County. His tune "Walk Mr. Bookar" may have been inspired by acquaintance with the Booker family, longtime black residents of the county; George Booker's mother received the aged Emmett in her home frequently.[38] Emmett also composed the "Seely Simpkins Jig," named after the county's first fiddler, born in 1799, who "frequented race tracks, and drew crowds and supplied hoe-downs on demand"; when Thomas Snowden acquired the land for his homestead in the 1820s, Simpkins's place was immediately adjacent.[39] Emmett's "Owl Creek Quickstep" named one of Knox County's earliest settlements.[40]

Emmett may well have had the opportunity to use material from the Snowdens, and he did refer to Mount Vernon themes in his compositions. Why, then, would he have failed to credit the black sources of "Dixie"? The simplest answer is that acknowledging collaboration or borrowing in what proved to be the hit song of America could only have damaged Emmett professionally. Bryant's Minstrels hired Emmett specifically to compose songs for the troupe, and as one of those songs, "Dixie" was to be credited as an Emmett creation pure and simple, whatever its inspiration. Furthermore, Emmett understood his precarious position as a delineator of black arts: however "authentic" white minstrels might claim to be, they were consigned forever to be imitations of the real McCoy. Why invoke comparison by identifying a particular family of blacks in regard to "Dixie"? The foremost white minstrel dancer of the 1840s, John Diamond, learned this lesson when the great black dancer William Henry Lane, known as Juba, beat him soundly in a series of dance competitions. Minstrels who made any claim of debuting material taken from blacks preferred to describe their sources in the most general of terms, repeating stories of chance meetings with unnamed riverboat workers or street performers. Beyond Lane, fewer than a handful of black artists associated with white minstrels were identified in their time, or even by later researchers.[41]

If an investment in seeming original could have been a barrier to identifying the Snowdens, so might have been its exact opposite: some early minstrels, like Emmett, may have been quite unconcerned with staking originality because they routinely borrowed and refashioned material for their purposes. Kathryn Reed-Maxfield refers to the "multiple versions of tunes and texts, the cross-breeding of songs within the repertory, and the presence of common textual and musical formulas" as evidence of minstrelsy's oral composition and transmission.[42] As a musician creating in the oral tradition, therefore, Emmett would not have felt compelled to identify which parts of "his" music he derived from other musicians, including the Snowdens.

Some of Mount Vernon's black residents address this question differently. They simply ascribe to Dan Emmett a certain shabbiness of character that would have enabled him to hide the song's source in the Snowden repertoire. Remembering him as an old man, some senior citizens retain an image of an impoverished eccentric who wandered around town with his coat tied shut with a rope. Vera Payne, age ninety-three when we spoke to her by phone at her home in Columbus, said that George Booker's family received Emmett in their home, a relationship furthered by the Bookers' renown as musicians; George's mother, Vera noted, was "quite a pianist," and his father was "a great singer." Vera "used to hear his [George's] mother talk about Dan Emmett, . . . told how he dressed: in wintertime had an old battered coat with a rope tied around his waist." Mount Vernon resident Stella Lee remembered Emmett as a drunk who "didn't take care of his family"; for her the idea that he could have failed to credit the Snowdens as sources for "Dixie" simply meshed with his questionable reputation.[43]

Finally, Mount Vernon's black people accept the idea that the Snowdens were responsible for "Dixie" because the song, notorious for its variety of meanings, can be read as a document of black experience in the hostile North. Frederick Douglass singled out Ohio, because of its "villainous black laws," as among the most inhospitable environments for blacks above the Mason-Dixon line.[44] William Diggs, born in 1912, a self-trained black historian of Charles County, Maryland, believes that the song recorded the personal stress of life up North and the grief of separation from family and friends still down South. Diggs maintains a private black history museum, housed in an elementary school only minutes from the place where Ellen Cooper was born. On the first visit with him, and well before we had announced to Diggs our interest in examining "Dixie" as an item of black experience, one of the authors noticed the display of sheet music for "Dixie" inside a showcase of nineteenth-century black memorabilia. As surprising as it was to find it there, even more surprising was Diggs's

immediate explanation, "You know that 'Dixie' was written by blacks."
On a later visit he elaborated on his idea, asserting that "Dixie" was born
from the "storm of prejudice" blacks encountered up North:

> Well, you see, to my opinion, which I know that my opinion is halfway
> right, if not entirely right, about the feeling of black people being taken
> away or driven away or have to run away from their home, and go to an-
> other strange place, and a cold place, and could not make a living there.
> And they were still treated, in a place that's called the Northern states,
> worse than they were in the Southern states. And therefore they ran into a
> storm of prejudice. A storm everywhere they went: "I don't want you to
> live in my community, I don't want you to work on my job, I don't want
> my children to play with your children." There was a storm, a prejudice
> storm. Therefore, when they got back in Dixie, where they came from, the
> children could play together, and the parents were happy, and they could
> sing their songs, and dance, and do whatever they wanted to do.[45]

George Booker likewise offers the South's warm climate, literally and
figuratively, and the music there as reasons why blacks might have written "Dixie":

> Well, South is warm. There were warm relationships there though they
> was suffering, and there were good times, too. Why wouldn't you, if maybe
> you were living in a cabin, and it was in the middle of winter, and you
> think about [Southern states] . . . and maybe through all the things you
> went through, you might be going through some tough times *here*, so
> might as well be *there* as be here. . . . Home's home, and maybe their roots
> were there, so to speak; even back in those days the old master let his peo-
> ple have land and so forth . . . and then the move came on and they got
> squeezed out a lot of times, they had no place to return to—yes, maybe
> they could have went, said, "I wish I was in the land of cotton, old times
> there are not forgotten," and they had a lot of good times. They had fiddle
> players, guitar players, banjo players, and hoedowns . . . a lot of laughter
> and good times. Yes, I can see why that song would be written.[46]

Hans Nathan decoded "Dixie" by establishing connections between
Emmett's lyrics and similar examples from the body of minstrel tunes,
treating the text as wholly a fiction.[47] Here, however, we shall take a different approach and read "Dixie" line by line against the biography of one
black woman, Ellen Cooper Snowden. Could "Dixie" be Ellen's protest?

She had endured more than her share of trials and separations at the hands of white folks, and, as Lawrence Levine notes (albeit in regard to the early twentieth century), "[African American] music has been a crucial and perhaps central vehicle for the expression of discontent and protest."[48] What, for example, was her state of mind on the morning in 1836 when Colonel John Greer read aloud a letter from her aging father, still a slave in Nanjemoy along with her brother and her old friends? How did it make her feel to read of the warm wishes from those people dearest to her, people she knew she would never see again? Did Ellen despair of her dislocation from the thriving black community of Nanjemoy, Maryland— the largest concentration of blacks in America—to an Ohio village in which she saw almost no black faces? Did she recall her girlhood days in Charles County, when she stepped around the crab carcasses along the Potomac and watched the boats sail off with a freedom she could only imagine? Beyond the bonds of affection, free blacks held legitimate fears for the well-being of family and friends still in slavery. Indeed, despite Alexander Greer's expressed intention to free Henry Cooper and his fellow slaves, by Greer's death in 1839 laws had been enacted against manumission in response to the Southampton revolt.

"Dixie" can also be read as protest by way of parody. Ellen was the direct inheritor of a tradition of using satire and irony in songs to comment on one's social environment. European travelers in Africa had long noted these elements of public singing.[49] On these shores enslaved African Americans used ironic language to ridicule those who controlled their lives, the master and mistress. The critic Henry Louis Gates, Jr., points out that in black song the producer has a crucial role in determining meaning; in effect, slave singing sometimes carried double meanings, understood differently by slave and nonslave listeners.[50] Where the master heard words of praise or burlesque, the slave intended critique, and other slaves heard that message. Among the earliest documentations of satirizing by Africans in America—and the first use of the word *banjo* to describe the gourdlike instrument used for accompanying songs—was Nicholas Cresswell's report of a "Negro ball" in Nanjemoy in 1774, the very place and era of Ellen's father's birth: "In their songs they generally relate the usage they have received from their Masters or Mistresses in a very satirical stile and manner." Frederick Douglass, an age peer to Ellen who was likewise enslaved in tidewater Maryland, recorded improvised dancing and music making at which "a sharp hit was given to the meanness of the slaveholders," citing as an example the following song:

> We raise de wheat,
> Dey gib us de corn;
> We bake de bread,
> Dey gib us de crust;
> We sif' de meal,
> Dey gib us de huss;
> We peel de meat,
> Dey gib us de skin;
> And dat's de way
> Dey take us in. . . .[51]

In placing Ellen Snowden in this tradition, we take it as significant that Gates identifies Cresswell's report as one of the earliest North American examples of *Signification,* the African American linguistic and poetic tradition (involving indirection, innuendo, satire, insult, and more) by which blacks "literally [define] themselves in language."[52] These strategies belong as much to speakers and singers as they do to writers, a point worth remembering in light of Ellen's illiteracy. As Joanne Braxton has observed: "Not all the texts in the literary tradition of black American women were written down. . . . 'Often in the most oppressive situations, it is the memories of mothers handed down through the daughters that keeps a community together. The mother tongue is not just the words or even the array of cultural symbols available to a people to resist its tormentors. The mother tongue *is* the oral tradition.'"[53]

It is surprisingly easy to read "Dixie" as a text composed from a girl's perspective, filled as it is with references to personalities and items in the domestic sphere—particularly food preparation and the life of the "Missus." However, this exercise is designed not to declare Ellen Snowden the author of "Dixie" but to examine this song text—once so familiar, now approaching obscurity—for its possible expression of an African American, female perspective on the Southern social world. And so we return to Charles County, land of Ellen's birth and seat of colonial aristocracy.

> *I wish I was in de land ob cotton,*
> *'Cimmon seed and sandy bottom,*
> *Look away—look 'way, away Dixie Land*[54]

"Cotton" was king in the Deep South, of course, but even within Charles County's tobacco economy it played an important role. Slaves used cotton for weaving, one of the tasks assigned to young girls, and sewed clothing from cotton raised on the farm. An 1866 atlas of Maryland noted, "And in the Southern counties—with a very mild climate—corn and other grain, and the more tender and early vegetables, large crops of sweet potatoes and considerable cotton for domestic use were raised."[55] "'Cimmon seed" refers to the persimmon, a fruit tree listed as early as 1800 as a regional fruit in Charles County and still prevalent; the current map of the county shows Persimmon Point jutting into the Potomac. Plantation children would collect persimmons for their seed after the frost, which turned the fruit sweet. "'Cimmon seed" could also be a corruption of *Simpson's seed*, a reference to Simpson, the Greer estate; the phrase thus might be using a metonym to identify the song maker as the seed of Alexander Greer. We have raised this speculation about Ellen Cooper previously, in the discussion of why Greer might have sent her north. "Sandy bottom" denotes wet lowland, common in Charles County and other farming regions in the South. Charles County's sandy bottomland was too soft to support the building of roads, rendering the homesteads relatively isolated and autonomous. Numerous references to the sandy soil in Nanjemoy can be found in local history and even on the map: Sandy Point Road runs east-west just above the road to Smith's Point, where Ellen Cooper was born; and the one-room Sandyfield School, now defunct, had stood at the heart of Nanjemoy "on a very sandy knoll. . . . The roads were a sea of mud during winter."[56] "Look away . . . Dixie Land" instructs us that the perspective is clearly from a Northern resident looking back toward home, toward the South. "Dixie Land" had a precise meaning for some blacks—not a general locale, as the white minstrels thought of it, but a particular place, probably the place of enslavement. In this Civil War–era anecdote, a black man expresses horror at the idea of going back to Dixie:

I sat in my tent-door thoughtfully, but very thoughtlessly humming "Dixie." I had not observed "Charles," a servant, or "contraband," here, who sat just within the tent.

"We stop a-singin' dat song now, massa!" said he, interrupting me.

"Why?" I inquired.

Charles was confused for a moment, but I pressed the question.

"Well," he replied hesitatingly, "it don't b'long to my perfession, sir; dat's all, I s'pose.—I don't wish I was in Dixie, I'se sure!" continued he.

"None o de niggers does; you may bet your soul o' dat!"

"Where is Dixie, Charles?"

"'S Norfolk—*dat's* what 'tis," was the indignant reply. "Kills de nig-gers in Dixie, jist like sheep, a-working in de batteries!"[57]

> *In Dixie land whar I was born in,*
> *Early on one frosty mornin;*

"Frosty mornin" echoes the autumn season invoked earlier by "'Cimmon seed." Slaves seldom knew their birth date and instead marked their birth by the agricultural seasons, as Africans did. Frederick Douglass noted: "I do not remember to have ever met a slave who could tell of his birthday. They seldom come nearer to it than planting-time, harvest-time, cherry-time, spring-time or fall-time. A want of information concerning my own was a source of unhappiness to me even during childhood."[58] "Early on one frosty mornin" is a similar date marker.

> *Den I wish I was in Dixie, Hooray, Hooray,*

This line may be ironic, remarkably like a couplet that Frederick Douglass transcribed from slaves in tidewater Maryland in 1845: "I'm going away to the Great House Farm, O yea, O yea / My old master is a good old master, O yea! O yea! O yea!" Douglass noted that whites routinely mis-understood the singing of plantation blacks as motivated by happiness when it actually stemmed from sadness: "I have often been utterly aston-ished, since I came to the north, to find persons who could speak of the singing among slaves, as evidence of their contentment and happiness. It is impossible to conceive of a greater mistake. Slaves sing most when they are most unhappy. The songs of the slave represent the sorrows of his heart; and he is relieved by them, only as an aching heart is relieved by its tears." Henry Louis Gates explains, "This great mistake of interpretation occurred because blacks were using antiphonal structures to reverse their apparent meaning, as a mode of encoding for self-preservation."[59] Fur-thermore, Ellen was immersed in a sentimental culture mad for nostalgic imagery. Some nineteenth-century black women resisted the dominant ex-pectations for feminine expression, as the autobiographical writings of Harriet Jacobs and Harriet Wilson show,[60] but Ellen could have chosen to express herself within the lexicon of the day.

> *In Dixie's land, we'll took our stand,*
> *To lib an die in Dixie,*

This interesting fragment suggests acts of cultural assertion. For African Americans of the time, to "take a stand" might mean to preserve the family unit, to preserve black cultural heritage—to *stand*, not fall, as a people, whether the outcome would be to live or to die.

> *Old missus marry Will de Weaber,*
> *William was a gay deceaber;*

These barbs come from an observer of the social whirl around the house, from someone who knows both the mistress and the artisans—someone in the position of, say, the child slave Ellen Cooper. "Will de Weaber" could be an enslaved black craft worker, like Ellen's father "Henry the Cooper," or a free white artisan in residence on the farm.[61] William Greer, for example, a weaver from Ireland, entered the port of Baltimore in 1822; his first step in resettling likely would have been to establish himself in the household of Greer relatives already in Maryland.[62] "Gay deceaber," dialect for "gay deceiver," is a stock phrase dating to the 1830s, indicating that the composer was conversant with popular music.[63] The Snowdens had many popular songs in their repertoire.

> *When he put his arm around 'er,*
> *He look as fierce as a forty pounder.*

A "forty pounder" was a cannonball, familiar to communities along the Potomac because the War of 1812 was largely fought in that area. Almost every house on the lower Potomac in Charles County was heavily plundered during the war.[64]

> *His face was sharp like a butchers cleaber,*
> *But dat did not seem to greab 'er;*

This analogy is one of many "kitchen" references that use food or food preparation as imagery. Kitchen and butchering chores were the domains of slave women and children.

> *Will run away missus took a decline, O'*
> *Her face was de color ob bacon rhine. O'*

Another "kitchen" image, this bit suggests that the mistress, enslaved by her affection, actually adopted a most obvious mark of enslavement: different coloration, perhaps "yellow."

> *While missus libbed she libbed in clover,*
> *When she died she died all ober;*

In an essentially humorous couplet, again focusing on the mistress, we are reminded that she lived as a wealthy woman, "in clover."

> *How could she act such a foolish part, O'*
> *An marry a man to break her heart. O'*

This is not the sentiment expected from a male perspective. Rather, this mild scold sounds like a sympathetic female's observation. Black enslaved women in the nineteenth century had a complex relationship with their mistresses. White slaveowning women were routinely jealous and dismissive of their female servants, yet blacks—both women and men—had a developed awareness of the conditions circumscribing women's lives, including the lives of white women.

> *Buckwheat cakes an stony batter,*
> *Makes you fat or a little fatter;*

Back in the kitchen again, the composer echoes a characteristically female attention to body image. Popular literature, from *Godey's Lady's Book* to temperance publications, campaigned for propriety in appearance as an analogue to behavior; women were urged to subordinate all sorts of desires in order to cultivate virtue within the family. Tavern keepers on the National Road, the route Ellen Cooper traveled to Ohio, delighted guests with their buckwheat cakes:

> It may seem a trifling thing to be written down in serious history, that the
> old taverns of the mountains excelled all others in the matter of serving
> buckwheat cakes; but it is germane and true. . . . There are men and
> women still living on the line of the National Road who often heard the
> great statesman, orator and patriot, Henry Clay, praising the good quali-
> ties of the buckwheat cakes furnished by the old mountain taverns with as

much fervor and more enthusiasm than he ever exhibited in commending his favorite measure, the Protective Tariff.[65]

"Stony Batter" also was the name of a land parcel (known as a "hundred") in Frederick County, Maryland, Thomas Snowden's place of origin.[66]

> *Here's a health to de next old missus,*
> *An all de galls dat wants to kiss us.*

This toast can be read as ironic. Ellen Cooper's father used a comparable expression in his letter of 1836: "Old master is I hope preparing to meet his Heavenly master as he devotes much time to religious duties in his Family." The "I hope" translates as a wish for the master's death or as concern for the man's spiritual preparation, depending on the receiver's disposition. "Here's a health . . ." closely resembles a parodic toast by North Carolinian slaves celebrating the African-based festivity of John Kunering: "May de good Lord bless old massa and missus and all de young massas, juba!"[67] "All de galls . . ." may be an alteration from an original phrasing as "all the boys . . ."; popular music writers often changed gender and other elements from a source piece (a practice still common). Minstrels used "gals" to mean females of any age, but if the lyric were "All the boys dat wants to kiss us," it might convey a young girl's understanding of sexuality.

> *Now if you want to drive 'way sorrow,*
> *Come an hear dis song to-morrow;*

To "drive 'way sorrow" perfectly captures the basic motif of the blues, that uniquely African American musical form born from the slavery experience. An expression of pain and betrayal told in the personal tale of woe, the blues paraphrases the brutal experience of all African Americans. The "remedy" offered, to participate in musical expression, is one that African Americans have always employed.

> *Den hoe it down an scratch yer grabble,*
> *In Dixies land I'm bound to trabble.*

The first of these lines suggests a location in the tobacco economy of the Upper South. In tobacco farming it was often the task of slave children to hoe down weeds and remove rocks (or gravel) from the tender new plants. Describing Africans brought to Maryland in the eighteenth century, historian Allan Kulikoff notes: "Nearly two-thirds of them arrived between June and August, when the tobacco plants had already been moved from seedbeds and were growing rapidly. The new slaves' first task was weeding between the rows of plants with hands, axes, or hoes. These jobs were similar to those that Ibos and other Africans had used in growing other crops in their native lands."[68] "Hoe it down an scratch yer grabble" also are dance figures in which the dancer moves down and around a line of stationary dancers.[69] "In Dixies land I'm bound to trabble [travel]" offers several conflicting meanings. "Bound" appears frequently in black spirituals of the nineteenth century in such expressions as "I am bound for the promised land" and "bound to go" (to a better place, in heaven or in Africa). The standard interpretation of *bound* is *want*, signifying hope and intention.[70] In this sense, "I'm bound to trabble" reprises "I wish I was in Dixie" and carries that line's ambiguous meanings. But another sense of *bound* obtains beyond the figurative: in the slave coffle, by which blacks were forcibly transported, they were actually in bonds, in chains.

The Snowden-Emmett "Dixie" story asks us to reexamine a pivotal question concerning blackface minstrelsy: the degree of authentic black arts represented onstage by the white minstrels. Some scholars of American culture, while acknowledging the distortions and demeaning characterizations in minstrelsy, fundamentally accept the minstrels' claims that they were authentic delineators of black arts. In 1971 ethnomusicologist Eileen Southern (herself African American), for example, expressed the influential view of minstrels as virtual folklorists of plantation life:

> To obtain materials for their shows, the white minstrels visited plantations, then attempted to recreate plantation scenes on the stage. They listened to the songs of the black man as he sang at work in the cotton and sugar cane fields, on the steamboats and river docks, and in the tobacco factories. The melodies they heard served as bases for minstrel songs, and they adapted the dances they saw to their needs. The musical instruments originally associated with plantation "frolics" became "Ethiopian instruments"—banjos, tambourines, fiddles, and bone castanets.[71]

Two decades of scholarship have not dismantled this perspective. Folklorist Roger Abrahams, in his 1992 book *Singing the Master*, mentions the variety of sources of the blackface show but ultimately concludes that it

> represented an ardent effort to bring to the stage studied imitations of slave styles of singing and dancing and celebrating. . . .
>
> Clearly, the minstrel show derives from outsiders' observations of the corn-shucking event and other slave holidays. For not only were the instruments, the songs, and the dances said by the performers to have been learned from observation and imitation of slaves, but the mock fights which the middlemen tried to control projected the very details of the plantation social order which could be seen in the accounts of the corn shucking.[72]

Hans Nathan also identified black tradition as the basis for minstrelsy, although he did not think to search out his own subject's possible connections to black musicians in the community. Nathan in fact perpetuated a blind spot in minstrelsy scholarship, namely, a focus on blacks in the South and nowhere else as models for blackface artists. In words that reveal his vision of the social scale, Nathan observed: "The minstrel band originated as a form of urban entertainment, but its roots lay deep in the lower strata of American society. The instruments of the early minstrel band—banjo, bones, tambourine, triangle, and fiddle—with the exception of the accordion, were a part of the life of southern slaves." Nathan also identified a mix of black and white sources for tune style in the 1830s and 1840s, the earliest era of minstrelsy: "Excessive repetition of single tones and of phrases of narrow compass derives from the Negro; on the other hand, the symmetry of phrase structure is a white concept."[73]

Other writers take the minstrels' Northern origins and the grotesqueries in visual and aural representation—the bug-eyed, big-lipped "blacks" rendered on minstrel sheet music covers, the ridiculous dialect in lyrics and "sermons," and so on—as evidence of the genre's fictionality. Alan W. C. Green, for example, likewise entrapped by the notion that black culture was bounded by the Mason-Dixon line, believes that the early minstrels had "at most a casual acquaintance with Negroes of any kind, and . . . all too often confused their black models with frontiersmen, Irishmen, or Germans." Green finds the roots of American blackface minstrelsy not in the black South but in the blackface tradition of English theater.[74]

Sam Dennison, similarly immune to the idea that whites might have interacted with black musicians or dancers outside the South, sees the racism of minstrelsy as proof of a lack of contact between blacks and whites. Familiarity would not have led to such damning stereotypes, he suggests, nor would blacks have disseminated such images about themselves:

> The notion that the fictional black as represented on the minstrel stage was based on the actual plantation slave is one of the enduring myths surrounding the form. Even today, writers occasionally resurrect stories of how white men absorbed the music and dance of plantation slaves, molding them into uniquely American forms. Facts contradict these theories[;] almost to a man, the minstrels were Northern whites with scant knowledge of black music and customs. Leading theaters in which the shows were produced were in the North, as were the larger music publishing firms. The paucity of plantation slaves on the streets of New York, where minstrelsy began, renders the theory of Southern origin absurd. . . . But there is still another, even greater reason for questioning the theory: the utter inconceivability of blacks using this form of expression to demean themselves so conclusively.[75]

We tread a middle path in this debate, using as our sources not the distant evidence of printed minstrel routines and sheet music but living community memory and artifacts of the actual lives of nineteenth-century black musicians. At least in some cases, we suggest, *Northern* black minstrels may well have inspired their Irish-American neighbors who left home for the minstrel stage. But to establish authentic exchange of music and sociability, as we do for the Snowdens and their white musical friends, is not, finally, to say that minstrelsy did not grossly distort the image of blacks and others. Familiarity does not inevitably breed fairness in representation. Presuming that the Snowden example is not an isolated case, and that black and white musicians in the minstrel era frequently interacted with some intimacy, we must ask how real contact and exchange nevertheless could result in undeniably racist and demeaning representations. The answer, which we can only broach here, may be found in examining the process by which traditional music, dance, lore, and oratory move from the context of home and community to arenas of popular consumption. Commercialization, we suspect, tends to pressure traditional arts toward more "consumable" forms; formula and stereotype usually accomplish this end.

But in interpreting "Dixie" with respect to Ellen Cooper Snowden's biography, we would be contributing only a spurious meaning if we could not show that the song and its reputed composer, Dan Emmett, actually impinged upon the Snowdens' lives. We have listened closely to the voices of aged community members who tell the Snowden-Emmett story; we have considered the many newspaper and magazine articles, national and regional, debating the authorship of "Dixie." But now we must dust off the eloquent evidence of the Snowdens' interest in this story. For here, in a narrow cardboard box holding seventy years' worth of letters and memorabilia, are two pieces meaningful to Ben and Lew Snowden. The first is a lengthy article in the *Mount Vernon Republican-News* of March 26, 1908, titled "Authorship of 'Dixie' and 'The Old Folks at Home,'" a reprint from the *New York World;* the second is a framed portrait of Dan Emmett, captioned "Author of 'Dixie!'"

The newspaper piece carried the subheads "Undoubted Proof of Emmett's Authorship Is Cited by the Writer" and "How Emmett Proved His Claim at Convention of Music Publishers." Will Hays of Louisville had joined the chorus of composers claiming "Dixie"; as the columnist observed, "This makes exactly thirty-seven persons to whom the authorship of 'Dixie' has been attributed, or by whom it has been claimed, every one of whose claims is spurious, up and down and all the way thru." The writer then recited the traditional story of the song's genesis on a rainy night in New York and offered a fond tribute to the late Emmett.[76]

These two items remained in the household until the death of the last Snowden, Lew, in 1923. People don't usually hold onto news clippings and photographs for fifteen years or more unless they hold some personal significance; we infer, then, that the brothers cared about Emmett, the authorship dispute, or both. Their interest, though, remains opaque. Did Ben and Lew carry a wound because Emmett never acknowledged their family as sources for "Dixie"? Were they simply interested in stories about local musicians? Or were they just conservers of materials about their trusted old friend?

We could speculate endlessly, but one ordinary, newsy letter from an elderly woman in Smyrna, a rural community in eastern Ohio, definitively links the Emmett and Snowden families. In the 1870s and 1880s, Ben and Lew raced horses at the county fairgrounds in Smyrna; there they met Eliza Campbell, a woman with strong connections to Mount Vernon, most likely a former resident herself. Eliza wrote to her "Dear Friends" in June 1883 to report on her progress for a quilt she was making them; she de-

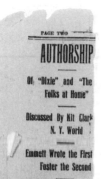

PAGE TWO

AUTHORSHIP

Of "Dixie" and "The Folks at Home"

Discussed By Kit Clark N. Y. World

Emmett Wrote the First Foster the Second

Undoubted Proof of Emm...
...ship is Cited B...

Ben and Lew Snowden's newspaper clipping from the March 26, 1908, Mount Vernon Republican-News *concerning the authorship debate surrounding "Dixie." It is suggestive, if elusive in meaning, that the men kept this article for the rest of their lives.*

Portrait of Dan Emmett as "Author of 'Dixie!'" kept by Ben and Lew Snowden until their deaths.

GRANDMOTHER SNOWDEN.

Death of an Estimable Colored Lady Widely Known and Loved.

"Grandmother" Snowden, a highly-esteemed colored lady, known to nearly every resident of this community, died on Sunday at her home north of town, at the age of 77 years, and was buried at the Lowery cemetery yesterday afternoon.

Mrs. Ellen Cooper Snowden, widow of Thomas Snowden, was born in the year 1817 near Port Tobacco, Charles county, Maryland, on the plantation of Alexander Greer. She was born in servitude, her master, Alexander Greer, liberating her at the age of ten years. In order to be certain of her freedom, Mr. Greer sent her out to this county in the year 1827 with Mrs. Mary Greer and her family, who always during her life time took especial interest in the child Ellen. Ellen continued to live with and was cared for by Mrs. Greer until she married Thomas Snowden in the year 1837. During the time she lived with Mrs. Greer she united with the Methodist Episcopal church in Danville. She was the mother of nine children, seven of whom have passed away, two only surviving her, Benjamin and Lewis. Some of her children died in childhood. The names of the dead were Oliver, Mary, Martha, Sophia, Phœbe, Anna and Elsie. Her husband died July 25, 1856, leaving to her the care and support of this large family. Mrs. Snowden was a woman of cheerful, kindly disposition, remembering with feelings of gratitude any kindness bestowed upon her. Her memory was retentive of the early events of her life. She remembered some of the early years of her bondage, which was in reality not bondage, for she never experienced any of the hardships of her race in slavery. Her master was of kind disposition. Before his death he liberated all who were under his control, with provisions of support to the old and infirm and to the young who were not capable of caring for themselves. Mrs. Snowden survived all the members of the family with which she came to this county. To use her own words, spoken to a friend just one week before she died, she said: "I am the last of that little colony that came out here from Maryland so many years ago." Her life in many respects was an eventful one, filled with the joys and sorrows that come to all the human family.

Her surviving sons cared for her very tenderly during her long widowhood and last illness, their filial affection being remarkable.

Obituary of Ellen Snowden as it appeared in the January 31, 1894, Mount Vernon Republican. The headline indicates that she received the community respect so important to her throughout her life. Ohio Historical Society, Columbus.

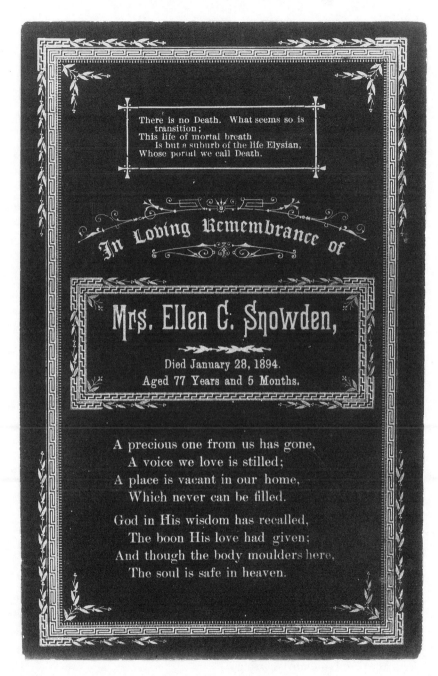

There is no Death. What seems so is transition;
This life of mortal breath
Is but a suburb of the life Elysian,
Whose portal we call Death.

In Loving Remembrance of

Mrs. Ellen C. Snowden,

Died January 28, 1894.
Aged 77 Years and 5 Months.

A precious one from us has gone,
A voice we love is stilled;
A place is vacant in our home,
Which never can be filled.

God in His wisdom has recalled,
The boon His love had given;
And though the body moulders here,
The soul is safe in heaven.

Death card of Ellen Snowden.

scribed her problems finding enough calico in the right shade of blue and noted that she had used parts of the quilt-in-progress to wrap "a piece of one of the jars that John Morgan broke while making the raid through Guernsey Co in 63," a reference to the famous Confederate general who stormed through eastern Ohio.[77] Eliza mentioned people in Fredericktown and Mount Vernon and said, recapping her correspondence with one Mary Scott, "I wrote about the Emmetts is Adam and Zarada and Mrs. Miller still living on a part of the farm."[78] Zarada and Mrs. Miller were Dan Emmett's cousin and aunt, respectively. Their home was the old Zerrick property, near the Snowdens. Martha Zerrick, sister of Sally Zerrick Emmett—Dan's mother—had become "Mrs. Miller" when she married James Miller of Mount Vernon. The couple had named their only child, a daughter, Zarada. Also living on the farm at this time was Edna Zerrick, Dan Emmett's other maternal aunt, who had never married.[79] Conclusively, this letter establishes that the Snowdens knew Dan Emmett's family, possibly over several generations, and that *others* knew that these families were connected in some sense.

Still, one more voice needs to be heard: that of the woman who kept alive her memories of family and heritage, who worked hard to maintain her sons and daughters materially and spiritually, who inspired and guided the music of her family. Perhaps the voice of Ellen Cooper Snowden speaks in the song we know as "Dixie"; certainly her words of encouragement and determination echo as the black community of Mount Vernon continues to honor her family so many years since their passing. Yet Ellen Snowden, an unlettered woman, was far from silent in her life. The January 31, 1894, issue of the *Mount Vernon Republican* ran an extensive obituary of this "estimable colored lady widely known and loved," written by "a gentleman familiar with her early history"—no doubt one of the Greers, since the families maintained a relationship throughout Ellen's lifetime. The writer summarized her connection to the Greer family, her marriage and children, and her benign experience in slavery as a child. In the only statement ever reputed to be Ellen's own words, spoken one week before her death, her sixty-seven years of life in Ohio were dwarfed by the memories of youth: "I am the last of that little colony that came out here from Maryland so many years ago."[80]

Epilogue
A Clinton Quadrille

By 1900 the Snowden Family Band had dwindled to two. It was different now, of course, not like the old days, when three fiddlers carried the lead, Ben, Sophia, and Annie—that was a powerful sound. In the old days, too, Lew's peppery banjo notes seemed to light a fire under Elsie's feet as she danced right up front, danced with her back to the musicians, danced to hit all the offbeats, so graceful in her flat-soled shoes. Folks loved that part the best, even more than the singing.

The strains of another fiddle could be heard in those same Clinton fields: that of Dan Emmett, who in April 1888 had retired to northern Mount Vernon after a lifetime in the theater. Emmett was seventy-three when he left Chicago for Ohio. He soon built a small frame house on the old Zerrick family homestead, no more than a quarter-mile walk from the Snowden place. The location brought back fond memories for Dan of early childhood days. But Mary, Emmett's second wife, quickly grew to

The elderly Lew Snowden, ca. 1920, posing outside his home with his dog and his chair.

The elderly Dan Emmett, ca. 1900, posing with one of the chairs he built for use with the Virginia Minstrels. Ohio Historical Society, Columbus.

hate their tiny cabin, the patch of ordinary flowers in front, and her coun-trified neighbors. After two years she moved back to Chicago, leaving Em-mett free to live as he pleased.[1]

Emmett's last years were spent quietly in Mount Vernon, punctuated only by a last tour with Al Field's Minstrels in 1895 and 1896. At home Emmett spent his time caring for his flock of chickens, enjoying a daily walk in the woods, and tending the garden. And, of course, Dan still played the fiddle. A neighbor, William McGee, recalled:

> One day in 1901 while playing around, we heard the strains of a violin in the distance. . . . We began . . . to go in the direction from which they came. . . . They were very attractive; we followed on, and over the fence and directly up to a beautifully neat little cabin surrounded by gar-dens. . . . We were a bit timid, but as the music continued we drew closer . . . to the little house from which the sounds came, when we discovered, through a doorway an old man swaying back and forth keeping perfect time to his playing. He came to the door and motioned us to come in, go-ing on with his playing. When he had finished he came out into the yard and in his kindly genial way with we shy boys, all were soon acquainted, and when we knew it was high time to skedaddle, we did it with great re-luctance, but made arrangements to "come again." You may be sure we did it too, not once, but probably hundreds of times, for he was the most delightful companion.[2]

Perhaps Emmett returned not only to his own homeplace but to the place of old friends. Living footsteps apart for more than fifteen years, from 1888 through 1904 (when Emmett died), Dan Emmett and the Snowden brothers likely spent many days playing music together. They shared a considerable repertoire, and Emmett had made his career imitat-ing black music on the minstrel stage, playing both banjo and fiddle. The retired minstrel was known to socialize with members of the black com-munity. A framed picture of the retired minstrel adorned the Snowden home—a memento, perhaps, of their friendship.

Clinton's reputation for music also drew a young fiddler, John Balt-zell, age twenty-eight when Emmett returned to Ohio. Baltzell, like Em-mett, had moved to Mount Vernon in April 1888; he found work as a boilermaker for the railroad. Like any country fiddler, Baltzell surely would have sought out the local master fiddler and composer. In Clinton he found two, Dan Emmett and Ben Snowden. Years later, Baltzell pro-claimed that he had been a partner of Dan Emmett's for many years.[3]

John Baltzell, prizewinning fiddler from Mount Vernon, in a publicity photo-graph made for the Edison phonograph company, ca. 1923. On the reverse side is noted, "All the music Mr. Baltzell plays is played by ear and he was a partner of Daniel Emmett for years." From the collections of Henry Ford Museum & Greenfield Village.

Baltzell, born in eastern Knox County in 1860, lived to see great technological and social changes that affected the careers of country fiddlers. He was a member of the first generation to participate in fiddling contests, a national craze Henry Ford introduced in 1923; he played regularly on radio stations throughout Ohio; and he was among the earliest fiddlers to take advantage of the new medium of sound recording. Unlike the great majority of young fiddlers who cut records in the early 1920s, he was already a mature artist in his sixties when he recorded some forty-two sides between 1923 and 1928. Baltzell had learned his fiddle style and repertoire in the nineteenth century.[4]

Baltzell's bowing style was authoritative and strong, well suited to the complex melodic phrases of many of his tunes. His left hand was equally precise, often moving up the neck to capture the high notes. Baltzell was undoubtedly "archaic" in playing pieces of various timings: jigs, quadrilles, hornpipes, schottisches, reels, and waltzes. Twentieth-century country fiddlers typically sped up the first four types of tunes, turning them into reels, and kept the waltzes.

In 1936 a young pianist and local historian named Ada Bedell Wootton told the story of Dan Emmett and John Baltzell to a national readership. The music magazine *Etude* published Wootton's "Something New about Dixie," in which she notated an instrumental interlude in "Dixie" that no longer appeared in the sheet music. This third part "had no words, simply action, when the singer could strut, twirl his cane, or mustache, and perhaps slyly wink at a girl on the front row." The author seemed to envision "Dixie" in the trappings of late minstrelsy and early burlesque, when mustaches and canes had displaced blackface and musical instruments as comic props. Beyond contributing an important musicological footnote about "Dixie," Wootton documented a relationship between fiddlers representing nearly one hundred years of American music, from blackface minstrelsy of the 1830s to sound recording and radio in the 1920s:

> The fact that this part had no words is probably the reason it never appears in the published song; yet Emmett's old crony and fellow fiddler, John Baltzell, still living in Mt. Vernon, was taught *Dixie*, by Emmett himself; and he assured me that the composer never failed to play the "walkaround" with the song.
>
> Emmett and Baltzell played together for dances, and in cafes for years, and many a Sunday found Emmett trudging across the fields to the

Ada Bedell Wootton, ca. 1930. A piano player who accompanied fiddler John Baltzell, Wootton wrote articles on the local origins of "Dixie." Courtesy Jean Bartlett.

Label of John Baltzell's recording of "Turkey in the Straw," made in 1927. Among the first country fiddlers to enter the recording studio, Baltzell recorded tunes well known in the area for generations as well as original compositions. Private collection.

Baltzell home, with his fiddle under one arm, and a chicken under the other—the latter to be transformed by Mrs. Baltzell into Emmett's favorite dish—chicken potpie.[5]

No one knows if Emmett's playing sounded swingy and black-tinged, with accentuated offbeats, or more Anglo, in strict time and with a studied sweetness of tone. Emmett died in 1904, before the new medium of sound recording documented fiddlers and former minstrels. The actual sound of early minstrel music therefore remains an educated guess, interpreted from contemporary accounts and sheet music.[6] But a clue to Emmett's style, and indirectly to the original sound of "Dixie," appears in a Baltzell recording very different from the rest of his music. Performing Emmett's

"Turkey in the Straw," a variation of the classic tune "Zip Coon," Baltzell used an uncharacteristically rhythmic, irregular, short bow stroke and a husky tone quality, suggesting African American musical influence. Baltzell's "Turkey," then, may capture Emmett's and the Snowdens' "Dixie" better than anything ever recorded.[7]

Like Emmett before him, Baltzell named tunes for the people and places that had shaped his fiddling. In the 1920s Baltzell's "Emmett's Quadrille" honored the area's most famous fiddler, and his "Clinton Quadrille" paid tribute to a community where four musicians shared tunes spanning from pioneer days to modern times: Dan Emmett, Ben and Lew Snowden, and John Baltzell.

In 1950 Ada Wootton published a second article exploring the mysteries of "Dixie," this time focusing not on missing music but on the missing *musicians* who had inspired Emmett. Wootton illustrated her article with two Snowden family photographs, portraits of Ben and Lew taken in the 1870s; evidently, she had talked about "Dixie" with Clyde Turner, who owned the photographs and other Snowden materials. "Where," she asked, "did Ohioan Daniel Decatur Emmett get his inspiration for such soul-stirring words that have thrilled millions and that are as potent today as when written? What did he know of 'de land ob cotton'? He had never been in the South." Wootton turned to Clinton for an answer, particularly to

> an old house a mile and a half north of Mount Vernon. It was just across a field from the home of Dan Emmett. It was the home of a remarkable family of Negroes in the 1850s, 60s, and 70s. They were musicians and were beloved by all who knew them. Elsie, Annie, Sophia, Ben and Lou Snowden all sang and played themselves into the hearts of all who heard them. Dan Emmett was a frequent visitor in this home, joining in with his fiddle in the ensemble of instruments. . . . Many songs and stories of the Southland were told to members of the family by the mother, Ellen Cooper Snowden. . . . Tenderness dwelt in the hearts of these gentle folk, associates and neighbors of Composer Daniel Decatur Emmett, who doubtless absorbed much Southern folklore around this fireside.[8]

Ellen died in January 1894, but her sons carried her memory reverently throughout their own long lives. Decades after her death, visitors to the home still found Ellen's Victorian dresses on view, hanging high on the door in a downstairs bedroom. Those old-fashioned, stiff dresses fascinated the youngsters especially; they invoked someone still present in

"Snowden Friends" nonchalantly holding chickens in their laps, ca. 1895. The photograph confirms the Snowdens' social and economic exchanges with whites. Ben and Lew raised and sold poultry, and cockfighting was an amusement with a considerable following.

spirit, loved and remembered. Marie Moorehead and Stella Lee, girls when they first saw Ellen's clothing and now elderly women, never forgot that room, as Lee described it: "I remember they taking us into the bedroom where their mother had died and they had her clothes just the way they had been—really interesting to me."[9]

Ben and Lew continued their bachelors' life of farming, making music, and racing their horses at county fairgrounds in central and eastern Ohio. The Mount Vernon track was nothing special, just a simple oval that any horse with speed and endurance could master. But a real challenge lay in the hilly coal country seventy-five miles to the east: Smyrna, in Harrison County.

Each year, in mid-September, the Smyrna Fair brought huge crowds to cheer the races and the baseball games. Infamous for its subtle uphill grading, the track was rough even for the best horses and drivers, and certainly for those who trained on the gentle track at Knox County. Ben and Lew tried to arrive at least a few days before fair time, to toughen up for the race.[10] In late August 1895 Lew had already gone on to practice, but Ben was stuck in Mount Vernon finishing up the chores. It always took work to leave the farm for two weeks straight, and Ben needed fresh shoes on his horse if he hoped to manage Smyrna's peculiar incline:

Friend Lew,
I thout that I Wood rite you a few lins to let no that i am all right and
hoap that these may find you the Same. I had every thing redey to Start
on thursday night But it raind all night and [I] Wood not start on
friday as i had Such Bad luck on laSt fryday But Will Start on monday
so donnt   easey i think that them Skivers mus be in Some your
things i cant find them I went and had Buell chang meay boys shoes
    I Must close for thi time hoping that i will got thare on tues day as the
rout is thirtey mils Shorter than the one that We come

from your Brother
B Snowden[11]

Black racehorse drivers were uncommon, making the Snowdens all the more visible in a region settled almost exclusively by Irish and English emigrants. Not surprisingly, the brothers developed friendships with whites in Smyrna who either were interested in horse racing or had connections to Mount Vernon. One long-lasting friendship was with the Lowther family. Robert C. Lowther, a farmer who signed his letters to Ben and Lew "from your true friend," corresponded about horses, races, crops,

The elderly Ben Snowden, ca. 1915.

and hard economic times. Expressing his regrets that the local "gang" had "used you mean" at the September 1895 race—probably referring to a racially motivated harassment—Lowther assured his friends that it would not happen again:

> friend lewis
> i have bin Delaying writing to you for Some time as i wanted to Send your money to you this time but as we have to pay on tax here by the 20 of this month i could not Send it this time So you will have to bear with me a little i will Send it in my next letter. . . .
> well i was at freeport the other day and Dr. Blacks Boys was asking if i had heard from you cince you left and wanted to know how fast the little Brown mare Could go i told them She Could go fast enough to give any thing there was there a horse Race yor mare is more Spoken of than any other Race horse on the Ground and you boys made lots of friends while the gang used you mean you acted the gentlemen you need not fear if that ever bother you any more when you Come back to the fair. . . . the boys was looking for Benny to Come and have a hunt about Christmast well i will Close for this time Sleepy tom was in 28 races this fall and took 26 first moneys and one Second and one third we have not had anny Cold wether yet one little Snow but it Did not last long
>
> > from your true friend
> > R. C. Lowther[12]

A letter from January 21, 1896, focused again on the upcoming race and the Snowdens' renowned brown mare:

> friend lewis
> i Received your letter and was Glad to hear from you but was Sorry to hear that you had bin unwell but i hope you have Gained your useal health by this time was Glad to hear that you Got your apples all Rite. we have had a nice warm winter here it was Down to zero one morning in Decembe. Cince that it has Run from 20 to 40 is 46 above to Day every thing is Dull here at this time there is talk of an oil Co. Comeing here to put Down Some test wells they Say there is plenty of oil here.
> Well Dave Says to tell you and Beny he is a going to Raise plety of millions and have them Reddy for you aGainst fair time he Sayes he is a going to bet Some money on Sewellen this time
> Well this leaves us all well and i hope it will find you both well and hearty

Lew Snowden as a racehorse driver, ca. 1890. Ben and Lew raced horses at county fairs throughout Ohio in the 1870s through the 1890s. Courtesy George Booker.

We all Goin in Sending our love to you and Beny

> write soon
> from your true friend
> R. C. Lowther

let me know how the little Brown mare is getting a long from your true friend R. C. Lowther write Soon[13]

In spring he again spoke of the "little Girl," telling Lew he was glad the horse had wintered over and was ready to race:

> friend Lewis
> i Receivd your letter yesterday and was Glad to hear from you i was afraid you was Sick
>   well this leaves us all well and i hope it will find you both well and hearty. We have Warm wether here now Warm as July and the heavest Bloom for a big Crop of all kindes fruit that i ever Saw i was Glad to hear

that the little Girl had winterd well and was in fine Condition i would like to See her march Down the line you bet tell Beny to Ship the potatoes to freeport times are hard here in Regeuard to money matters the hardest Cince I have been liveing here

well i will Close for this time we all Goin in Sending our love to you and Benny

from your true friend write Soon
R. C. Lowther

i will Do Better next time from your true friend R. C. Lowther write Soon[14]

Ben and Lew did not make it to Smyrna that September. Lowther reported the unexciting results, asking how the brothers had fared at the fall races elsewhere:

friend lewis
i thought i would write you a few lines to let you know about our fair. It was not worth a Cuss there was no Show of nothing there was no Races to amount any thing but one and that was betwen Grosio and Besie B Grosio paced in 2.22 that is the Best time that ever was made on Smyrna track in a Race Grosio is all the horse that where this year that was here last year. Sleepy tom went in a big Race over in pensylvania on last Thursday time 2. nine. toms three year old Colts are Showing up well on the track Sleepy tom wone the Race in three Strate heates.

Well this leaves us all well and I hope it will find you both well and hearty i want you to write and let me know how you got along at the Races this fall

Well i will close for this time by giveing our love to you both

from your true friend
R. C. Lowther write Soon write Soon[15]

In August 1897 Lew received a letter from W. A. Lowther, his friend's son, telling of Robert's death and their poor financial situation. In the course of asking the Snowdens for a loan, the young Lowther mentioned a mutual family friend, Eliza Campbell, whose letters to the Snowdens had mentioned the Emmett family. News of horse racing filled even this sad letter:

I seat myself to answer your kind and welcome letter which we re-cieved so long ago.

$500.⁰⁰ SMYRNA FAIR. $500.⁰⁰

Thirty-Sixth Annual

TWO DAYS EXHIBITION AND RACES TWO DAYS

September 15, 16 & 17 '96.

THE MANAGEMENT takes pleasure in announcing the following liberal purses and the statement that our expenditure of $1800.00 upon the track and grounds has produced an excellent speed course. Every dollar of the purse will be paid in full.

Wednesday 1:00 P. M.

No. 1. 2:29 Pace. Purse $100.00
First Premium..................$50.00
Second Premium..................25.00
Third Premium..................15.00
Fourth Premium..................10.00

1:30 P. M.

No. 2. 2:40 Trot. Purse $60.00
First Premium..................$30.00
Second Premium..................15.00
Third Premium..................9.00
Fourth Premium..................6.00

No. 3. 3:00 Trot or Pace. $Purse 30.00
First Premium..................$15.00
Second Premium..................7.50
Third Premium..................4.50
Fourth Premium..................3.00

Thursday 1:00 P. M.

No. 4. 2:28 Trot. Purse $100.00
First Premium..................$50.00
Second Premium..................25.00
Third Premium..................15.00
Fourth Premium..................10.00

1:30 P. M.

No. 5. 2:18 Trot or Pace. Purse $150.00
First Premium..................$75.00
Second Premium..................37.50
Third Premium..................22.50
Fourth Premium..................15.00

1:00 P. M.

No. 6. 2:45 Pace. Purse $60.00
First Premium..................$30.00
Second Premium..................15.00
Third Premium..................9.00
Fourth Premium..................6.00

Conditions: Entries in speed classes close September 9, 1896. All racing shall be mile heats, 3 in 5 with five to enter and three to start. With "Old Rule" distancing all trotting and pacing shall be governed by rules of "American Trotting Association," of which the Stillwater Union Industrial Association is a member. Entrance fee 5 per cent. at time of making entry with 5 per cent. additional from money winners, which will admit owner or driver and groom during fair, with stall for horse without additional cost. A horse distancing the field is entitled to first money only. A record made on or after September 9, '96. No bar to above races.

The Snowdens' advertisement for the 1896 Smyrna Fair in Harrison County. This fair was one of Ben and Lew's major competitions as racehorse drivers.

I should have answered sooner, but somehow I just could not.

Since you wrote I have passed throug one of the saddest experiences allotted to man, that is, the sickness and death of a parent.

On Sunday morning Aug. 1 at 3 oclock A.M. my father quietly passed away.

He had been ailing for some time but not so much as to cause any uneasyness untill about five weeks before his death.

He spoke of you and Bennie while he was sick and was much pleased to hear that you won that race July 4th

. . . . You can tell his old friends, as you know them all, and I do not.

I wish you caould have seen him once more before he passed away.

Ma wanted me to speak to you of the financial situation in which we are left. There is a preferred claim of $45.00 again the place for the funeral expenses of Eliza J Campbell which Pa had not paid. . . . We have tried and cannot find that much around here and thought possbly you could lend us that much till spring when we will make some arrangement so as to get out of this embarrassing fix.

Have you been taking anymore races. accept my congratulations for taking that race July 4th. Smyrna fair will be held Sept. 14, 15 and 16 this fall. can you come. please write soon and tell me all about how you are getting along.

W A Lowther[16]

Racing horses was a way to have some fun, even to earn some money, but it was just one part of life. There were still peaches and potatoes to raise and sell, hens to feed, hay to thresh, firewood to cut and haul.[17] And people still wanted to hear the music. They came by buggy and motorcar up the old stagecoach route, Mansfield Road. Turning onto Clinton Road, they often stopped first at Smith's Tavern to buy whiskey and beer; then, strolling over the lawn toward the Snowdens' place, they spread blankets to sit on, opened the picnic hamper, and gazed up at the duo playing fiddle and banjo in the gable.[18]

Isabelle Wintermute, a grande dame who inherited her deceased husband's renowned collection of Dan Emmett memorabilia, attended picnics with other upper-class whites at the Snowdens' home. Sunday was the (black) cook's day off, and, after church, her group often headed out to the Snowden farm for a day of socializing and entertainment. (They skipped the tavern stop on Sundays.) The social distance between these visitors and the entertainers was, of course, great.[19]

Blacks recall similar gatherings, but with a profound difference of

George Booker as a boy of about five (first row), seated at the foot of the elderly Lew Snowden during a family reunion, ca. 1920. The black community regularly held gatherings at the Snowden farm. Courtesy George Booker.

social meaning. Farmers and trade workers, sharers of a distinctive African American culture and history, the Snowdens and the black families of Knox County were social kin. Never was the relationship between artists and audience closer than when black families visited the Snowdens.

George Booker remembers the family reunions he attended at the Snowdens' farm. It was a place blacks always felt welcome, unlike other public spaces:

> It was a church-related Sunday school thing, picnic. They'd take the children out there; . . . it was nice and plenty of water, and they could turn the children loose and let them run and get stung by the bees and anything else they wanted to get stung by, and it was just a nice place, and at that particular time it was difficult to find. We did have Riverside Park, but sometimes it was often filled, so in a way you were always welcome at the Snowdens out there. . . . They had music and singing and preaching really, and then after that, why, then it was you feel free to socialize and do whatever you wanted to do.[20]

Ben Snowden died in 1920 at the age of eighty. Lew died in 1923, age seventy-five. People mention the brothers in regard to "Dixie," but the Snowden family's reach extends much further than one song. For many the Snowdens shared and continued "a spiritual heritage," as George Booker phrased it, symbolizing the early years of black life on the free soil of Ohio. Their struggles and successes belong not to one family alone but to the black community as a whole.

George Booker once sat at the feet of the elderly Lew Snowden during a family reunion, circa 1920. To that little boy, and to the man he has become, Lew Snowden was a figure of grace and dignity, even of royalty: "He'd come out of the house and everybody would greet him and so forth and treat him like a king, because that's what he was, a king. It was his place."[21]

Appendix
A Sampler of the Snowden Family Band Repertoire

The Appendix includes songs mentioned in the Snowdens' correspondence and songs from their sheet music collection, scrapbook, and manuscripts. These sources confirm only part of their repertoire, since they learned and passed on much of their music orally. Titles follow the spellings of the originals; in brackets we include, where known, the song's formal title, lyricist, and composer.

America and Old Glory! [William H. Barnes and Henry S. Sawyer]
Annie Laurie [anon.-Lady John Scott; arr. P. K. Moran]
Arnnetta [Iowen M. Lawson]
Belle Brandon ["Bell Brandon"; T. Ellwood Garrett and Francis Woolcott]
Captain Jinks ["Captain Jinks of the Horse Marines"; William Horace Lingard and T. Maclagan]
Comrades, Fill No Glass for Me [Stephen C. Foster]
Curnell Ellsworth ["Colonel Ellsworth"]
Dan Cupid [Frederic N. Bartley]

Farewell to America [C. P. Cranch and Goldschmidt]
Father's Come Home [sequel to "Come Home, Father" by Henry Clay Work]
Forty Years Ago [John C. Baker]
Gathering Up the Shells
Golden Slippers, The ["Oh, Dem Golden Slippers"; James A. Bland]
Goodby ["Good-Bye"; trad.]
Croon Palmo [J. Faure]
Greshen [Grecian] Bend Song, The
"has a trol lol to it" [title unknown]
Home, Sweet Home [John Howard Payne and Henry Rowley Bishop]
Hupde Duden Do ["Hop de Dood'n Doo"; M. A. I.]
In the Morning by the Bright Light [James A. Bland]
Jacob Gets the Mitten [George P. Knauff]
Marching through Georgia [Henry Clay Work]
My Last Cigar ["'Twas Off the Blue Canaries; or, My Last Cigar"; James M.
  Hubbard]
"New Words to an Old Tune" [to melody "Old Uncle Ned" by Stephen C. Foster]
Non è ver [Frank H. Evans and Titto Mattei]
Oh I Would Like to Marry [G. W. Goodwin]
Oh! No I'll Never Mention Him
O How I Wish I Was Singgle Again
Old Kentucky Home ["My Old Kentucky Home"; Stephen C. Foster]
Old Oaken Bucket, The
Old Sweetheart of Mine, An [Frederic Chapin]
She Heard a Strain of Music
Spanish Gipsy, The [Michael Watson]
Sweetest Girl of All, The [John Winsler Hayes]
There Is Danger in the Town
There's a Meeting Here Tonight [trad.; arr. Pete Devonear]
Tobacco Song
Uncle Tom's Cabin [J. M. Orr]
Unfinished Letter, An [George W. Sharp]
Until Then [George M. Vickers]
We Are Coming Sister Mary [Henry Clay Work]
We Are Goin to Leave Knox County [Snowden family]
When the Angels Have Lifted the Veil [Emma Pitt and Pemberton Pierce]
When the Moon Shines Bright [Felix F. Feist and Joe Nathan]
When the 76 Comes Around

Notes

INTRODUCTION: SEARCHING FOR DIXIE

1. The Emmett marker was one of many efforts to honor Emmett suitably after his death; others included proposals for a United States stamp featuring Emmett and a Dixie National Memorial in Columbus, Ohio. See Frederick N. Lorey, *History of Knox County, Ohio*, 2d ed. (Mount Vernon, Ohio: Knox County Historical Society, 1992), pp. 433–37; "The Dixie National Memorial, Honoring Daniel Decatur Emmett, in Columbus, Ohio in 1935," Emmett archives, folder OVS 851, Ohio Historical Society, Columbus.

2. Dan Bartlett, interview with authors, Fredericktown, Ohio, Jan. 1, 1988.

3. *New York Clipper*, Aug. 10, 1861, cited in David Ewen, ed., *American Popular Songs from the Revolutionary War to the Present* (New York: Random House, 1966), s.v. "Dixie." The status of "Dixie" as one of America's most widely known songs is affirmed in no less than a letter to Dear Abby. A music appreciation teacher at Marin Community College in California asked her students which

songs are the most widely known among the American population. The list of responses included "Dixie" along with "Happy Birthday," "Take Me Out to the Ball Game," and "Yankee Doodle." "Dear Abby," *Mount Vernon News*, May 28, 1991.

4. "Cat and Dog Fight," *New York Clipper*, Sept. 8, 1872, cited in Hans Nathan, *Dan Emmett and the Rise of Early Negro Minstrelsy* (Norman: University of Oklahoma Press, 1962), pp. 265–66. See also pp. 266–69 for a discussion of the delays in the copyrighting of "Dixie" and its preemptive publication and attribution to one J. C. Viereck. The issue of copyright was, of course, important to Emmett, but he signed away all rights for a sum even then considered small, $300. For the host of claimants by the time of Emmett's death, see "Authorship of 'Dixie' and 'The Old Folks at Home,'" *Mount Vernon Republican-News*, Mar. 26, 1908.

5. Constance Rourke, *American Humor: A Study of the National Character* (1931; reprint, New York: Harcourt Brace Jovanovich, 1959), p. 87.

6. George Bird Evans, the great-grandson of Emmett's second wife, Mary Brower Bird, recounted the Davis inauguration in "Original Copy of 'Dixie' Identified," *Civil War Times*, Nov. 1961, p. 14.

7. Charles Reagan Wilson and William Ferris, eds., *Encyclopedia of Southern Culture* (Chapel Hill: University of North Carolina Press, 1989), pp. 277, 604.

8. The "cult of the Lost Cause" was aligned with but not identical to Southern racist ideology; see Melvin Patrick Ely, *The Adventures of Amos 'n' Andy: A Social History of an American Phenomenon* (New York: Free Press, 1991), p. 20.

9. "3 Georgia Lawmakers Leave Chamber as Dixie Is Sung," *Jet* 75 (Feb. 13, 1989): 4.

10. Sam Dennison, *Scandalize My Name: Black Imagery in American Popular Music* (New York: Garland Publishing Co., 1982), p. 188.

11. Tony Russell, *Blacks Whites and Blues* (New York: Stein and Day, 1970), p. 21.

12. For a general discussion of the minstrel show, see Robert C. Toll, *On with the Show: The First Century of Show Business in America* (New York: Oxford University Press, 1976). Regarding Dan Emmett's contribution to minstrelsy, see Nathan, *Dan Emmett.*

13. Robert Lloyd Webb, "Confidence and Admiration: The Enduring Ringing of the Banjo," in his *Ring the Banjar! The Banjo in America from Folklore to Factory* (Cambridge, Mass.: MIT Museum, 1984), pp. 4–11; Dale Cockrell, "Of Gospel Hymns, Minstrel Shows, and Jubilee Singers: Toward Some Black South African Musics," *American Music* 5 (1987): 417–32.

14. For a discussion of black stereotypes in minstrel lyrics, see Dennison, *Scandalize My Name*, pp. 87–155.

15. Dena J. Epstein, *Sinful Tunes and Spirituals: Black Folk Music to the Civil War* (Urbana: University of Illinois Press, 1977), p. xviii.

16. Robert C. Toll, *Blacking Up: The Minstrel Show in Nineteenth-Century America* (New York: Oxford University Press, 1974), p. 40. We discuss these positions in depth in chapter 5.

17. Today, Knox County's back roads still follow the 640-acre boundaries established by its initial survey; drivers across the rural landscape confront a grid of ninety-degree turns that bear no relation to the topography.

18. For a general discussion of the Northwest Ordinance and of early Ohio history, see Henry Howe, *Historical Collections of Ohio* (Cincinnati: E. Morgan & Co., 1851), pp. 9–15. On the early settlement of Knox County, see A. Banning Norton, *A History of Knox County, Ohio, from 1779 to 1862 Inclusive* (Columbus, Ohio: Richard Nevins, 1862), pp. 7–34.

19. The earliest evidence of blacks in Knox County is a story of two men who had escaped slavery, taking up residence with native Indians. Their masters had been pursuing them from Virginia, and the two were first spotted at the banks of Owl Creek. The master's son perished in the scuffle that followed, and his black assailant was subsequently murdered by those remaining in the party. The surviving black man, fleeing to safety farther north, recounted the tragedy years later. Albert B. Williams, *Past and Present of Knox County, Ohio*, vol. 1 (Indianapolis: B. F. Bowen & Co., 1912), p. 311.

20. Norton, *History of Knox County*, p. 62, recounts a fight—"a little incident, illustrating the sports of the pioneers in 1807"—that included Knuck Harris, "a 'colored gemmen,' the first one ever in Mount Vernon." Norton documents Enoch Harris's working with horses in a story regarding the selection of Mount Vernon as county seat, told by a town founder, Benjamin Butler: "The next morning the Commissioners got ready to start, and I had got Knuck Harris, the only nigger in the country then, to sleek their horses off, and they came out looking first rate" (pp. 93–94). Jonathan Hunt confirmed Enoch Harris's early presence in Mount Vernon in a letter written February 18, 1850: "In 1806 when I came out . . . the persons then living in cabins on what is now Mt. Vernon were . . . *Enoch Harris*, Colored man." *Ohio Records and Pioneer Families* 3, no. 3 (July–Sept. 1962): 136.

21. Epstein, *Sinful Tunes and Spirituals*, p. 360, notes Cresswell's mention of *banjo* as the first use of the term.

22. Third census of the United States (1820), Knox County.

23. William Loren Katz, *The Black West*, 3d ed. (Seattle: Open Hand Publishing, 1987), p. 48. For a general discussion of the restrictions facing blacks in Ohio and the antebellum North, see Leon F. Litwack, *North of Slavery: The Negro in the Free States, 1790–1860* (Chicago: University of Chicago Press, 1961).

24. W. E. B. Du Bois, *The Souls of Black Folk* (1903; reprint, New York: Penguin Books, 1982), p. 45. Du Bois identified revolt against oppression, adjustment to the will of the dominant group, and striving to achieve self-development as common responses to racism among African Americans.

25. For an account of fiddle playing and instruction among slaves, see Epstein, *Sinful Tunes and Spirituals*, pp. 80–81, 112–17, 147–53. Epstein discusses the African origins of the banjo and its playing by slaves in America (pp. 30–38, 145–47); see also Webb, "Enduring Ringing of the Banjo," pp. 2–4.

26. For a general discussion of European and African musical traditions, see Bruno Nettl, *Folk and Traditional Music of the Western Continents*, 2d ed. (Englewood Cliffs, N.J.: Prentice Hall, 1973), pp. 37–81 (European), 125–55 (African).

27. Peter Guralnick, *Lost Highways: Journeys and Arrivals of American Musicians* (New York: Vintage Books, 1982), pp. 123–26; Peter Watrous, "White Singers + Black Style = Pop Bonanza," *New York Times*, Mar. 11, 1990, sec. 2, pp. 1, 34.

28. On the experience of African Americans in the Great Migration to northern cities in the twentieth century, see Nicholas Lemann, *The Promised Land: The Great Black Migration and How It Changed America* (New York: Alfred A. Knopf, 1991).

29. Vera Payne, telephone interview with authors, spring 1984.

30. Joseph Greer McMillan, interview with authors, Columbus, Ohio, Mar. 11, 1992.

31. Jean Irwin McMillan, *The Greer Family Genealogy: Descendants of Robert and Ann Emerson Greer* (Columbus, Ohio: J. I. McMillan, 1978), p. 1.

32. H. Ogden Wintermute, *Daniel Decatur Emmett* (Columbus, Ohio: Heer Printing Co., 1955). The Wintermute collection of Emmett materials is now the property of the Knox County Historical Society.

33. Ada Bedell Wootton, "How 'Dixie's' Composer Learned about the South," *Columbus Dispatch*, Sunday magazine, Oct. 29, 1950.

34. "Snowden Family Gained Fame as Musicians," *Mount Vernon News*, Sept. 4, 1976, sec. F, p. 4.

35. Howard L. Sacks, "John Baltzell, a Country Fiddler from the Heartland," *Journal of Country Music* 10, no. 1 (1985): 18–24, 33–35.

36. We have visited regularly with Marie Moorehead since 1982. Bud Moorehead died in 1988.

37. The flute, tambourine, and scrapbook are in the collection of the Knox County Historical Society. The remainder of the materials are privately owned.

38. Toll, *Blacking Up*, pp. 281–82.

39. Information from the Greers is drawn from written correspondence, phone conversations, and visits with Dwight and Mildred Greer from 1987 to 1992. Jim Burgess talked with us by phone in the spring of 1987.

40. C. Wright Mills, *The Sociological Imagination* (New York: Oxford University Press, 1959), p. 6.

41. Lorey, *History of Knox County*, pp. 391 (Snowden), 433–40 (Emmett).

CHAPTER 1. 'CIMMON SEED AND SANDY BOTTOM

1. Henry Cooper to Ellen Snowden, Charles County, Md., Feb. 14, 1836. Letters cited retain the original spellings, capitalizations, and punctuation. In some places we have inserted clarifications in brackets.

2. Simon J. Martinet, *Martinet's Map of Maryland*, atlas ed. (Baltimore: Simon J. Martinet, 1866).

3. Daniel W. Lord, "Journal of a Trip from Baltimore to Savannah and Return, Feb. 12–ca. May 20, 1824," file 82-93815, Manuscripts Division, Library of Congress. For additional descriptions by travelers alluding to the region's natural beauty, see Frances Trollope, *Domestic Manners of the Americans* (1832; reprint, New York: Oxford University Press, 1984), p. 199; Adam Hodgeson, *Letters from North America* (London: Hurst, Robinson, & Co., 1824), p. 18; Carl David Arfwedsen, *The United States and Canada in 1832, 1833, and 1834*, vols. 1 and 2 (1834; reprint, New York: Johnson Reprint Corp., 1969), p. 312.

4. Ellen Cooper's and Frederick Douglass's experiences would have been most similar in childhood, when few distinctions were made on the basis of gender. Until about the age of twelve, slave children dressed alike, accomplished similar chores, and enjoyed common indulgences as they played around the manor house. See Jacqueline Jones, *Labor of Love, Labor of Sorrow: Black Women, Work, and the Family from Slavery to the Present* (New York: Vintage Books, 1986), pp. 23–24; Deborah Gray White, *Ar'n't I a Woman? Female Slaves in the Plantation South* (New York: W. W. Norton & Co., 1985), pp. 92–94; Eugene D. Genovese, *Roll, Jordan, Roll: The World the Slaves Made* (New York: Vintage Books, 1976), p. 505.

5. Frederick Douglass, *Narrative of the Life of Frederick Douglass an American Slave* (1845; reprint, Cambridge: Belknap Press of Harvard University Press, 1960), pp. 95–97.

6. For a detailed discussion of the rise of the Maryland slave economy, see Allan Kulikoff, *Tobacco and Slaves: The Development of Southern Cultures in the Chesapeake, 1680–1800* (Chapel Hill: University of North Carolina Press, 1986), pp. 23–161. The discussion presented here draws on his work.

7. For a discussion of the transition from servitude to slavery, see Edmund Sears Morgan, *American Slavery, American Freedom: The Ordeal of Colonial Virginia* (New York: W. W. Norton & Co., 1975).

8. U.S. Bureau of the Census, *Negro Population in the United States, 1790–1915* (New York: Arno Press, 1968), p. 783; U.S. Bureau of the Census, *A Century of Population Growth: From the First Census of the United States to the Twelfth, 1790–1900* (1909; reprint, Baltimore: Genealogical Publishing Co., 1969), p. 198. Of the 20,613 inhabitants of Charles County enumerated in the 1790 census, 10,085 were listed as slaves and 404 as free persons of color.

9. Nicholas Cresswell, *The Journal of Nicholas Cresswell, 1774–1777* (Port Washington, N.Y.: Kennikat Press, 1924), pp. 18–19.

10. Henry Louis Gates, Jr., discusses the Cresswell quote as an early documentation of *Signification,* his term for black rhetorical practices based in African tradition, in *The Signifying Monkey: A Theory of African-American Literary Criticism* (New York: Oxford University Press, 1988), pp. 66–67.

11. Margaret Brown Klapthor and Paul Dennis Brown, *The History of Charles County Maryland* (La Plata, Md.: Charles County Tercentenary, 1958), p. 119.

12. Josiah Henson, *Father Henson's Story of His Own Life* (Boston: John P. Jewett and Co., 1858), p. 6. For additional references to black musical expression in Maryland, see George P. Rawick, *The American Slave: A Composite Autobiography,* vol. 16, *Maryland Interviews* (Westport, Conn.: Greenwood, 1972), pp. 8, 56.

13. Kulikoff, *Tobacco and Slaves,* pp. 341–42, observes: "From just north of the Patuxent to just south of the James, plantations were large, black population density was high, few whites were present, and road networks were well developed. Slaves in these areas could create a rudimentary cross-plantation society." Jean Butenhoff Lee challenges Kulikoff's assertions of a cross-plantation slave society in tidewater Maryland; see "The Problem of Slave Community in the Eighteenth-Century Chesapeake," *William and Mary Quarterly* 43 (July 1986): 333–61. Lee's argument underscores the difficulties African Americans faced in establishing and maintaining broadly based communities. Still, on large estates like that of Alexander Greer, black sociability and cultural community were most likely. Our elaboration of black demographics and kin relations on the Greer farm provides, in part, the evidence that Lee finds lacking in arguments for sustained slave communities. For additional background regarding black population patterns and community life in Charles and surrounding counties, see Russell R. Menard, "The Maryland Slave Population, 1658 to 1730: A Demographic Profile of Blacks in Four Counties," *William and Mary Quarterly* 32 (Jan. 1975): 29–54.

14. Federal census records document the relative stability in the number of slaves on Alexander Greer's estate: Slaves numbered thirty-nine in 1810, twenty-nine in 1820, thirty-four in 1830. The inventory of property taken at his death in 1839 included thirty-six slaves.

15. Lee, "Slave Community in the Chesapeake," p. 352. In 1820, three years after Ellen Cooper's birth, the black population on the Greer farm included five females and nine males under fourteen years of age, two females and two males age fourteen to twenty-six, two females and two males age twenty-six to forty-five, and five females and two males over forty-five. This pattern of full representation across age and gender continued through the following two decades.

16. References to family members are not uncommon in slave letters; see, for

example, Randolph B. Campbell and Donald K. Pickens, "'My Dear Husband': A Texas Slave's Love Letter, 1862," *Journal of Negro History* 65 (Fall 1980): 361–64; Robert S. Starobin, *Blacks in Bondage: Letters of American Slaves* (New York: New Viewpoints, 1974), pp. 64–65. Kulikoff, *Tobacco and Slaves*, pp. 360–71, notes the existence of stable families in the Chesapeake by the latter part of the eighteenth century, particularly on large estates. For a general discussion of multigenerational families in slavery, see Herbert G. Gutman, *The Black Family in Slavery and Freedom, 1750–1925* (New York: Pantheon, 1976).

17. Greer's marriage was most fortuitous, since opportunities had become as depleted as the soil worked consistently for nearly a century and a half. In 1773 Samuel Graham, a Scottish visitor to Charles County, wrote home to his father about economic prospects along the tobacco coast: "I have heard of several people marrying advantageously with great industry in making good Crops come from nothing to something, but I have heard too of more whose predecessors have a long while in the Country and are yet in straiting enough circumstances." Chancery Records 26:68–69, Maryland Hall of Records; reprinted in Kulikoff, *Tobacco and Slaves*, p. 131.

18. Klapthor and Brown, *History of Charles County Maryland*, pp. 89–90; J. Richard Rivoire, "Stoddert Family Cemetery (at Southampton)," Inventory Form for State Historic Sites Survey CHAS-168 (Annapolis: Maryland Historical Trust, 1980). Alexander Greer's status as one of the elite planters of the region is indicated, too, by his associates. In his will Greer appointed "my esteemed friends" John T. Stoddert, Walter H. I. Mitchell, and William B. Stone as executors; all were prominent Charles County planters who counted military leaders and United States congressmen among their kin. See John M. Wearmouth, *Charles County Helps Shape the Nation* (La Plata, Md.: Charles County Board of Education, 1986); Sarah L. Barley et al., *A Window on the Past: The Mitchells of Linden, 1845–1870* (La Plata, Md.: Charles County Community College, n.d.).

19. Shad and herring fishing was a lucrative business along the Potomac in the early 1800s. "Sixty fish stands" were listed in the inventory taken upon Alexander Greer's death in 1839. In a May 10, 1828, letter to Dr. Morgan Harris, Robert Fowke of Nanjemoy noted that "if H. doesn't succeed in negotiations with Maj. Greer, the Fishing Shore at Thornsgut will be to rent next year"; Maryland Historical Society, Baltimore. For a general discussion of fisheries along the Potomac in Charles County, see Fredrick Tilp, "A Potomac River Shad Fishery, 1814–1824," *Chronicles of St. Mary's: Monthly Bulletin of the St. Mary's County Historical Society* 23, no. 4 (Apr. 1975): 1–8.

20. These holdings, enumerated in the Greer estate inventory, typified what was to be found on the Greer farm; see "Alexander Greer Inventory," Charles

County Inventory Book, 1837–1841, pp. 289–96, Maryland Hall of Records, Annapolis (microfilm WK-254-255-1).

21. Kulikoff, *Tobacco and Slaves,* pp. 276–77.

22. These possessions marked Greer as a "gentleman." Drawing the distinction between gentlemen and ordinary planters, Kulikoff, *Tobacco and Slaves,* p. 277, virtually describes Alexander Greer's personal inventory: "A middling planter lived in a two- or three-room house, and owned a couple of sheets and a tablecloth; a gentleman lived in a mansion and stocked a linen closet. Gentlemen used tea and coffee regularly and ate from fine china; other planters drank tea or coffee only intermittently and used earthenware utensils. Every planter owned a horse or two and often a simple cart, and gentlemen raised racing steeds and drove fine carriages to church or courthouse."

23. Ibid., p. 373; see also pp. 388, 396, 403; Douglass, *Narrative,* p. 40.

24. We base our discussion of slave life, especially the experiences in the manor house, upon several general studies. Drawing on slave narratives and a range of other historical documents, these volumes provide a valuable composite picture of slave life in the antebellum South. See, in particular, Genovese, *Roll, Jordan, Roll;* White, *Ar'n't I a Woman?;* Elizabeth Fox-Genovese, *Within the Plantation Household: Black and White Women of the Old South* (Chapel Hill: University of North Carolina Press, 1988); Leslie Howard Owens, *This Species of Property: Slave Life and Culture in the Old South* (New York: Oxford University Press, 1976); Sterling Stuckey, *Slave Culture: Nationalist Theory and the Foundations of Black America* (New York: Oxford University Press, 1987); George P. Rawick, *From Sundown to Sunup: The Making of the Black Community* (Westport, Conn.: Greenwood Publishing Co., 1972); John W. Blassingame, *The Slave Community: Plantation Life in the Antebellum South,* rev. 2d ed. (New York: Oxford University Press, 1979); Kenneth M. Stampp, *The Peculiar Institution: Slavery in the Ante-Bellum South* (New York: Vintage Books, 1956). Life on the tobacco farms of the Upper South, however, differed from that on the cotton plantations of the Deep South; hence, general statements regarding slave culture and consciousness must be viewed with caution. For discussions of antebellum life focused on the Upper South, see Kulikoff, *Tobacco and Slaves;* George W. McDaniel, *Hearth and Home: Preserving a People's Culture* (Philadelphia: Temple University Press, 1982); Mechal Sobel, *The World They Made Together: Black and White Values in Eighteenth-Century Virginia* (Princeton, N.J.: Princeton University Press, 1987); Barbara Jeanne Fields, *Slavery and Freedom on the Middle Ground: Maryland during the Nineteenth Century* (New Haven, Conn.: Yale University Press, 1985); James M. Wright, *The Free Negro in Maryland, 1634–1860* (New York: Columbia University Press, 1921); Jeffrey R. Brackett, *The Negro in Maryland: A Study of the Institution of Slavery* (1889; reprint, New York: Negro Universities Press, 1969).

25. Josiah Henson, cited in Genovese, *Roll, Jordan, Roll,* p. 344.

26. Margaret Klapthor, telephone conversation with authors, 1990.

27. A compilation of the wealthiest Maryland planters in 1790 noted that "Charles county starts off in a more pretentious way, for Elizabeth Hanson owned 115 slaves." Listed second was Gerald B. Causen with seventy-five, and the chronicle then cited a number of planters with between thirty and forty slaves. Almy D'Arcy Wetmore, "Maryland Slave Owners in 1790," n.p., n.d., subject file "Slavery–Owners of Slaves," Maryland Historical Society, Baltimore.

28. Sobel, *World They Made Together*, pp. 128–29.

29. Douglass, *Narrative*, p. 41; Jones, *Labor of Love, Labor of Sorrow*, pp. 26–28.

30. Inventory values may have been figured conservatively to decrease the estate taxes and therefore may not reflect actual market values. For example, the valuation of the skilled blacksmith, Tom, at $850 was probably low, since at that time a male unskilled field-worker in good health would have brought about $1,500. The authors thank Will Scott for this information.

31. Genovese, *Roll, Jordan, Roll*, p. 338.

32. Blassingame, *Slave Community*, p. 316.

33. Genovese, *Roll, Jordan, Roll*, pp. 338–42; Owens, *Species of Property*, pp. 112–13.

34. Robert Starobin, *Blacks in Bondage*, p. xiv, considering the historical value of slave correspondence, cautions readers of the difficulties posed by letters dictated to whites: "The letters have to be read with extreme care, for they are loaded with subtleties of meaning, irony, double entendres, and outright put-ons." Despite the apparent closeness between Henry Cooper and John Greer, Henry likely thought it wise to exercise caution in expressing his feelings to Ellen.

35. Black servants who interacted frequently with whites publicly adopted whites' standards of acceptable behavior, as observer Adam Hodgson noted in his travels along the Potomac: "I have hitherto conversed with but few slaves, comparatively, in the plantations; but I have been surprised with the ease, cheerfulness, and intelligence of the domestic slaves. Their manners, and their mode of expressing themselves, have, generally, been decidedly superior to those of many of the lower classes in England." Hodgson, *Letters from North America* (London: Hurst, Robinson, and Co., 1824), p. 24.

36. "Alexander Greer's Will & Codicil," Charles County Book of Wills, p. 179, Maryland Hall of Records, Annapolis (microfilm WK-246-247-2).

37. Fourth and fifth censuses of the United States, Charles County, Md.

38. Fields, *Slavery and Freedom*, p. 32; Brackett, *Negro in Maryland*, pp. 149–55.

39. "The [Maryland] legislators were seized by the frenzy that followed the Southampton insurrection in Virginia and by reports of a similar plot in Anne Arundel County, Maryland." Wright, *Free Negro in Maryland*, p. 122. See also

Brackett, *Negro in Maryland*, pp. 66–69. For a general account of the insurrection, see Thomas C. Parramore, *Southampton County, Virginia* (Charlottesville: University Press of Virginia, 1978), pp. 81–104; Stephen B. Oates, *The Fires of Jubilee: Nat Turner's Fierce Rebellion* (New York: Harper & Row, 1975).

40. "Resolutions Adopted by a Meeting of the Citizens of Charles County, Maryland, at Port Tobacco, in Relation to the Free People of Color," 1831, Maryland Department, Enoch Pratt Free Library, Baltimore, Md.

41. "Greer's Will & Codicil," pp. 180–81.

42. Obituary of Ellen Snowden, *Mount Vernon Democratic Banner*, Feb. 1, 1894.

43. Levi Coffin, cited in White, *Ar'n't I a Woman?* p. 36.

44. Jones, *Labor of Love, Labor of Sorrow*, p. 29; Blassingame, *Slave Community*, p. 171; Rawick, *From Sundown to Sunup*, p. 77; Stampp, *Peculiar Institution*, p. 58; Kulikoff, *Tobacco and Slaves*, p. 377.

45. These chores were typical for children in slavery. The tasks noted relate to specific items in Alexander Greer's estate inventory.

46. Douglass, *Narrative*, p. 51. It was generally not until the age of ten that children were committed to daily labor in the fields; see Kulikoff, *Tobacco and Slaves*, p. 373; Jones, *Labor of Love, Labor of Sorrow*, p. 23; Blassingame, *Slave Community*, p. 185; Stampp, *Peculiar Institution*, p. 280. See also Blassingame, *Slave Community*, pp. 183–84, and Douglass, *Narrative*, p. 39, for further descriptions of slave children's daily life.

47. Annie L. Burton, *Memories of Childhood's Slavery Days* (Boston: Ross Publishing Co., 1909), pp. 3–4. Slave children, like all in bondage, were hardly immune from harsh treatment, and even youths accustomed to relative freedom from responsibilities received abuse for misdeeds. Burton recalled that older children were sent each day with food to the workers in the fields: "Of course, I followed, and before we got to the fields, we had eaten the food nearly all up. When the workers returned home they complained, and we were whipped" (p. 4). But Ellen was protected, to some degree, by her father's status within the Greer household.

48. Traveling in tobacco country in 1829, James Stuart remarked that "much of that part of Virginia, through which I passed in travelling by the stage, forty-five miles from Washington to Annapolis, has been deteriorated by being over-cropped with tobacco. It is a dry and sandy soil. I hardly observed a white person working out of doors in that part of the country. Slaves do all the drudgery in Virginia and Maryland, and are in many places most obsequious." James Stuart, *Three Years in North America* (1833; reprint, New York: Arno Press, 1974), pp. 253–54. The value of property and money to leave Charles County and neighboring St. Mary's County in one eighteen-month period was nearly $1.5 million; see Amy Odelle Craver, *Soil Exhaustion as a Factor in the Agricul-*

tural History of Virginia and Maryland, 1606–1860 (Gloucester, Mass.: Peter Smith, 1926), p. 123.

49. Obituary of Ellen Snowden, *Mount Vernon Democratic Banner,* Feb. 1, 1894.

50. Jean Irwin McMillan, *The Greer Family Genealogy: Descendants of Robert and Ann Emerson Greer* (Columbus, Ohio: J. I. McMillan, 1978), p. 1.

51. Wright, *Free Negro in Maryland,* p. 25, indicates that blood relation was one cause for manumission in Maryland. Genovese, *Roll, Jordan, Roll,* p. 416, notes that "throughout the history of the slave regime there were planters who openly or surreptitiously accepted responsibility for the paternity of mullatoes, educated them, freed them, and, when manumission became difficult, made special provisions for their care."

52. Henson, *Father Henson's Story of His Own Life,* p. 7. Henson described being sold South as "an object of perpetual dread to the slave of the more northern States" (p. 47).

53. Charles County Land Records, Libre IB 17, Dec. 12, 1827.

54. Henson, *Father Henson's Story of His Own Life,* pp. 58–59.

55. Jack D. Brown et al., *Charles County Maryland: A History* (South Hackensack, N.J.: Custombook, 1976), p. 17; Brackett, *Negro in Maryland,* pp. 40–41. With many operations maintained on the plantation and direct access to trade via the Potomac and its navigable creeks, many planters, such as Greer, had little need for a central port town. In 1810 only eleven families resided in the county seat of Charlestown, renamed Port Tobacco in 1820. The county's first newspaper was not published until 1843, and as late as 1865 a regional mapmaker noted that Charles County included "no villages of any importance." Martinet, *Martinet's Map of Maryland.* See also Lee, "Slave Community in the Chesapeake," p. 344.

56. *Religious Folk Songs of the Negro As Sung on the Plantations* (Hampton, Va.: Hampton Normal and Agricultural Institute Press, 1918), p. 86.

57. Hope H. Grace to authors, Mar. 23, 1988.

58. The National Road first opened to the public in 1818, reaching as far as Wheeling, Va. (present-day W.Va.), on the border with Ohio. Philip D. Jordan, *The National Road* (New York: Bobbs-Merrill Co., 1948), p. 55; Thomas B. Searight, *The Old Pike: A History of the National Road, with Incidents, Accidents, and Anecdotes Thereon* (Uniontown, Pa.: T. B. Searight, 1894), pp. 13–16.

59. Searight, *Old Pike,* p. 354.

60. Ibid., p. 109.

61. Ibid., p. 337.

62. Ibid., pp. 223–24.

63. Ibid., p. 202.

64. Ibid., p. 109.

65. Ibid., pp. 149–50.

66. N. N. Hill, Jr., *History of Knox County, Ohio: Its Past and Present* (Mount Vernon, Ohio: A. A. Graham, 1881), p. 493. Searight, *Old Pike*, pp. 112–13, described an 1838 wagon trip from Baltimore to Mount Vernon as having taken thirty days.

67. Peter Neilson, *Recollections of a Six Years' Residence in the United States of America* (Glasgow: David Robertson, 1830), p. 162.

68. Isaac Holmes, *An Account of the United States of America* (1823; reprint, New York: Arno Press, 1974), p. 125.

69. Ibid., p. 132. Neilson, *Recollections*, pp. 163–64, echoed Holmes's sentiments: "An industrious man who can pay his expenses to America, and have £100, or even £50 in his pocket on his arrival there, may, in a very few years, be the proprietor of a small farm, provided he is saving, and commences operations in one shape or other immediately upon his arrival there. There are, however, in America, thousands of farmers and mechanics who arrived out [*sic*] literally without a dollar in their pocket, and are now possessed of considerable property."

70. Robert Emerson to Robert Greer, Nov. 30, 1853. Collection of Dwight Greer.

71. In the early decades of settlement in the Northwest Territory, it was common for Ohio's pioneers to purchase woodlands from the government, building a log house and clearing a small plot for a first planting of crops. This improved lot would be sold at a profit to later immigrants, who might further improve the property by enlarging the house, adding outbuildings, or erecting fences. Years later a third settler might buy this fully cleared farm, thereby avoiding the arduous tasks of early settlement. A traveler in the vicinity of John Greer's homestead in 1832 described such an improved property: "a cultivated farm, three quarters of a mile long, and half a mile wide; about 60 acres fenced and improved,—a dwelling house, barn, other outhouses; orchard and garden, for 900 dollars." William O'Bryan, *A Narrative of Travels in the United States of America* (London: William O'Bryan, 1836), p. 129.

72. A. Banning Norton, *A History of Knox County, Ohio, from 1779 to 1862 Inclusive* (Columbus, Ohio: Richard Nevins, 1862), pp. 313–14.

73. Hill, *History of Knox County*, p. 676.

74. Martin Welker, *Farm Life in Central Ohio Sixty Years Ago* (Wooster, Ohio: Clapper's Print, 1892), p. 12.

75. Ibid., p. 35.

76. William McKendree, Enoch George, and Robert R. Roberts, *The Doctrines and Discipline of the Methodist Episcopal Church*, 19th ed. (New York: John C. Totten, 1817), pp. 211–12.

77. O'Bryan, *Narrative*, pp. 143, 161.

78. R. R. Griffith, *Genealogy of the Griffith Family: The Descendants of Wil-*

liam and Sarah Maccuben Griffith (Baltimore: William K. Boyle & Son, 1892), pp. 171, 175.

79. J. Thomas Scharf, *History of Western Maryland*, 2 vols. (1882; reprint, Baltimore: Regional Publishing Co., 1968), 1:361–64, 369.

80. Ibid., p. 364.

81. Ibid. 2:1553–54.

82. Ibid. 1:421–22.

83. Brackett, *Negro in Maryland*, pp. 52, 60; Kenneth L. Carroll, "An Eighteenth-Century Episcopalian Attack on Quaker and Methodist Manumission of Slaves," *Maryland Historical Magazine* 80 (Summer 1985): 139–50; Wright, *Free Negro in Maryland*, p. 46.

84. Grace L. Tracey and John P. Dern, *Pioneers of Old Monocacy: The Early Settlement of Frederick County, Maryland, 1721–1743* (Baltimore: Genealogical Publishing Co., 1987), pp. 233–36.

85. Lucy Dupuy Plummer, "History of Plummer Family," typescript, ca. 1935, p. 5, Maryland Historical Society, Baltimore.

86. Scharf, *History of Western Maryland* 1:605–6.

87. Knox County Probate Court Marriage Records (GR 2867), p. 315.

CHAPTER 2. THE SNOWDEN FAMILY! ARE COMING!

1. Renfind E. Withrew to Snowdens, Kanawha County, Va., June 10, 1855.

2. Seventh census of the United States (1860), Knox County, Morris Township, p. 16. The census taker overlooked Annie, age five in 1860, but identified Ellen, Sophia, Ben, Phebe, Martha, Lew, and Elsie.

3. Only one other entry in the federal census for Knox County approaches the Snowdens' in its uniqueness. In 1900 the occupational listing for Dan Emmett read "author of Dixie."

4. John W. White, comp., *White's Mount Vernon Directory, and City Guide*, vol. 1, *1876–1877* (Gambier, Ohio: Argus Book and Job Office, 1876), p. 121.

5. Robert C. Toll identifies only four black minstrel troupes before 1860, noting that there is no evidence any of them lasted more than a month. Robert C. Toll, *Blacking Up: The Minstrel Show in Nineteenth-Century America* (New York: Oxford University Press, 1974), p. 275. Writing about early black musical shows, Henry T. Sampson similarly notes that before the Civil War there were "a few nomadic minstrel and jubilee entertainers who somehow managed to eke out a precarious living . . . but very little is known about these performers." Henry T. Sampson, *Blacks in Blackface: A Source Book on Early Black Musical Shows* (Metuchen, N.J.: Scarecrow Press, 1980), p. 1.

6. By the time the handbill appeared, Martha or Phebe may have died; hence the reference to "six in number."

7. Ada Bedell Wootton, "How 'Dixie's' Composer Learned about the South," *Columbus Dispatch*, Sunday magazine, Oct. 29, 1950.

8. William D. Piersen, *Black Yankees: The Development of an Afro-American Subculture in Eighteenth-Century New England* (Amherst: University of Massachusetts Press, 1988), p. 98.

9. Barbara Jeanne Fields, *Slavery and Freedom on the Middle Ground: Maryland during the Nineteenth Century* (New Haven, Conn.: Yale University Press, 1985), p. 45. A white traveler in Lynchburg, Va., in 1859 recorded his encounter with black boys who gathered in the street and whistled local plantation tunes "with an accuracy, and even sweetness, which the instrument cannot always achieve." Alexander J. Patten, cited in Dena J. Epstein, *Sinful Tunes and Spirituals: Black Folk Music to the Civil War* (Urbana: University of Illinois Press, 1977), p. 184.

10. E. C. L. Adams, cited in Sterling Stuckey, *Slave Culture: Nationalist Theory and the Foundations of Black America* (New York: Oxford University Press, 1987), p. 19.

11. For a general introduction to Ohio fiddle music in print and sound recording, see album notes for *Seems Like Romance to Me: Traditional Fiddle Tunes from Ohio*, Gambier Folklore Society GFS-901 (1985).

12. Fortescue Cuming, *Sketches of a Tour to the Western Country . . . 1807–1809* (Pittsburgh, 1810). Reprinted in *An Ohio Reader: 1750 to the Civil War*, ed. Thomas H. Smith (Grand Rapids, Mich.: William B. Eerdmans, 1975), p. 106.

13. For an overview of early musical life in Ohio, including fiddling, see Elizabeth Baer, "Music: An Integral Part of Life in Ohio, 1800–1860," *Bulletin of the Historical and Philosophical Society of Ohio* 14 (1956): 197–210; Donald I. Sonnedecker, "Early Musical Life in Wooster, Ohio, and Vicinity (1830–1870)," *Northwest Ohio Quarterly* 29 (1956–57): 46–55.

14. N. N. Hill, Jr., *History of Licking County, Ohio* (Newark, Ohio: A. A. Graham & Co., 1881), p. 230.

15. Martin Welker, *Farm Life in Central Ohio Sixty Years Ago* (Wooster, Ohio: Clapper's Print, 1892), pp. 49–50.

16. Rhea Mansfield Knittle, "Early Ohio Taverns," *The Ohio Frontier Series*, no. 1 (Ashland, Ohio: Privately printed, 1976), p. 18.

17. Elijah Hart Church, *Early History of Zanesville*, ed. Jeff Carskadden (Zanesville, Ohio: Muskingum Valley Archaeological Survey, n.d.), pp. 67–68, 145.

18. African American fiddling can be heard on *Altamont: Black Stringband Music from the Library of Congress*, Rounder Records 0238 (1989), featuring field recordings made in Tennessee in the 1940s. Andrew and Jim Baxter's 1927

recording of "The Moore Girl" is included on *Songs of Migration & Immigration,*
Folk Music in America Series, vol. 6, Library of Congress LBC 6 (1977). The
Baxters also recorded in the 1920s with a white string band, the Georgia Yellow
Hammers; see *The Georgia Yellow Hammers: "The Moonshine Hollow Band,"*
Rounder Records 1032 (1979). The contemporary fiddle and banjo music of Joe
and Odell Thompson of North Carolina can be heard on *Old Time Music from
the North Carolina Piedmont,* Global Village C217 (1989).

19. Richard Nevins, album notes for *Old Time Fiddle Band Music from Kentucky,* Morning Star Records 45003 (1980), 3 discs. Recordings of "Soldier's
Joy," "Grey Eagle," and "Forked Deer" by Taylor's Kentucky Boys can be heard
on vol. 1, *Wink the Other Eye.*

20. E. D. Root to Sophia Snowden, Pataskala, Ohio, n.d.

21. James Battle Avirett, cited in Epstein, *Sinful Tunes and Spirituals,* p. 156.
Epstein provides detailed accounts of the African and African American origins
of the instruments named.

22. John Work, cited in Charles Wolfe, album notes for *Altamont: Black
Stringband Music.*

23. Wolfe, album notes about the John Lusk band for *Altamont: Black
Stringband Music.* David Evans describes the older, African-derived aspects of
black banjo playing as "the use of a high bridge, fretless neck, neutral third in
the tuning, and a high degree of percussion and syncopation"; Evans, album
notes for *Afro-American Folk Music from Tate and Panola Counties, Mississippi,*
Library of Congress AFS L67 (1987), p. 13. Evans recorded banjoist Lucius
Smith in 1971, some thirty years after Alan Lomax had recorded him. On this album Smith played solo and with black fiddler Sid Hemphill. Field recordings
made in the 1930s and 1970s of Virginia banjo players Irvin Cook, Jimmie
Strothers, "Uncle" Homer Walker, "Big Sweet" Lewis Hairston, and John Law-
son Tyree can be heard on *Virginia Traditions: Non-Blues Secular Black Music,*
BRI Records BRI-001 (n.d.). Contemporary guitarist John Jackson of Fairfax,
Va., played banjo on *Blues and Country Dance Tunes from Virginia,* Arhoolie F
1025 (1969).

24. Wootton, "How 'Dixie's' Composer Learned about the South."

25. George Root to Snowdens, Harrison, Ohio, n.d.

26. Arthur Kirby to Ben Snowden, Knox County, July 1876. "Suinging" probably is *swinging,* indicating a dance party. The swing is still the favorite dance
figure among Knox County's square dancers.

27. Alta Scott to Ben and Lew Snowden, Gallatin, Mo., June 9, 1883.

28. Toll, *Blacking Up,* pp. 216–29.

29. A. Banning Norton, *A History of Knox County, Ohio, from 1779 to 1862
Inclusive* (Columbus, Ohio: Richard Nevins, 1862), p. 153. Public singing was a
regularly scheduled part of local Independence Day celebrations as well. In 1816
Mount Vernon's first newspaper noted that "all those who are completely ac-

quainted with all or either of the parts of vocal music, are requested to make it known some time previous to forming for the march, as it is intended to practice certain tunes." *Ohio Register,* June 19, 1816.

30. George Booker, interview with authors, Mount Vernon, Ohio, July 10, 1991.

31. Welker, *Farm Life in Central Ohio,* pp. 64–65. For a discussion of early camp meetings in the West, see William Warren Sweet, *The Rise of Methodism in the West* (Nashville: Smith and Lamar, 1920), pp. 20–21, 56, 68; see also Wallace Guy Smeltzer, *Methodism on the Headwaters of the Ohio* (Nashville: Parthenon Press, 1951), pp. 107–9.

32. Records of the Methodist church in the Danville area described one of its early pastors, a Rev. Shaffer, as a great evangelist and noted singer; Albert B. Williams, *Past and Present of Knox County, Ohio,* vol. 1 (Indianapolis: B. F. Bowen & Co., 1912), p. 152.

33. William McKendree, Enoch George, and Robert R. Roberts, *The Doctrines and Discipline of the Methodist Episcopal Church,* 19th ed. (New York: John C. Totten, 1817), pp. 81–83.

34. William O'Bryan, *A Narrative of Travels in the United States of America* (London: William O'Bryan, 1836), p. 159.

35. Welker, *Farm Life in Central Ohio,* pp. 50–51.

36. Stuckey, *Slave Culture,* pp. 93–94.

37. Fredrika Bremer, cited in Epstein, *Sinful Tunes and Spirituals,* p. 223.

38. William Francis Allen, Charles Pickard Ware, and Lucy McKim Garrison, comps., *Slave Songs of the United States* (New York: A. Simpson, 1867), pp. iv–v.

39. Epstein, *Sinful Tunes and Spirituals,* pp. 217–29.

40. Allen, Ware, and McKim, *Slave Songs,* p. v.

41. Ibid., p. 52. Songs identified as part of the Snowden repertoire are those requested in correspondence, pasted in their family scrapbook, or included in their sheet music collection. A complete list of these songs appears in the Appendix.

42. Laurence Oliphant, cited in Epstein, *Sinful Tunes and Spirituals,* pp. 226–28. "There's a Meeting Here Tonight" also appears in Allen, Ware, and McKim, *Slave Songs,* no. 11.

43. Fredrika Bremer found the service at "a negro Baptist Church belonging to the Episcopal creed" that she visited in Cincinnati "quiet, very proper and a little tedious"; Bremer, cited in Epstein, *Sinful Tunes and Spirituals,* p. 223.

44. Rev. J. F. Shaffer, *Sermon on Dancing* (Springfield, Ohio: Republic Printing Co., 1867), p. 1.

45. R. Carlyle Buley, *The Old Northwest, Pioneer Period, 1815–1840,* vol. 1 (Indianapolis: Indiana Historical Society, 1950), p. 327.

46. Nan Simpson to Ben Snowden, Newville, Ohio, Dec. 7, no year.

47. George Booker, interview with authors, Mount Vernon, Ohio, July 10, 1991.

48. We draw much of the general discussion on nineteenth-century popular music from two books by Nicholas Tawa: *A Music for the Millions: Antebellum Democratic Attitudes and the Birth of American Popular Music* (New York: Pendragon Press, 1984) and *Sweet Songs for Gentle Americans: The Parlor Song in America, 1790–1860* (Bowling Green, Ohio: Bowling Green University Popular Press, 1980).

49. Richard Crawford, ed., *The Civil War Songbook: Complete Original Sheet Music for 37 Songs* (New York: Dover Publications, 1977), pp. v–vi; Richard Jackson, *Popular Songs of Nineteenth-Century America* (New York: Dover Publications, 1976), p. vi; Tawa, *Sweet Songs for Gentle Americans*, p. 102; Tawa, *Music for the Millions*, p. 33.

50. "New Words to an Old Tune," n.d., clipping in Snowden scrapbook, Snowden collection.

51. Tawa, *Sweet Songs for Gentle Americans*, p. 66, notes that popular tunes were so familiar that people could enjoy them even amid the distractions of outdoor concerts.

52. "Father's Come Home," n.d., clipping in Snowden scrapbook, Snowden collection. The parody is based on Henry Clay Work's "Father, Dear Father, Come Home with Me Now" (1864), cited in Roger Lax and Frederick Smith, *The Great Song Thesaurus* (New York: Oxford University Press, 1984), p. 210. Robert C. Toll discusses the play in *On with the Show: The First Century of Show Business in America* (New York: Oxford University Press, 1976), pp. 149–50.

53. T. E. Garrett and Francis Woolcott, "Bell Brandon" (St. Louis: Balmer and Webe, 1854), clipping in Snowden scrapbook, Snowden collection; see Tawa, *Music for the Millions*, pp. 114–15, 160.

54. Carl Bode, *The Anatomy of American Popular Culture, 1840–1861* (Berkeley and Los Angeles: University of California Press, 1959), p. 38.

55. John C. Baker, "40 Years Ago" (New York: Firth, Pond & Co., 1857).

56. Crawford, *Civil War Songbook*, p. vii.

57. George Root to Ben Snowden, Harrison, Ohio, n.d.

58. Mrs. Sam Cowell, *The Cowells in America, Being the Diary of Mrs. Sam Cowell during Her Husband's Concert Tour in the Years 1860–1861*, ed. M. Willson Disher (London: Oxford University Press, 1934), pp. 372–75.

59. Stephen C. Foster, "Comrades, Fill No Glass for Me" (Baltimore: Miller & Beacham, 1855), clipping in Snowden scrapbook, Snowden collection; see William W. Austin, *"Susanna," "Jeanie," and "The Old Folks at Home": The Songs of Stephen C. Foster from His Time to Ours* (New York: Macmillan, 1975), pp. 104–5.

60. "My Last Cigar" (1848), clipping in Snowden scrapbook, Snowden collection; see Tawa, *Music for the Millions*, pp. 149–50.

61. The details of Thomas's death were noted in an obituary in the *Mount Vernon Republican*, Aug. 5, 1856.

62. Herman and Lucy Benedict deeded eight acres of land to Thomas Snowden for $800 on Oct. 31, 1854. Deed Record, vol. VV, p. 136, Knox County Recorder's Office.

63. The Snowden collection includes five promissory notes from Thomas Snowden to Herman Benedict, Oct. 31, 1854. On the reverse side of these notes, Herman Benedict guaranteed "the payment of the within to H. Curtis for value." The Snowdens signed over the deed to their property to Herman Benedict as collateral against the mortgage. Deed conveyance, "Thomas and Ellen Snowden to Herman Benedict," Mar. 21, 1855, bk. 4, pp. 223–24, Knox County Recorder's Office.

64. Petition, "Hosmer Curtis vs. Eleanor Snowden and Others," Sept. 11, 1857, file box 105, Knox County Courthouse. Final judgment was rendered Dec. 10, 1859; see *Minutes, Knox County Court of Common Pleas, 1858–1860*, vol. V, p. 352.

65. Loan agreement between Ellen Snowden and Potter and Richards, July 2, 1859, Snowden collection.

66. Ledger sheet, Snowden collection.

67. "We Are Goin to Leave Knox County," a "Composed Song by the Snowden Family on Leaving Knox County," n.d., Snowden collection.

68. D. C. Montgomery purchased two acres of the Snowden property at the sheriff's sale on Aug. 13, 1864; see "D. C. Montgomery (Trustee) to Riley Jenkins," Knox County Record Book, vol. 54, p. 56. Final disposition of the case took place on Oct. 25, 1864; see "Hosmer Curtis vs. Eleanor Snowden, widow, of Thomas Snowden, et al.," *Minutes, Knox County Court of Common Pleas, 1862–1867*, bk. 10, p. 195.

69. "D. C. Montgomery, Deed to Eleanor Snowden, Widow, and Others," Nov. 21, 1864, Snowden collection.

70. Toll, *On with the Show*, p. 3; William Lawrence Slout, *Theatre in a Tent: The Development of a Provincial Entertainment* (Bowling Green, Ohio: Bowling Green University Popular Press, 1972), p. 12.

71. In response to suspicions about the morality of performers, theatrical facilities adopted such phrases as "academy of music," "opera house," and "town hall." Upon its renovation in 1883, Woodward Hall was renamed the Woodward Opera House, although operatic performance onstage was certainly a rarity. See M. B. Leavitt, *Fifty Years in Theatrical Management* (New York: Broadway Publishing Co., 1912), p. 6; Toll, *On with the Show*, pp. 30, 53; Slout, *Theatre in a Tent*, p. 3.

72. Toll, *On with the Show*, p. 141; Slout, *Theatre in a Tent*, pp. 3–5. On one wall of the decaying hall, visitors can still make out a painted scoreboard.

73. Philip C. Lewis, *Trouping: How the Show Came to Town* (New York: Harper & Row, 1973), p. 13; Slout, *Theatre in a Tent*, pp. 8–10.

74. Tawa, *Sweet Songs for Gentle Americans*, pp. 73–74.

75. *Mount Vernon Democratic Banner*, Feb. 29, 1853; ibid., Dec. 20, 1859.

76. Ibid., Feb. 26, 1856. A general description and photograph of the Alleghanians can be found in Leavitt, *Fifty Years in Theatrical Management*, pp. 3–4.

77. *Mount Vernon Democratic Banner*, Nov. 23, 1852; ibid., Nov. 30, 1852.

78. The *Mount Vernon Democratic Banner* regularly printed advertisements for circuses touring Mount Vernon from 1852 to 1860. Performances included Raymond and Company and Van Amburgh and Company's Menageries United (Apr. 28, 1852), Johnson and Company's Empire Circus (June 24, 1852), P. T. Barnum's Grand Colossal Museum and Menagerie (Sept. 16, 1852), Rivers Circus (July 8, 1853), Whitbeck's Circus (Aug. 8, 1854), Herr Driessen and Company's Circus and Menagerie (Apr. 22[?], 1856), R. Welch's National Circus and L. B. Lent's New York Circus (Oct. 1, 1856), Spalding and Rogers' Three Circuses (Aug. 8, 1857), National Circus (June 16, 1859), Van Amburgh's Zoological and Equestrian Company (Aug. 11, 1860).

79. In a letter to the editor of the *Mount Vernon News* (Apr. 17, 1984), Fred Hayes recalled that calliopes with the circus "could be heard as far away as Gambier."

80. Advertisement, *Mount Vernon Democratic Banner*, Apr. 27, 1852.

81. Toll, *On with the Show*, pp. 51–52.

82. Advertisement, *Mount Vernon Democratic Banner*, June 15, 1852.

83. Toll, *On with the Show*, pp. 41–44.

84. Ibid., p. 31. Barnum's success stimulated others to apply his formula. One of his chief competitors successfully toured the Wild Men of Borneo, "twin sons of the emperor of Borneo." The two were in fact brothers Hiram and Barney Davis, dwarfs from Gambier, a few miles east of Mount Vernon. They are buried in Mound View Cemetery, not far from Dan Emmett's grave.

85. Hans Nathan, *Dan Emmett and the Rise of Early Negro Minstrelsy* (Norman: University of Oklahoma Press, 1962), pp. 109–12.

86. *Mount Vernon Democratic Banner*, Dec. 21, 1858.

87. In 1852 W. M. Cunningham advertised his new wholesale bookstore in Mount Vernon, offering instruments including guitars, violins, and flutes—"for sale cheap"—and five thousand pieces of sheet music; *Mount Vernon Democratic Banner*, July 27, 1852. Bourne & Torrey of Sandusky City, Ohio, advertised in 1853 to offer local residents guitars, violins, flutes, banjos, and tambourines; *Norton's Daily True Whig*, Mar. 28, 1853. In 1857 H. Kleber and Brother offered Nunn and Clark pianos, Carhart and Needham melodeons, and Martin guitars,

in addition to brass instruments and strings for violin, guitar, and banjo; *Mount Vernon Democratic Banner*, May 19, 1857. According to Jim Bollman of the Music Emporium, Cambridge, Mass., Lew Snowden's engraved banjo was likely made by the Buckbee company in the late 1860s or early 1870s. Buckbee was one of the first commercial manufacturers of banjos.

88. Lewis, *Trouping*, pp. 52–53, 117–18; Slout, *Theatre in a Tent*, p. 7; Toll, *On with the Show*, p. 76.

89. Leavitt, *Fifty Years in Theatrical Management*, pp. 511–12.

90. Andrew and Gabriela Lewis, telephone interview with authors, Nov. 7, 1984; Stella Lee, interview with authors, Mount Vernon, Ohio, Apr. 13, 1984; John Payne, telephone interview with authors, Jan. 15, 1984; James Payne, telephone interview with authors, Dec. 6, 1984; Vera Payne, telephone interview with authors, Dec. 6, 1984; George Booker, interview with authors, Mount Vernon, Ohio, July 10, 1991.

91. Mr. and Mrs. Samuel Albert to Ben, Lew, and Ellen Snowden, Mount Vernon, Ohio, Jan. 20, 1879. The 1880 Knox County census listed Samuel Albert, age fifty-seven, as a white farmer.

92. Sarah and Bell Blair to Sophia Snowden, Mount Vernon, Ohio, Sept. 23, 1858; E. D. Root to Sophia Snowden, Pataskala, Ohio, n.d.

93. Nan Simpson to Ben Snowden, Newville, Ohio, n.d.

94. Epstein, *Sinful Tunes and Spirituals*, pp. 150–51.

95. Nan Simpson to Ben Snowden, Newville, Ohio, n.d.; Reuben Oliver to Ben Snowden, Cardington, Ohio, Jan. 21, 1860. The 1860 census listed Reuben Oliver as twenty years old, white, and married. The "Tobacco Song" likely described tobacco as a vice.

96. Sarah and Bell Blair to Sophia Snowden, Mount Vernon, Ohio, Sept. 23, 1858.

97. Almeda Lewis to Sophia Snowden, Mount Vernon, Ohio, n.d.

98. "Hop de Dood'n Doo" (Philadelphia, 1854). A version of the song, titled "Hoop De Dooden Doo," appeared in the *Mount Vernon Democratic Banner* on July 20, 1858; "Hoop-de-Dooden Do" appears in a Dan Emmett songbook, box 3, Emmett archives, Ohio Historical Society, Columbus. William Horace Lingard, "Grecian Bend" (New York: William A. Pond and Co., 1868). For a photograph of fashion associated with the Grecian bend, see Priscilla Harris Dalrymple, *American Victorian Costume in Early Photographs* (New York: Dover Publications, 1991), p. 33.

99. Alta Scott to Ben and Lew Snowden, Gallatin, Mo., June 9, 1883.

100. Ibid., June 14, 1883.

101. George Root to Ben Snowden, Harrison, Ohio, n.d.

102. Amateur musicians in Knox County could take formal musical instruction from Charles Dommall, whose twenty years of professional experience as a teacher of music had been obtained "in the principal cities Colleges and Seminar-

ies of fifteen states of the Union." In 1853 Dommall offered musical instruction "on the flute, violin, guitar—with singing—piano forte, melodeon, and thorough bass or the principals of harmony." Pupils from the countryside could take two or more lessons in a single day in order to complete the course with fewer sojourns to Mount Vernon. *Mount Vernon Democratic Banner,* Nov. 22, 1853.

103. To this day most country fiddlers play by ear rather than by reading music, and many fiddlers believe that a tune's subtleties of phrasing and inflection cannot be learned from sheet music or even from sound recordings. Most fiddlers know who the masters are in their area, and they seek them out to learn their tunes. Noting the importance of oral transmission in fiddle music, contemporary Ohio fiddler John Hannah remarked: "As far as reading music, I couldn't read, never tried to read music, but that wouldn't be too hard. . . . I can learn the tune a lot faster than I could try to learn the music. If you start depending on learning from a sheet, I imagine that would take away from your ear, you know. If you're not depending on a sheet then you have to depend on listening to the tune. I try to play it just by memory then. I don't think old-time music was meant to be played from a music sheet, anyway; I think it was just meant to be played by ear." Album notes for *Seems Like Romance to Me,* p. 11.

104. George Root to Ben Snowden, Harrison, Ohio, n.d.

CHAPTER 3. I AM SITTING SAD AND LONELY

1. Bert James Loewenberg and Ruth Bogin, eds., *Black Women in Nineteenth-Century American Life: Their Words, Their Thoughts, Their Feelings* (University Park: Pennsylvania State University Press, 1976), p. 282.

2. Carter G. Woodson, *The Education of the Negro prior to 1861* (1919; reprint, New York: Arno Press and the New York Times, 1968), p. 237. By 1860 the proportion of black schoolchildren had risen to 15 percent; adult illiteracy stood at 17 percent (p. 240).

3. Matilda A. Jones to Miss Dewey, Washington, D.C., June 25, 1855. Reprinted in Dorothy Sterling, ed., *We Are Your Sisters: Black Women in the Nineteenth Century* (New York: W. W. Norton & Co., 1984), p. 191. For an additional discussion of the importance of education to African Americans in the nineteenth century, see Angela Y. Davis, *Women, Race & Class* (New York: Vintage Books, 1983), pp. 99–109.

4. The United States censuses of 1850 and 1860 listed the Snowden children as having attended school within the last year.

5. White Hall Library Association certificate, July 1, 1855, Snowden collection.

6. Lizzie Hicks to Annie Snowden, Fredericktown, Ohio, n.d.; Jan. 10, 1867.

7. Ibid., n.d.

8. Ibid., n.d.

9. Mary E. Hicks to Martha and Annie Snowden, Fredericktown, Ohio, month and day illegible, 1865.

10. Lizzie Hicks to Annie Snowden, Fredericktown, Ohio, n.d.

11. Ibid.

12. Rowland Berthoff, *An Unsettled People: Social Order and Disorder in American History* (New York: Harper & Row, 1971), p. 260.

13. Undated manuscript, ca. 1865, Snowden collection.

14. For a general discussion of the changes occurring in America during the first half of the nineteenth century and the rise of popular culture, see Berthoff, *Unsettled People;* Carl Bode, *The Anatomy of American Popular Culture, 1840–1861* (Berkeley and Los Angeles: University of California Press, 1959).

15. Ann Douglas, *The Feminization of American Culture* (New York: Alfred A. Knopf, 1977), pp. 50–51.

16. Elizabeth Pearson, *A Walking Tour of Mount Vernon's Historic East Gambier, East High and North Main Districts* (Mount Vernon, Ohio: Mount Vernon/Knox County Chamber of Commerce and the Knox County Historical Society, 1990).

17. N. N. Hill, Jr., *History of Knox County, Ohio: Its Past and Present* (Mount Vernon, Ohio: A. A. Graham & Co., 1881), pp. 399–401. Mount Vernon's development was typical of towns throughout the West; see Richard Lingeman, *Small Town America: A Narrative History, 1620–the Present* (New York: G. P. Putnam's Sons, 1980), pp. 107–68; Jerome Blum, ed., *Our Forgotten Past: Seven Centuries of Life on the Land* (London: Thames and Hudson, 1982), pp. 184–96.

18. Douglas, *Feminization of American Culture*, pp. 56–62; Bode, *Anatomy of American Popular Culture*, p. 261.

19. The scrapbook does not identify its compiler. Based on the subject matter and publication dates of the contents and on the Snowden children's ages, we attribute the scrapbook's creation to Sophia.

20. For a general discussion of the relationship between sentimental culture and the problem of sincerity, see Karen Halttunen, *Confidence Men and Painted Women: A Study of Middle-Class Culture in America, 1830–1870* (New Haven, Conn.: Yale University Press, 1982).

21. Unless otherwise noted, all extracts that follow are drawn from the Snowden scrapbook.

22. *Mount Vernon Democratic Banner*, Aug. 7, 1860; Sept. 20, 1859; Mar. 28, 1854.

23. This practice continued well into the twentieth century. The renowned country music stars the Carter Family, as old-fashioned (even in the thirties) and God-fearing as they come, felt obliged to advertise that "the Show is Morally

Good"; see John Cohen and Mike Seeger, eds., *Old-Time String Band Songbook* (New York: Oak Publications, 1976), p. 45.

24. Several undated letters of recommendation for the Snowden Family Band survive. John Springer of Shanesville (now known as Sugarcreek)—a town some sixty miles northeast of Mount Vernon, in Tuscarawas County—wrote: "I reckemend those folks to you for there Worthy of the Reckomenddatuon I want you to do all for them that you can." Geo. Hart, S. W. Brown, and Hugh Hamilton, Esq., acknowledged that "This is to certify that we attended the Concert of the above Family and was Satisfactorily Entertaind."

25. The Snowdens' appeal to "Preachers, Lawyers, Doctors" as respected citizens reflected the high status of these professions in a modernizing America. Writing about the growth of towns across America, Page Smith notes, "In the nineteenth century the lawyer became, with the teacher and minister, one of the three leading figures in the town." Page Smith, *As a City upon a Hill: The Town in American History* (New York: Alfred A. Knopf, 1966), p. 140.

26. Renfind E. Withrew to Snowden family, Kanawha County, Va., June 10, 1855. Bode, *Anatomy of American Popular Culture*, p. 171, notes that the expression of sentimentality was allowed for men as well as women.

27. Davis, *Women, Race & Class*, pp. 31–32; Douglas, *Feminization of American Culture*, pp. 50–55.

28. Douglas, *Feminization of American Culture*, pp. 44–66.

29. In popular verse marriage and the family were typically viewed through the eyes of a child; see Nicholas Tawa, *A Music for the Millions: Antebellum Democratic Attitudes and the Birth of American Popular Music* (New York: Pendragon Press, 1984), p. 88.

30. Public education for women offered instruction on virtue in addition to the three *R*s. The Mount Vernon Female Seminary, which opened in 1844, offered a course of study including "conversation on common things," "exercises in composition," and "moral science." Elective programs in the "ornamental branches" provided instruction in instrumental music, drawing, painting, and ornamental needlework. *Twenty-first Catalogue of the Instructors and Pupils of the Mount Vernon Female Seminary, Mount Vernon, Ohio* (Cleveland: Fairbanks, Benedict & Co., 1865).

31. Douglas, *Feminization of American Culture*, p. 200.

32. Halttunen, *Confidence Men and Painted Women*, p. 124; Tawa, *Music for the Millions*, pp. 101–33.

33. Tawa, *Music for the Millions*, p. 127.

34. Eliza Jane Campbell to Ellen and Sophia Snowden, Smyrna, Ohio, Apr. 17, 1872.

35. Ibid.

36. Beth Maclay Doriani, "Black Womanhood in Nineteenth-Century America:

Subversion and Self-Construction in Two Women's Autobiographies," *American Quarterly* 43, no. 2 (June 1991): 199–222; Davis, *Women, Race & Class*, pp. 30–45; Douglas, *Feminization of American Culture*, pp. 58–71; Patricia Hill Collins, *Black Feminist Thought: Knowledge, Consciousness, and the Politics of Empowerment* (New York: Routledge, 1991).

37. Valerie Smith, introduction to Harriet Jacobs, *Incidents in the Life of a Slave Girl: Written by Herself* (1861; reprint, New York: Oxford University Press, 1988), p. xxxii.

38. Erlene Stetson, "Studying Slavery: Some Literary and Pedagogical Considerations on the Black Female Slave," in *But Some of Us Are Brave*, ed. Gloria T. Hull, Patricia Bell Scott, and Barbara Smith (Old Westbury, N.Y.: Feminist Press, 1982), pp. 68–69.

39. Smith, introduction to Jacobs, *Incidents in the Life of a Slave Girl*, p. xxxvi.

40. Anthony G. Barthelemy, *Collected Black Women's Narratives* (New York: Oxford University Press, 1988), p. xlvi. See also Hull, Scott, and Smith, *But Some of Us Are Brave*, p. xxi.

41. Almeda Lewis to Sophia Snowden, Mount Vernon, Ohio, n.d.

42. Seventh census of the United States, Knox County, Ohio.

43. Untitled poem by Phebe Snowden, n.d., Snowden collection.

44. Helen P. Snowden to Sophia Snowden, Warsaw, N.Y., Sept. 11, 1869. Information on Helen's later life comes from the obituary of Benjamin Snowden in the *Western New-Yorker* (Warsaw, N.Y.), Mar. 15, 1893.

45. Elizabeth Higginbotham, "Two Representative Issues in Contemporary Sociological Work on Black Women," in Hull, Scott, and Smith, *But Some of Us Are Brave*, p. 95.

46. John Edward Philips, "The African Heritage of White America," in *Africanisms in American Culture*, ed. Joseph E. Holloway (Bloomington: Indiana University Press, 1990), p. 233; Davis, *Women, Race & Class*, pp. 30–45.

47. Benjamin Snowden escaped from Maryland to New York by way of the Underground Railroad, according to his obituary. The Fugitive Slave Act of 1850 legislated the capture and return of blacks to their former masters.

48. Carter G. Woodson, ed., *The Mind of the Negro As Reflected in Letters Written during the Crisis, 1800–1860* (1926; reprint, New York: Negro Universities Press, 1969), pp. 508–9.

49. Ibid., pp. 509–10.

50. For a discussion of the importance of religion in the lives of nineteenth-century African American women, see Loewenberg and Bogin, *Black Women in Nineteenth-Century American Life*, pp. 126–80.

51. Ibid., pp. 15–19.

52. Nan Simpson to Ben Snowden, Newville, Ohio, June 25, 1878.

CHAPTER 4. OHIO'S NOT THE PLACE FOR ME

1. Quoted words from "Away to Canada!" *Voice of the Fugitive* 1, no. 2 (Jan. 15, 1851): 4. The final refrain of this song is quite close to the words conveyed in a letter written by fugitive slave John H. Hill: "Come Poor distress men women and come to Canada where colored men are free." Cited in Carter G. Woodson, ed., *The Mind of the Negro As Reflected in Letters Written during the Crisis, 1800–1860* (1926; reprint, New York: Negro Universities Press, 1969), p. 583. The song continued in oral tradition in central Ohio a century after its composition. In 1957 folklorist Anne Grimes collected a version from Reuben Allen, a descendant of a free black family in Zanesville. Carol Bishop Myers, "The Musical Expression of Anti-Slavery Sentiment in Ohio," *Sonneck Society Bulletin* 18, no. 1 (Spring 1992): 8–11.

2. Frederick Jackson Turner, *Rise of the New West, 1819–1829* (New York: Harper & Brothers, 1906), pp. 68–69. Robert Chaddock, in his 1908 history of Ohio before 1850, similarly affirmed frontier democracy: "The freedom of the individual and the broad basis for democratic representative government in the United States developed not in the older states but for the first time on the extending frontier of the Middle West." Robert Chaddock, *Ohio before 1850* (New York: Columbia University, 1908), p. 5.

3. Leon F. Litwack, *North of Slavery: The Negro in the Free States, 1790–1860* (Chicago: University of Chicago Press, 1961), p. vii; Frank U. Quillin, *The Color Line in Ohio: A History of Race Prejudice in a Typical Northern State* (Ann Arbor, Mich.: George Wahr, 1913), p. 59. By 1850 white liberals in Ohio had joined a "Free Soil Movement" to rid the state and the nation of a legacy of political and economic discrimination against blacks. See Eric Foner, *Free Soil, Free Labor, Free Men: The Ideology of the Republican Party before the Civil War* (New York: Oxford University Press, 1970).

4. Articles on women's suffrage appeared in the *Mount Vernon Republican* on Mar. 1, Mar. 22, and Mar. 29, 1870, just before ratification of the Fifteenth Amendment. The Ohio legislature turned down a resolution on women's suffrage on Mar. 16, 1870, by the slimmest of margins, 52 to 54; editor Bascom noted, "So that probably ends the subject for this year"; *Mount Vernon Republican*, Mar. 22, 1870.

5. Ibid., Jan. 25, 1870. Harper referred to Republicans as "Radicals" and their cause as "Radicalism"; Bascom taunted his adversaries with the label "Copperheads."

6. Ibid., Feb. 1, 1870; *Mount Vernon Democratic Banner*, Apr. 15, 1870. Although it appeared two weeks after ratification, the phrase "The White Man's Party" clearly characterized the Democrats' posture in the months of weekly debate.

7. *Mount Vernon Republican*, Apr. 19, 1870; ibid., May 10, 1870. Zouaves, French soldiers who fought on the side of the North during the Civil War, were famed for their exotic "oriental" costuming, featuring a tasseled turban or fez, baggy trousers, and gaiters, and for their precise, dramatic drill formations. *Zouaves* eventually became the term for a number of volunteer regiments who adopted the Zouave traditions of style and battle performance.

8. Ibid., May 17, 1870; Knox County census of 1870.

9. *Mount Vernon Democratic Banner*, Apr. 15, 1870.

10. "The Grand Summation," *Mount Vernon Republican*, Apr. 5, 1870.

11. For a discussion of local government in pioneer towns, see Richard Lingeman, *Small Town America: A Narrative History, 1620–the Present* (New York: G. P. Putnam's Sons, 1980), p. 123.

12. *Mount Vernon Democratic Banner*, Apr. 8, 1870. Information on the broadside's dissemination and on the Snowdens' appearance at the polling place with Grant's speech in hand is from the *Mount Vernon Republican*, Apr. 12, 1870.

13. *Snowden* v. *Young* et al., Knox County Court of Common Pleas, file no. 27 (16353), Apr. 6, 1870.

14. "Blind Prejudiced Judges," *Mount Vernon Republican*, Apr. 12, 1870 (emphasis in original).

15. *Mount Vernon Democratic Banner*, Apr. 8, 1870. Public response to blacks exercising their right to vote varied with the community. In Chillicothe, Ohio, the novelty of black voters and the anticipation of possible disturbances drew crowds at some polling places. But black citizens voted early to avoid possible confrontations or avoided any demonstrations that might arouse their opponents. See Quillin, *Color Line in Ohio*, p. 103.

16. Republicans' concern for the Snowdens continued well beyond their first attempt to vote. A handwritten letter from one A. T. Wikoff and J. C. Donaldson to the family, dated Oct. 16, 1876, encouraged them to vote for the reelection of Rutherford B. Hayes as governor in November and reported Republican victories in recent state elections; letter in Snowden collection.

17. Cited in Quillin, *Color Line in Ohio*, p. 98.

18. Richard Albert Folk, "Black Man's Burden in Ohio, 1849–1863" (Ph.D. diss., University of Toledo, 1972), pp. 130–31; Quillin, *Color Line in Ohio*, pp. 13–14, 19, 63–64, 75–80, 97–102; Joseph P. Smith, ed., *History of the Republican Party in Ohio*, vol. 1 (Chicago: Lewis Publishing Co., 1898), pp. 230–39. A few African Americans did vote in Ohio before ratification of the Fifteenth Amendment. Some light-skinned black men cast ballots in the 1830s and 1840s, when courts were inclined to interpret "white" to mean individuals with more than 50 percent white ancestry. In central Ohio's Muskingum County, a light-skinned black man denied the right to vote in 1864 successfully sued the voting officials and was awarded damages of $240. Wayne L. Snider, *Guernsey County's Black Pioneers, Patriots, and Persons* (Columbus: Ohio Historical Society,

1979), pp. 31–33. See also C. Peter Ripley, ed., *The Black Abolitionist Papers*, vol. 4, *The United States, 1847–1858* (Chapel Hill: University of North Carolina Press, 1991), p. 225.

19. Farmers had planted tobacco as a cash crop in the hilly regions of central and eastern Ohio since the 1820s, and by the 1830s Knox County had become a leading producer. Despite the vagaries of the market and the cumulative effects of soil exhaustion, local farmers included tobacco among their program of general farming well after the Civil War. Francis A. Walker, comp., *The Statistics of the Wealth and Industry of the United States* (Washington, D.C.: Government Printing Office, 1872), p. 224. However, tobacco production declined steadily from the time of its initial boom in the 1820s and 1830s. By the Civil War, Knox County was only a minor producer. Robert Leslie Jones, *History of Agriculture in Ohio to 1880* (Kent, Ohio: Kent State University Press, 1983), pp. 250–58.

20. *Snowden* v. *Cummins and Sturtz*, Knox County Court of Common Pleas, file box 119 (13740), Aug. 23, 1866.

21. Jones, *Agriculture in Ohio*, p. 257.

22. Jacqueline Jones, *Labor of Love, Labor of Sorrow: Black Women, Work, and the Family from Slavery to the Present* (New York: Vintage Books, 1986), p. 58.

23. The Northwest Ordinance prohibited slavery within the territory, a position the territorial legislature opposed from its inception in 1799. The debate over slavery resumed as Ohio prepared a state constitution in 1802. Ultimately, the framers forbade slavery in the new state, fearing that the United States Congress would reject their petition for statehood if slavery was not disallowed. Charles Thomas Hickok, *The Negro in Ohio, 1802–1870* (Cleveland: Williams Publishing & Electric Co., 1896), pp. 9–31.

24. "Hordes of Negroes Coming!" *Mount Vernon Democratic Banner*, Feb. 12, 1861. Articles in the *Banner* frequently reported alleged idleness, incompetence, and unwillingness to work among blacks who had escaped to Canada; see "The Fugitive Negroes in Canada," Feb. 17, 1860; "Fugitive Slaves in Canada," Jan. 10, 1860; "Condition of Fugitive Slaves in Canada," Aug. 22, 1854.

25. Eugene H. Berwanger, *The Frontier against Slavery: Western Anti-Negro Prejudice and the Slavery Extension Controversy* (Urbana: University of Illinois Press, 1967), pp. 33–35; Quillin, *Color Line in Ohio*, p. 50; David A. Gerber, *Black Ohio and the Color Line, 1860–1915* (Urbana: University of Illinois Press, 1976), p. 7.

26. Woodson, *Mind of the Negro*, p. 482; see also pp. 483–84.

27. Hickok, *Negro in Ohio*, pp. 32–76; Quillin, *Color Line in Ohio*, pp. 21–34; Folk, "Black Man's Burden in Ohio," pp. 4–5; "Race Hate in Early Ohio," *Negro History Bulletin* 10 (June 1947): 203–4, 206–8, 210; Charles Jay Wilson, "The Negro in Early Ohio," *Ohio History* 39 (1930): 717–68. For an early discussion of the impact of the black laws in Ohio, see A. D. Barber, *Report on the Condi-*

tion of the Colored People of Ohio; Read before the Ohio Anti-Slavery Society at Its Fifth Anniversary, at Massillon (n.p., May 27, 1840).

28. Gerber, *Black Ohio and the Color Line*, p. 14, notes that instead of posting bond, "the word of an established white resident or a respected black minister might suffice as a guarantee of good behavior."

29. In a few larger cities, black communities attempted to raise funds for separate schools, but with meager results. Quillin, *Color Line in Ohio*, pp. 23, 45–66, 82–85.

30. Reverdy C. Ransom, *The Pilgrimage of Harriet Ransom's Son* (Nashville, Tenn.: Sunday School Union, 1949), pp. 22–23. On legislation regarding black education in Ohio, see Hickok, *Negro in Ohio*, pp. 90–91; Quillin, *Color Line in Ohio*, pp. 82–93; Folk, "Black Man's Burden in Ohio," p. 127. Information on the Snowden children's schooling comes from the Knox County census of 1850.

31. Folk, "Black Man's Burden in Ohio," pp. 3, 6.

32. The federal census of 1850 indicated that of Knox County's black residents, nine were born in Pennsylvania, seven in Virginia, five in Maryland, and one each in New York, Georgia, and Canada. The remainder were born in Ohio. Gerber, *Black Ohio and the Color Line*, p. 15, notes that, like Knox County, Ohio's black population before 1860 came primarily from the Upper South, made up of "recently emancipated slaves and the more established, older group of free people of color."

33. In other sections of the state, larger groups of African Americans settled together in a particular area. In some cases, a group of manumitted slaves settled on land purchased for their relocation by their former master. Less often, groups of African Americans formed utopian communities. These collective settlements often fared worse than did the small black communities that grew by accretion. Group settlements became the focus of more intense and vocal prejudice and were perceived as a greater source of economic competition with whites. Folk, "Black Man's Burden in Ohio," pp. 3, 6–13; Snider, *Black Pioneers, Patriots, and Persons*, pp. 1, 29. For an example of one master's efforts to relocate his slaves in Ohio, see Edgar F. Love, "Registration of Free Blacks in Ohio: The Slaves of George C. Mendenhall," *Journal of Negro History* 69, no. 1 (Winter 1984): 38–47. To this day the county's African American residents have never lived in an identifiably black district.

34. Gerber, *Black Ohio and the Color Line*, pp. 67–68. Similar occupations were noted for African Americans in Guernsey County, Ohio; Snider, *Black Pioneers, Patriots, and Persons*, p. 8.

35. For a general discussion of religious and fraternal organizations within Ohio's black communities, see Gerber, *Black Ohio and the Color Line*, pp. 20–22, 140–58. First established in Philadelphia in 1787 by African American churchmen dissatisfied with their ill treatment from the white Methodist church,

the African Methodist Episcopal Church developed a mission dedicated to promoting racial solidarity and improving the condition of the nation's black citizenry. Under Bishop Richard Allen's leadership, the A.M.E. Church fought against colonization and for the cause of abolition; in 1830 Allen organized the first of the "Negro Conventions" to unite black leadership in the fight against slavery. Believing that education was fundamental to black social advancement, the A.M.E. Church established several academic institutions, including Ohio's Wilberforce University in 1856. See Richard Allen, *The Life, Experience and Gospel Labors of the Rt. Rev. Richard Allen* (New York: Abingdon Press, 1983); Howard D. Gregg, *History of the African Methodist Episcopal Church* (Nashville, Tenn.: AMEC Sunday School Union, 1980); Daniel A. Payne, *History of the African Methodist Episcopal Church* (1891; reprint, New York: Arno Press and the New York Times, 1969). A brief summary of A.M.E. Church history can be found in C. Eric Lincoln and Lawrence H. Mamiya, *The Black Church in the African American Experience* (Durham, N.C.: Duke University Press, 1990), pp. 50–56.

36. N. N. Hill, Jr., *History of Knox County, Ohio: Its Past and Present* (Mount Vernon, Ohio: A. A. Graham & Co., 1881), pp. 419–20; Johanna Holbrook, "A History of Wayman Chapel African Methodist Episcopal Church" (Unpublished paper, 1992).

37. J. B. T. Marsh, *The Story of the Jubilee Singers*, rev. ed. (New York: S. W. Green's Son, 1883), pp. 26–27.

38. Holbrook, "History of Wayman Chapel," pp. 19–20, 23.

39. "What Makes the Negro Black," *Mount Vernon Democratic Banner*, May 4, 1858; "A Negro Turning White," ibid., July 27, 1858; "Black Siamese Twins," *Mount Vernon Republican*, Mar. 31, 1857.

40. "A Nigger Head and a Locomotive," *Mount Vernon Democratic Banner*, Oct. 18, 1859; "The Nigger," ibid., Apr. 30, 1860.

41. "Horrible Murder—A Master Killed and Burned by His Slaves," ibid., Feb. 14, 1860; "A Horrible Murder in Tennessee—A Planter Killed by His Slave," ibid., Jan. 8, 1861; "Diabolical Design," ibid., Jan. 29, 1856. Other articles of this type include "Horrible Rape by a Negro," ibid., June 1, 1858; and "Murdered by His Slaves," ibid., Nov. 15, 1853.

42. "A Negro Slave Shot by His Clergyman," ibid., Apr. 27, 1858. Articles sympathetically documenting the murder of blacks were commonplace in the *Mount Vernon Democratic Banner:* "Two Negroes Hung—One Burnt at the Stake," Aug. 2, 1859; "Judge Lynch—Negro Roasted Alive," Feb. 8, 1859; "Lynch Law in Ohio," Dec. 9, 1856; "Burnt Alive," Jan. 29, 1856; "Brutal Murder," June 6, 1854. The article concerning the "negro roasted alive" was included in the regular column entitled "Interesting Variety."

43. "Disgraceful Row," ibid., Jan. 27, 1857. Representations of African Ameri-

cans in Mount Vernon's newspapers were typical of publications throughout the state; for a general description of black images in Ohio newspapers, see Folk, "Black Man's Burden in Ohio," pp. 65–75, 80–98.

44. "Another Judson Case—A Negro Runs Away with a White Girl—Disgusting Developments," *Mount Vernon Democratic Banner*, Mar. 6, 1860; "A White Heiress Elopes with a Negro," ibid., Jan. 18, 1859,

45. "The Editor of the Republican Carrying Out His Principles, by Marrying a Negro to a White Woman!" ibid., June 15, 1858.

46. For a discussion of regional variations in prejudice against African Americans within Ohio, see Quillin, *Color Line in Ohio*, pp. 65–72. A case study of Quaker activity supporting blacks elsewhere in the Midwest can be found in George K. Hesslink, *Black Neighbors: Negroes in a Northern Rural Community*, 2d ed. (Indianapolis: Bobbs-Merrill Co., 1974), pp. 29–46.

47. "Africa for Fremont!" *Mount Vernon Democratic Banner*, Aug. 12, 1856.

48. "The Official Returns," ibid., Dec. 2, 1856. Debates about the status of African Americans apparently continued with regard to the Kansas question. The Kansas-Nebraska bill, submitted to Congress in 1857, sought to repeal the Missouri Compromise banning slavery in territories north of 36° 30′. Local dissension on this issue stimulated publication of a humorous lampoon by J. W. White, *The First Book of Chronicles Humorously Illustrated: Being a Faithful History of the Dissensions among the Harmonious Democracy! of the County of Knox upon the Kansas Question!* (Mount Vernon, Ohio: National Book and Job Office, 1858).

49. For a general discussion of the conflicts between abolitionists and those favoring colonization in the three decades before the Civil War, see C. Peter Ripley, ed., *The Black Abolitionist Papers*, vol. 3, *The United States, 1830–1846* (Chapel Hill: University of North Carolina Press, 1991), pp. 3–69.

50. "Colonization," *Mount Vernon Democratic Banner*, Jan. 31, 1854. *Banner* articles reported news of colonization efforts and of the American Colonization Society: "Interesting from Liberia," Mar. 15, 1859; "The African Repository," Feb. 8, 1859; "Past and Present Condition of the Negro," Mar. 17, 1857; "Emigrants for Liberia," June 6, 1854.

51. Howard H. Bell, "The Negro Emigration Movement, 1849–1854: A Phase of Negro Nationalism," *Phylon* 20, no. 2 (1959): 132–42. See also Folk, "Black Man's Burden in Ohio," pp. 163–206.

52. "The Christian Anti-Slavery Movement," *Mount Vernon Republican*, Dec. 12, 1859, announced the upcoming visit of "Rev. Lucas Matlack of Syracuse, N.Y., [who] has been appointed the General Agent for this state." A critical review of his address appeared in the *Mount Vernon Democratic Banner*, Dec. 27, 1859. The *Banner*, vigilant in its opposition to the antislavery cause, documented many local abolitionist meetings: "The Abolition Meeting on Friday," Aug. 20, 1859; "Tom Corwin to Be Here," Sept. 14, 1858; "Abolition County

Convention," Sept. 9, 1856; "The Abolition Farce on Saturday," June 13, 1854. Abolitionists had long been active in the area; twelve citizens of Mount Vernon attended one of Ohio's first antislavery conventions in 1836. The Ohio Anti-Slavery Society was officially formed in 1835. For Knox County's involvement, see Robert Price, "The Ohio Anti-Slavery Convention, 1836," *Ohio State Archaeological and Historical Quarterly* 45, no. 2 (Apr. 1936): 177–78; Wilbur H. Siebert collection, boxes 100–116, Ohio Historical Society.

53. Elwell O. Mead, "Historical Sketch," in *Manual of the First Congregational Church* (Mount Vernon, Ohio, 1924), pp. 52–53.

54. The extent of this network and the number of African Americans aided are subjects of some debate. Wilbur H. Siebert, who collected documents and reminiscences of those familiar with the Underground Railroad, estimated that not less than forty thousand fugitives escaped slavery through the system between 1830 and 1860; Wilbur H. Siebert, *The Underground Railroad from Slavery to Freedom* (New York: MacMillan Co., 1898), p. 46. Among the materials collected by Siebert was a letter from J. H. Leasure, who identified sites in Knox County: "I well remember that a line of this road was through Knox Co. Richland Co. and Huron Co., Ohio, and I well remember of meeting a number of colored men on the road in wagons driven by white men, strangers to me, and it was hard to find out where stations were kept." Siebert collection, boxes 100–116, OHS. Siebert himself identified one station as located in the Owl Creek Friends settlement, two miles north of Fredericktown.

More recent scholarship suggests that Siebert accepted the estimates of participants uncritically and appraised the operation's significance through a scrim of romanticism; see Larry Gara, *The Liberty Line: The Legend of the Underground Railroad* (Lexington: University of Kentucky Press, 1961), pp. 17–18, 190; Charles L. Blockson, ed., *The Underground Railroad* (New York: Prentice Hall Press, 1987). We thank Heath Bair for sharing his research with us.

55. Helen Snowden, a cousin and age peer to Sophia, wrote to the Ohio Snowdens about schooling and job prospects there. Benjamin Snowden, brother of Thomas, died in 1893 at age 101. The Warsaw paper, the *Western New-Yorker*, published a notice on Mar. 15 detailing his life:

Benjamin Snowden died at his residence in this village March 13th. He was born a slave in Maryland, but came north when a young man, and was cared for by agents of the "underground railway," at Whitestown, the residence of Gerrit Smith. He attended school and was married there, and his four children were born there. Mr. Snowden's wife died some years ago. Since then his daughter Ellen [Helen] has been his house-keeper. Two sons also survive him, Jerome, of Oleau, and Theodore, of Warsaw. Mr. Snowden had reached a great age, but just how many years, he did not know. He lost a son James several years ago. Both father and son were at that

time at work in the New-Yorker office. Mr. Snowden will be buried this afternoon at 3 o'clock from his residence on Jefferson Street. The Rev. Mr.
McKinley will officiate.

56. Folk, "Black Man's Burden in Ohio," pp. 313–42.

57. "A Kidnapping Case," *Mount Vernon Republican*, Nov. 5, 1859.

58. F. D. Root to Sophia Snowden, Pataskala, Ohio, n.d.

59. Northern communities often reacted to interracial marriages with hostility,
even after legal barriers had been removed. A case in point is the marriage of
James Bromley to Elizabeth Willett in Monroe, Mich., on Dec. 17, 1888. Although Michigan's antimiscegenation law had been repealed in 1882, the marriage of a black man to a white woman created a furor; following the wedding
Bromley was afraid to walk through the streets for fear of being mobbed. The
community gradually accepted the couple, but townspeople generally viewed the
marriage as a "big mistake." James E. DeVries, *Race and Kinship in a Midwestern Town: The Black Experience in Monroe, Michigan, 1900–1915* (Urbana: University of Illinois Press, 1984), pp. 118–19.

60. The 1880 Richland County census identified Nancy J. Simpson of Newville
as a twenty-five-year-old white female, and her mother Rebecca as a sixty-year-
old widow. According to the census, Rebecca's father was born in Ireland.

61. Nan Simpson to Ben Snowden, Newville, Ohio, n.d.

62. Ibid., Dec. 7, no year; ibid., June 11, no year.

63. Ibid., n.d.

64. Ibid., n.d.

65. Commenting on interracial courtships in the early twentieth century,
Mount Vernon resident Isabelle Wintermute said that black women, not white
women, usually ended the affairs: "It was the colored women who were sensible;
the white women just threw up their hands." Isabelle Wintermute, interview with
authors, Mount Vernon, Ohio, May 22, 1989.

66. Nan Simpson to Ben Snowden, Newville, Ohio, n.d.; ibid., June 12, no
year.

67. An essay in the Snowden scrapbook, titled "Tobacco—What It Costs," asserted that "if you pay five cents per day for the filthy trash men chew and
smoke you will spend $18.25 in one year." Noting that "even the ladies(?) some-
times snuff, and smoke, and chew the filthy weed!" the article closed with the
call for "a temperance epoch, antinarcotic in type. God speed the day when it
shall come."

68. Nan Simpson to Ben Snowden, Newville, Ohio, n.d.

69. Ibid., June 19, no year.

70. Ibid., Apr. 11, no year.

71. Taken about 1870, when blacks formed the Mount Vernon Zouaves and
paraded in honor of the Fifteenth Amendment's ratification, the photo shows

costuming similar to Zouave costume of the Civil War era. Lew wore a typical Zouave tasseled turban, and his unusual kneepads might have been part of an improvised, homemade Zouave effect. Another possibility is that his clothing was the ceremonial garb of a fraternal club. Black Freemasonry began in Ohio about 1847, and Mount Vernon's Lodge No. 43 was warranted in 1883. See Charles H. Wesley, *The History of the Prince Hall Grand Lodge of Free and Accepted Masons of the State of Ohio, 1849–1971* (Washington, D.C.: Associated Publishers for the Association for the Study of Negro Life and History, 1972), pp. 2, 92. Prince Hall founded black Freemasonry when the white Masonic organization rejected African Americans.

72. In eighteenth-century New England, African Americans used charms for protection against disease, accident, and human enemies. William D. Piersen suggests that "while magical talismans may not have destroyed the power of the white master class, they probably did reduce the anxieties of the slaves. By protecting bondsmen from fears of mistreatment, charms made their lives more comfortable. The whites were rarely aware of this counterforce, which made the covert use of magic far safer than more open acts of rebellion." William D. Piersen, *Black Yankees: The Development of an Afro-American Subculture in Eighteenth-Century New England* (Amherst: University of Massachusetts Press, 1988), p. 152.

CHAPTER 5. I WISH I WAS IN DIXIE

1. Ken Burns's series "The Civil War" aired on PBS in spring 1990.

2. Marshall Frady, "If They Wouldn't Play 'Dixie' So Much . . . ," *Mademoiselle* 36 (1966): 333.

3. Marshall Ingwerson, "'Dixie' Anthem, Confederate Flags Demean Citadel's Black Cadets," *Christian Science Monitor*, Mar. 6, 1967, National ed.; Sam Dennison, *Scandalize My Name: Black Imagery in American Popular Music* (New York: Garland Publishing Co., 1982), p. 530 n. 3. In this footnote Dennison also cites a 1970 protest of the song by civil rights leader Whitney Young, Jr., and another in 1971 by the 75th U.S. Army Band.

4. Robert McG. Thomas, Jr., "Tradition Brings Controversy," *New York Times*, Sept. 18, 1989.

5. Robert C. Toll, *Blacking Up: The Minstrel Show in Nineteenth-Century America* (New York: Oxford University Press, 1974), pp. 104–33, discusses the minstrels' complex responses to the Civil War. Union sympathizers because antisecessionist, minstrels nevertheless ridiculed abolitionists and the cause of equal opportunity for blacks.

6. Charles Burleigh Galbreath, "Song Writers of Ohio," *Ohio Archaeological Quarterly* 13 (Oct. 1904): 533–34.

7. Clipping titled "The Author of Dixie," n.p., n.d. (ca. 1895), Emmett archives, VFM 2246, Ohio Historical Society (hereafter OHS), Columbus; "How 'Dan' Emmett's Song Became the War Song of the South," New York *Tribune*, ca. 1908, Emmett archives, VFM 2246, OHS.

8. Charles Burleigh Galbreath, *Daniel Decatur Emmett: Author of "Dixie"* (Columbus, Ohio: Heer Printing Co., 1904), p. 524,

9. W. H. Smith, "The Story of Dixie and Its Picturesque Composer," *Etude* 52 (Sept. 1934): 524.

10. *Craft* 49, no. 6 (Dec. 1989/Jan. 1990): 67. Comments on the event's success and the lack of reaction about the use of "Dixie" are from Sarah Stengle, Metropolitan Council staffer, telephone conversation with authors, July 30, 1991.

11. Hans Nathan, *Dan Emmett and the Rise of Early Negro Minstrelsy* (Norman: University of Oklahoma Press, 1962), p. 262. Nathan summarizes the etymology of "Dixie" on pp. 262–66.

12. Frank Moore, *The Civil War in Song and Story, 1860–1865* (1865; reprint, New York: Johnson Reprint Corp., 1970), p. 46.

13. Nathan, *Dan Emmett*, pp. 247–48.

14. Toll, *Blacking Up*, p. 12; John G. Blair, "Blackface Minstrels in Cross-Cultural Perspective," *American Studies International* 28, no. 2 (Oct. 1990): 57, 59.

15. On black composers in minstrelsy, see Thomas L. Riis, *Just before Jazz: Black Musical Theater in New York, 1890–1915* (Washington, D.C.: Smithsonian Institution Press, 1989).

16. Information on the commissioning of the headstone comes from an interview with township trustee Dan Bartlett, who is in charge of the graveyard; Dan Bartlett, interview with authors, Fredericktown, Ohio, Jan. 1, 1988. The stone is not actually above Ben and Lew's graves; their individual burial sites are topped with plain, untitled slabs.

17. Norm Cohen, album notes for *Minstrels and Tunesmiths: The Commercial Roots of Early Country Music*, John Edwards Memorial Foundation JEMF 109 (1981), p. 5.

18. Nathan, *Dan Emmett*, p. 247, cites the traditional version, which first appeared in 1872 in the show business newspaper the *New York Clipper*; David Ewen, ed., *American Popular Songs from the Revolutionary War to the Present* (New York: Random House, 1966), s.v. "Dixie"; clipping "The Author of Dixie"; "War Song of the South"; "The Author of 'Dixie' Passes to Great Beyond," *Mount Vernon Democratic Banner*, July 1, 1904.

19. Nathan, *Dan Emmett*, p. 247, describes the Minnesota report as "wholly uncorroborated." Pushing the date of composition even further back, the *Washington Post* had reported that "Dixie" was written in 1843, seventeen years before the song was copyrighted; see clipping "The Author of Dixie."

20. Toll, *Blacking Up*, p. 45.

21. George Booker, interview with authors, Mount Vernon, Ohio, July 10, 1991.

22. Marie Moorehead, interview with authors, Mount Vernon, Ohio, May 14, 1982; Ethel Hammond, cited in "Local Woman Recalls Times of Dan Emmett," *Mount Vernon News*, Aug. 2, 1967.

23. Marie Moorehead, interview with authors, Mount Vernon, Ohio, May 14, 1982; George Booker, interview with authors, Mount Vernon, Ohio, July 10, 1991.

24. Marie Moorehead, interview with authors, Mount Vernon, Ohio, May 14, 1982.

25. George Booker, interview with authors, Mount Vernon, Ohio, July 10, 1991; Ethel Hammond, "Local Woman Recalls Times of Dan Emmett."

26. Dena J. Epstein, *Sinful Tunes and Spirituals: Black Folk Music to the Civil War* (Urbana: University of Illinois Press, 1977), p. 173; Eileen Southern, ed., *Readings in Black American Music* (New York: W. W. Norton & Co., 1971), p. 148; Eugene D. Genovese, *Roll, Jordan, Roll: The World the Slaves Made* (New York: Vintage Books, 1976), p. 317. Epstein discusses the improvisatory nature of song making among African peoples throughout her book; see, for example, pp. 174, 181, 228.

27. Nathan, *Dan Emmett*, p. 104, recounts, "He must have excelled in writing, for his manuscripts throughout his life show clear, well-rounded letters and notes, carefully drawn with a quill." Note 16 on p. 104 also cites another such admiring reference.

28. Stella Lee, interview with authors, Mount Vernon, Ohio, Jan. 15, 1984.

29. We thank Joe Wilson for this observation.

30. May McClane, "Daniel Decatur Emmett, Author of 'Dixie,' Pioneer and Son of Pioneers" (Unpublished manuscript in the Wintermute collection, Knox County Historical Society, ca. 1935).

31. The Knox County census of 1850 recorded Abraham Emmett as a fifty-nine-year-old blacksmith.

32. H. Ogden Wintermute, Dan Emmett's local biographer, located the Emmett home and shop on two lots at Front and Mulberry streets; he also told the story of the boy and the traveling musician. H. Ogden Wintermute, *Daniel Decatur Emmett* (Columbus, Ohio: Heer Printing Co., 1955), pp. 16, 27.

33. One report does place Emmett in Mount Vernon sometime between 1835 and the early 1840s, when he was in his twenties: Smith, "Story of Dixie," p. 524. See Nathan, *Dan Emmett*, for Emmett's whereabouts from the 1830s through 1859.

34. McClane, "Daniel Decatur Emmett."

35. Toll, *Blacking Up*, p. 42; Dan Emmett, cited in Clifford Wayne, "Notes of Early Burnt Cork Opera," *Antiques Journal* (July 1962): 14.

36. Epstein, *Sinful Tunes and Spirituals*, pp. 241–42; see also Lawrence W. Levine, *Black Culture and Black Consciousness: Afro-American Folk Thought from Slavery to Freedom* (New York: Oxford University Press, 1979), pp. 192–93.

37. Emmett archives, OHS.

38. "Walk Mr. Bookar," song in "Sayings" booklet, box 1, Emmett archives, OHS. Information on the Booker family's relationships with Dan Emmett and the Snowdens came from Vera Payne, telephone interview with authors, June 1988.

39. "Seely Simpkins Jig," box 1, Emmett archives, OHS. Renamed a fancy quickstep, the tune appears in Emmett's manual of military and popular fife music; Daniel Decatur Emmett, *Fife Instructor* (1862; reprint, Chicago: Photopress Publishing Co., n.d.), p. 78. Seeley Simpkins was renowned in pioneer times as an extraordinary fiddler and whistler. Knox County historian A. Banning Norton devoted an entire chapter to Simpkins in his 1862 volume: "He was a great favorite with the squaws and pappooses, by reason of his uncommon musical talent. He could mimic any sound of varmint or human, surpassed the lute of Orpheus, and out-whistled all creation. He furnished *the* music for early musters, and when it took four counties to make a regiment he gave them a challenge to out-whistle any man within them." A. Banning Norton, *A History of Knox County, Ohio, from 1799 to 1862 Inclusive* (Columbus, Ohio: Richard Nevins, 1862), p. 422.

40. Emmett, *Fife Instructor*, p. 60.

41. Toll, *Blacking Up*, pp. 43–47, reviews statements by the early minstrels about their black sources; see p. 43 for the contest between Diamond and Lane.

42. Kathryn Reed-Maxfield, "Emmett, Foster, and Their Anonymous Colleagues: The Creators of Early Minstrel Show Songs" (Paper presented at the annual meeting of the Sonneck Society for American Music, Pittsburgh, Apr. 4, 1987), p. 4.

43. Vera Payne, telephone interview with authors, Dec. 6, 1984; Stella Lee, interview with authors, Mount Vernon, Ohio, Apr. 13, 1984. Nathan, *Dan Emmett*, p. 282, cites a similar physical description of the elderly Emmett from a Mount Vernon postmaster.

44. Frederick Douglass, letter in *The Mind of the Negro As Reflected in Letters Written during the Crisis, 1800–1860*, ed. Carter G. Woodson (1926; reprint, New York: Negro Universities Press, 1969), p. 482.

45. William Diggs, interviews with authors, La Plata, Md., Mar. 14, 1988, July 2, 1991.

46. George Booker, interview with authors, Mount Vernon, Ohio, July 10, 1991.

47. Nathan, *Dan Emmett*, pp. 255–62.

48. Levine, *Black Culture and Black Consciousness*, p. 246. For a useful dis-

cussion of songs expressing protest and the synthetic nature of African American music, see his chapter "The Rise of Secular Song."

49. John Atkins, an English traveler to Sierra Leone in 1721, noted, "Sometimes they are all round in a Circle laughing, and with uncouth Notes, blame or praise somebody in the Company." A later visitor to that region, Thomas Winterbottom, wrote in 1803 about both the improvisational and satirical songs he heard from canoe rowers on the Gold Coast: "One of the rowers sings a couplet, somewhat in a recitative voice, which is closed by a chorus in which they all join. . . . The subject of the song is either a description of some love intrigue, the praise of some woman celebrated for her beauty, &c. or it is of a satirical cast. . . . They are commonly impromptu, seldom the result of much study, and frequently describe the passengers in a strain either of praise or of the most pointed ridicule." Epstein, *Sinful Tunes and Spirituals*, pp. 5, 6.

50. Henry Louis Gates, Jr., *The Signifying Monkey: A Theory of African-American Literary Criticism* (New York: Oxford University Press, 1988), p. 67.

51. Nicholas Cresswell, *Journal, 1774–1777*, quoted in Miles Mark Fisher, *Negro Slave Songs in the United States* (1953; reprint, New York: Citadel Press, 1990), p. 11; Frederick Douglass, cited in Genovese, *Roll, Jordan, Roll*, p. 581. Levine, *Black Culture and Black Consciousness*, p. 194, comments: "Antebellum white Southerners may have delighted in such songs as harmless and amusing burlesques and found in them relief for any repressed feelings of guilt and ambivalence they might have had concerning slavery. For the blacks who sang them, they were clearly outlets for a quite different complex of emotions." See also Epstein, *Sinful Tunes and Spirituals*, pp. 187–88.

52. Gates, *Signifying Monkey*, pp. 66, 67. Gates uses the capitalized *Signification* to denote black tradition. Roger D. Abrahams has been the seminal investigator of signifying in black urban settings; see, for example, his *Deep Down in the Jungle: Negro Narrative Folklore from the Streets of Philadelphia* (New York: Aldine Publishing Co., 1970) and *Talking Black* (Rawley, Mass.: Newbury House, 1976).

53. Joanne M. Braxton, *Black Women Writing Autobiography: A Tradition within a Tradition* (Philadelphia: Temple University Press, 1989), p. 5. Braxton here is quoting Temma Kaplan; see Kaplan, introduction, *Barnard Occasional Papers on Women's Issues* 3, no. 2 (1988): 2–3.

54. We draw our text of "Dixie" from the sheet music that appeared in the 1895 *Confederate Veteran* 3 (Sept.): 268–69. Hans Nathan suggested that this version most closely resembles the original manuscript, now lost; see Nathan, *Dan Emmett*, pp. 250–51. The manuscript reproduced in 1895 is owned by George Bird Evans, whose great-grandmother was Emmett's second wife; see George Bird Evans, "Original Copy of 'Dixie' Identified," *Civil War Times*, Nov. 1961, pp. 13–15.

55. Simon J. Martinet, *Martinet's Map of Maryland*, atlas ed. (Baltimore: Simon J. Martinet, 1866), intro.

56. Jane G. Wheeler, "Sandyfield School," in *A Legacy: One- and Two-Room Schools in Charles County* (La Plata, Md.: Charles County Retired Teachers Association, 1984), p. 43.

57. Moore, *Civil War*, p. 58.

58. Frederick Douglass, *Narrative of the Life of Frederick Douglass an American Slave* (1845; reprint, Cambridge: Belknap Press of Harvard University Press, 1960), p. 23. Mechal Sobel reviews African Americans' marking of time by the crops in *The World They Made Together: Black and White Values in Eighteenth-Century Virginia* (Princeton, N.J.: Princeton University Press, 1987), pp. 34–36.

59. Frederick Douglass, *My Bondage and My Freedom . . .* (New York: Miller, Orton & Mulligan, 1855), pp. 97–98; Douglass, *Narrative*, p. 368; Gates, *Signifying Monkey*, p. 67. Gates emphasizes repetition and reversal as key features of Signification.

60. Beth Maclay Doriani advances this thesis in "Black Womanhood in Nineteenth-Century America: Subversion and Self-Construction in Two Women's Autobiographies," *American Quarterly* 43, no. 2 (June 1991): 199–222.

61. Barbara Jeanne Fields cites free white artisans on Maryland slaveholding farms: "the well-digger, the carpenter, the pump-maker, even the seamstress"; Barbara Jeanne Fields, *Slavery and Freedom on the Middle Ground: Maryland during the Nineteenth Century* (New Haven, Conn.: Yale University Press, 1985), p. 88.

62. William Greer, age twenty-four, arrived in Baltimore on Sept. 30, 1822, with his wife, two children, and parents; *Passengers Who Arrived in the United States, September 1821–December 1823* (Washington: U.S. Department of State, 1969), pp. 149–50.

63. "Gay deceiver" appears in the minstrel song "Gumbo Chaff" from the 1830s; see Nathan, *Dan Emmett*, pp. 260–62.

64. Margaret Brown Klapthor and Paul Dennis Brown, *The History of Charles County Maryland* (La Plata, Md.: Charles County Tercentenary, 1958), p. 101.

65. Thomas B. Searight, *The Old Pike: A History of the National Road, with Incidents, Accidents, and Anecdotes Thereon* (Uniontown, Pa.: T. B. Searight, 1894), p. 245.

66. J. Thomas Scharf, *History of Western Maryland*, 2 vols. (1882; reprint, Baltimore: Regional Publishing Co., 1968), 1:378.

67. Sterling Stuckey, *Slave Culture: Nationalist Theory and the Foundations of Black America* (New York: Oxford University Press, 1987), p. 72. Stuckey interprets the toast as ironic.

68. Allan Kulikoff, *Tobacco and Slaves: The Development of Southern Cultures in the Chesapeake, 1680–1800* (Chapel Hill: University of North Carolina Press, 1986), p. 325.

69. Information on these terms as dance figures comes from Joe Wilson.

70. Fisher, *Negro Slave Songs*, pp. 111–19.

71. Eileen Southern, *The Music of Black Americans: A History* (New York: W. W. Norton & Co., 1971), p. 102.

72. Roger D. Abrahams, *Singing the Master* (New York: Pantheon, 1992), pp. 133, 136.

73. Nathan, *Dan Emmett*, pp. 153, 187. Describing Emmett's walk-arounds, Nathan, p. 236, writes: "The most tangible Negro element in his walk-arounds is the solo-ensemble alternation in their first part and the repetitiousness of its melodic and textual phrases. Another one is the interval of the minor third, upward and downward, which, as in Negro spirituals, often appears in a pentatonic formula (that is, with a preceding major second), while its larger context is regulated by a major or minor tonality. A few more specific relations to Negro music exist, but they are rather tenuous." Based on an examination of minstrel sheet music, Constance Rourke concluded that "Emmett's walkarounds—'Dixie' was a walkaround—are particularly significant as suggesting Negro origins"; Constance Rourke, *American Humor: A Study of the National Character* (1931; reprint, New York: Harcourt Brace Jovanovich, 1959), p. 312.

74. Alan W. C. Green, "'Jim Crow,' 'Zip Coon': The Northern Origins of Negro Minstrelsy," *Massachusetts Review* 11 (1970): 391.

75. Dennison, *Scandalize My Name*, p. 89.

76. "Authorship of 'Dixie' and 'The Old Folks at Home,'" *Mount Vernon Republican-News*, Mar. 26, 1908.

77. Eliza Campbell to Snowdens, Smyrna, Ohio, June 14, 1883. Morgan's raid into Smyrna is recounted in William G. Wolfe, *Stories of Guernsey County, Ohio* (Cambridge, Ohio: W. G. Wolfe, 1943), p. 318.

78. Eliza Campbell to Snowdens, Smyrna, Ohio, June 14, 1883.

79. McClane, "Daniel Decatur Emmett."

80. Obituary in the *Mount Vernon Republican*, Jan. 31, 1894.

EPILOGUE: A CLINTON QUADRILLE

1. For biographical information on Dan Emmett's later life, see H. Ogden Wintermute, *Daniel Decatur Emmett* (Columbus, Ohio: Heer Printing Co., 1955), pp. 45–57; and Hans Nathan, *Dan Emmett and the Rise of Early Negro Minstrelsy* (Norman: University of Oklahoma Press, 1962), pp. 276–84.

2. May McClane, "Daniel Decatur Emmett, Author of 'Dixie,' Pioneer and Son of Pioneers" (Unpublished manuscript in the Wintermute collection, Knox County Historical Society, ca. 1935).

3. Howard L. Sacks, "John Baltzell, a Country Fiddler from the Heartland," *Journal of Country Music* 10, no. 1 (1985): 21–24, 33–35. Much of our discussion of Baltzell is based on this article.

4. Baltzell was also among the earliest fiddlers to be recorded. Music scholars consider his style and repertoire "Northern," as opposed to the "Southern" rhythmic, short-bowed stroke and distinctive repertoire of the southern Appalachians. We accept this distinction only in part. Regionality is hard to document in the first era of recording. It is possible that nineteenth-century fiddlers were more alike stylistically, regardless of their region, than musicians of subsequent eras. For example, fiddler Allen Sisson of Tennessee, a man of Baltzell's generation, played in a style similar to Baltzell's, not like a "Southern" fiddler; Sacks, "John Baltzell," pp. 33–34.

5. Ada Bedell Wootton, "Something New about Dixie," *Etude* 54 (Dec. 1936): 809.

6. Thomas Edison invented the phonograph in 1877. By the mid-1890s commercial recordings were available, but the first records of folk fiddlers were made in 1923. See Norm Cohen, album notes for *Minstrels and Tunesmiths: The Commercial Roots of Early Country Music*, John Edwards Memorial Foundation JEMF 109 (1981), p. 2. For a contemporary re-creation of early minstrel music, see *The Early Minstrel Show*, New World Records NW 338 (1985).

7. For a discography of John Baltzell, see Simon Bronner, "John Baltzell: Champion Old Time Fiddler," *Old Time Music* 27 (Winter 1977/78): 14.

8. Ada Bedell Wootton, "How 'Dixie's' Composer Learned about the South," *Columbus Dispatch*, Sunday magazine, Oct. 29, 1950.

9. "Musical Snowdens Were Known by Local Woman," *Mount Vernon News*, May 27, 1968; Stella Lee, interview with authors, Mount Vernon, Ohio, Jan. 15, 1982. Moorehead and Lee saw the display some twenty-five years after Ellen's death.

10. Information on the Smyrna track's uphill grade comes from Mrs. A. E. Hibbs of Smyrna, age ninety-four, telephone conversation with authors, July 2, 1992. Smyrna is now no more than a crossroads, and the fair died out fifty years ago.

11. Ben Snowden to Lew Snowden, Mount Vernon, Ohio, Aug. 30, 1895. On another occasion Lew wrote Ben from Piedmont, a town near Smyrna, telling him, "Start Sunday night as thay ar trying to fix up a job." The brothers may have performed or done farm work, aside from racing. Lew Snowden to Ben Snowden, Piedmont, Ohio, Mar. 14, no year.

12. R. C. Lowther to Lew Snowden, Smyrna, Ohio, Dec. 18, 1895.

13. Ibid., Jan. 21, 1896.

14. Ibid., Apr. 19, 1896.

15. Ibid., Sept. 20, 1896.

16. W. A. Lowther to Lew Snowden, Smyrna, Ohio, Aug. 26, 1897.

17. Several letters document Lew's purchase of registered poultry: Phil Wittmer to Lew Snowden, Cannelton, Ind., Apr. 8, 1896; Thomas Hogshead to Lew Snowden, Staunton, Va., Aug. 11, 1899; F. G. Henry & Co. to Lew Snowden,

Marietta, Ohio, Feb. 28, 1907. E. J. Marana of Fredericktown wrote to ask if "Mr Snodon" had peaches, in exchange for which he offered to make a vest "well made worth three dollars" (Sept. 21, no year). A Mount Vernon woman, Mrs. J. Lewis, wrote Oct. 29, 1902, to ask Lew to deliver firewood.

18. Smith's Tavern was built in 1808 to serve overnight guests traveling by stagecoach from Zanesville to Mansfield. Formerly directly across the street from the Snowden homestead, the tavern was demolished in 1947. George Booker thought the Snowdens might have made their drop-door performance gable to entertain stagecoaching guests: "Maybe that's one reason why they had that black farm and let it [the gable door] down and entertain people. . . . So maybe at that particular time, why, they done most of the entertainment for thirty years or more." George Booker, interview with authors, Mount Vernon, Ohio, July 10, 1991.

19. Isabelle Wintermute, interview with authors, Mount Vernon, Ohio, May 22, 1989.

20. George Booker, interview with authors, Mount Vernon, Ohio, July 10, 1991.

21. Ibid.

Index

Page numbers in italics indicate illustrations

Abolitionism, 7, 29, 31, 41, 53, 56, 77, 78, 119–21, 127, 134, 143, 145–46, 159, 235n3, 239n35, 240n52, 243n5
Abrahams, Roger D., 181, 247n52
Accordion, 181
African Americans. *See* Black community, Knox County, Ohio; Blackface minstrelsy; "Dixie"; Music; Race relations, Knox County, Ohio; Slavery; Snowden Band; Songs
African Methodist Episcopal (A.M.E.) Church, 12, 70–71, 73, 136, 137–40, 162, 166, 239n35
Albert family, 88
Allen, William Frances, 71
Antislavery movement. *See* Abolitionism
Antrim, Ireland, 17, 42, 49–50

Baltimore, 46, 54, 56, 60, 77, 177
Baltzell, John, 18, 192, *193*, 194–97, 250n4
Banjo, *2*, 3, 5, 6, 7, 9, 14–16, 17, 19, 30, 31, 59, 63–64, *65*, 84, *86*, 87, 129, *141*, *151*, 152, 165, 172, 173, 180, 181, 189, 192, 214n25, 225nn18, 23, 229n87
Barnum, P. T., 84, 102, 139, 229n84
Bartlett, Dan, 244n16
Bascom, William, 126–28, 235nn4, 5
"Bell Brandon," 75
Black community, Knox County, Ohio: church life, 12, 137–39, 140, 162, 166; demographics, 1, 9, 11, 12, 115, 122,

128, 136–37, 238nn32, 33; employment, 137; social networks, 19, 68, 127–28, 137, 139, 141, 207. *See also* Race relations, Knox County, Ohio; Slavery
Blackface minstrelsy: black artists in, 67, 77, 85, 159, 169, 170, 223n5; black sources of, 3, 5, 7–8, 15, 20, 85, 160–61, 166–71 passim, 180–82, 246n41, 249n73; described, 5–7, 14, 77, 78, 84, 85, 159, 160, 164, 170, 177, 180, 181, 182, 194, 249n73; and popular culture, 6, 85–86, 158–59, 169, 194, 196–97; racial stereotypes in, 7, 8, 15, 77, 78, 158–59, 180–82. *See also* "Dixie"; Emmett, Daniel Decatur; Songs; *and individual instruments*
Blair, Sarah and Bell, 89, 90, 161
Bland, James, 77, 85, 169
Blind Tom (Thomas Bethune), *82*
Bogin, Ruth, 94
Bollman, Jim, 230n87
Bones (castanets), 5, 7, 14, 63, 180, 181
Booker family, 19, 68, 88, 170, 171
Booker, George, 19, 68, 73, 88, 162, 164, 170, 171, 172, *206*, 207, 251n18
Bremer, Frederika, 71, 226n43
Brower, Frank, 5, 84. *See also* Virginia Minstrels
Brown, John, 12, 19, 101, 119, *120*, 121, 128
Bryant's Minstrels, 3, 160, 167, 170. *See*

Bryant's Minstrels (*continued*)
  also Blackface minstrelsy; "Dixie"; Emmett, Daniel Decatur
Burgess family, 54, 112
Burgess, Jim, 22
Burton, Annie, 42, 220n47

Campbell, Eliza, 112, 183, 188, 203, 205
Camp meetings, 68, 139, 140
Canada, 124, 146, 235n1, 237n24
C. & E. Cooper Company, 100, 137
"Captain Jinks of the Horse Marines," 169
Captina, Ohio, 137, 139
Carroll, Charles, 34
Casey (slave), 34, 36, 39, 41
Chaddock, Robert, 235n2
Charles County, Md., 9, 25, *28*, 27–45, 54, 55, 171, 173, 174–80, 215n8, 217n17, 219n27, 220n48, 221n55
Chesapeake Bay, 29, 30, 32, 46
Cincinnati, 71, 74, 136–37, 145, 146
Circus, 3, 5, 83–84, 158, 167, 229nn78, 79
Civil War, 41, 66, 76, 122, 126, 133, 134, 243n5; era, 12, 29, 52, 59, 60, 67, 70, 84, 85, 101, 108, 122, 124, 127, 134, 143, 157, 175, 223n5, 243n71
Clay, Henry, 49, 121, 178–79
Clinton, Ohio, 2, 11, 22, 87, 166, 189, 192, 197
"Clinton Quadrille," 197
Cochran, William H., 143, 144, 146
Cohen, Norm, 160
Cole, Rose, 19
"Colonel Ellsworth," 76
Colonization, African, 40, 145, 239n35, 240n50
Columbus, Ohio, 127, 128, 134, 145, 146, 162, 164, 171
"Comrades, Fill No Glass for Me," 77
Cooper, Ellen. *See* Snowden, Ellen Cooper
Cooper, Harry, 27, 32, 34, 39–41
Cooper, Henry, 21, 25–27, 30, 31, 33–41, 43, 56, 173, 179
Corwin, Thomas, 49
Cotton, 32, 35, 43, 174–75, 180
Cresswell, Nicholas, 9, 30–31, 173, 174
Culp's schoolhouse, 66, 75
Curtis, Hosmer, 78, 80, 228nn63, 68

Dancing, 3, 5–7, 17, 30–31, 59, 61, 73, 77, 83, 85, 89, 102, 159, 160, 168, 170, 172, 173, 180, 182, 189, 194, 225n26. *See also* Blackface minstrelsy; Snowden Band
Dan Emmett Grange, 23
Danville, Ohio, 51, 53, 68, 69–70
Davis, Jefferson, 4, 159
Delaware, Ohio, 128
Democratic party, 126, 128–29, 133, 139, 142, 143–45, 159, 235nn5, 6. *See also* Colonization, African; Race relations, Knox County, Ohio; Slavery
Dennison, Sam, 4, 182, 243n3
Diamond, John, 170
"Dixie": black origins of, 3, 8, 16–18, 22, 159–88, 197, 207, 249n73; as Confederate symbol, 3–5, 16, 23, 153, 155–58, 243n3; earliest version of, 247n54; in minstrel show, 3, 5, 6, 16, 80, 158, 160–61, 166; popularity of, 3–5, 16, 156–59, 211n3; on sound recordings, 194, 196, 197; as term, 157, 175–76, 244n11. *See also* Blackface minstrelsy; Emmett, Daniel Decatur; Snowden, Benjamin (Ben); Snowden, Ellen Cooper; Snowden, Lewis (Lew)
Douglass, Frederick, 12, 29, 34, 36, 42, 101, 122, 171, 173, 176, 215n4
Drum, 15, 63, 168
Du Bois, W. E. B., 13, 213n24
Dulcimer, 63

Education, 11, 13, 52, 53, 88, 93, 94, 96, 98–100, 114, 118, 129, 135, 136, 231n2, 233n30, 238n29. *See also* Literacy
Ellender (slave), 27, 32, 34, 36, 38
Emmett, Catherine, 168
Emmett, Daniel Decatur, 1–8 passim, 17, 18, 21, 22, 84, 155–72, 183, *185*, 188, 189, *191*, 192–97, 205, 211n1, 212n4, 223n3, 230n98, 245n33, 249n73. *See also* Blackface minstrelsy; "Dixie"
Emmett family, 161, 166–68, 183, 188
Emmett, Mary, 189–90
"Emmett's Quadrille," 197
Epstein, Dena, 214n25, 225n21, 245n26

Evans, David, 225n23
Evans, George Bird, 212n6, 247n54

Farming, 11–14, 52, 80, 88, 90, 93, 100, 102, 135, 137, 148, 199, 202, 203, 205, 237n19, 250n11. *See also* Cotton; Slavery; Tobacco
"Father's Come Home," 75
Fiddle. *See* Violin
Fields, Barbara Jeanne, 248n61
Fife, 3
Fifteenth Amendment, 14, 126–33, 235n4, 236nn15, 18. *See also* Race relations, Knox County, Ohio
First Congregational Church, 138, 143
Fishing, commercial, 33, 217n19
Flute, 19, 63, 229n87, 231n102
"Forty Years Ago," 76, 90, 169
Foster, Stephen, 57, 74, 75, 169
Frederick County, Md., 54–56, 143
Fredericktown, Ohio, 56, 96, 127, 143, 188
Freemasonry, black, 243n71
Frontier. *See* West, the

Gates, Henry Louis, Jr., 173, 174, 176, 247n52, 248n59
"Gathering up the Shells," 90, 161
Genovese, Eugene, 38, 165, 221n51
Gerber, David A., 238nn28, 32
"Good-Bye," 71–72, 90, 161
Grant, Ulysses S., 122, 128, 129
"Grecian Bend," 90, 230n98
Green, Alan W. C., 181
Greenville, Ohio, 9, 47, 133
Greer, Alexander, 25, 27, 28, 31–45 passim, 175, 216nn13–15, 217nn17–19, 218n22, 219n30, 220n45
Greer, Dwight, 21
Greer, James, 17, 43, 44
Greer, John, 25, 26, 27, 38, 41, 42, 51, 52, 56, 173, 219n34, 222n71
Greer, Mary, 17, 42–43, 50, 51, 54
Greer, Mildred, 21
Greer, Robert, 21, 50–52
Greer, William, 177
Guernsey County, Ohio, 136, 188
Guitar, 14, 30, 60, 81, *113*, 172, 225n23, 229n87, 231n102

Hammond, Ethel, 162, *163*, 164
Harper, Lecky, 126, 134, 235n5
Harper's Ferry, Va., 120
Harris, Enoch, 9, 213n20
Harrison County, Ohio, 199
Harrison, Ohio, 64, 93
Henson, Josiah, 31, 35, 45, 221n52
Hicks, Lizzie, 96, 98
Hicks, Mary, 96, 98
Higginbotham, Elizabeth, 119
Hill, N. N., 61
Holmes, Isaac, 50
"Home, Sweet Home," 76
"Hop de Dood'n Doo," 90, 169, 230n98
Horse racing, 9, 18, 130, 166, 183, 199, 201–5

Improvisation, 31, 62, 164–65, 173, 245n26, 247n49
Industrialization, 99–101, 103, 105, 112, 233n25. *See also* Sentimental culture
"In the Morning by the Bright Light," 77, 91, 161
Irony, 173–74, 176, 179, 219n34. *See also* Parody; Signification

Jacobs, Harriet, 114, 176
Jefferson Township (Knox County, Ohio), 50–52
Johnson, Mess (Samuel), 61–62
Jones, Jacqueline, 134
Juba (William Henry Lane), 170

Kanawha County, Va., 57
Kentucky, 62, 68, 136, 143, 146
Kersands, Billy, 85
Kirby, Arthur, 66
Knox County, Ohio, 1, 9–13, 42, 49–52, 56, 122, 126–52, 170, 213n17, 223n3, 237n19, 238nn32, 33, 240n48, 241nn52, 54. *See also* Black community, Knox County, Ohio; Race relations, Knox County, Oh; West, the
Kulikoff, Allan, 180, 216n13, 218n22

Lee, Jean Butenhoff, 32, 216n13
Lee, Stella, 87, 171, 199, 250n9
Levine, Lawrence W., 173, 247n51
Lewis, Almeda, 90, 115

Lewis, Andrew, 87
Lewis, Gabriela, 87
Lewis, John Newton, 168
Lewis, Martha Emmett, 168
Liberia, 40, 145
Lincoln, Abraham, 121, 122, 126, 128, 135, 159
Literacy, 11, 52, 70, 79, 94, 96, 101, 134, 165, 174, 188, 231n2. *See also* Education
Litwack, Leon, 124
Lloyd, Colonel, 34, 36
Loewenberg, Bert James, 94
Lord, Daniel W., 27
Lowther, Robert A., 199, 201–3
Lowther, W. A., 203

McClane, David Rittenhouse, 168
McClane, May, 168
McIntire, John, 61–62
McMillan, Joseph Greer, 17
Mansfield, Ohio, 81, 88
Manuel (slave), 34, 39–41
Maryland, 9, 17, 25, 27–46, 54–56, 134, 146, 147, 171, 173–80, 188, 248n61. *See also* Charles County, Md.; Slavery; Tobacco
Melodeon, 81, 229n87, 231n102
Methodism, 53, 68–70, 122. *See also* African Methodist Episcopal (A.M.E.) Church
Mills, C. Wright, 22
Minstrel shows. *See* Blackface minstrelsy
Missouri, 67, 90
Moorehead, Marie, 19, *20*, 21, 152, 162, 164, 199, 250n9
Moorehead, Myron (Bud), 19
Morris Township (Knox County, Ohio), 96, 129, 131–32
Morrow County, Ohio, 146
Mount Gilead, Ohio, 146
Mount Vernon Democratic Banner, 81, 102, 126, 128–29, 133, 134–35, 139, 142–45, 229nn78, 87. *See also* Democratic party
Mount Vernon News, 20, 162, 163, 229n79
Mount Vernon, Ohio, 1, 11, 23, 54, 59, 81–85, 100–101, 129, 137, 145, 150, 166, 170, 183, 213n20, 229n78,

232n17. *See also* Black community, Knox County, Ohio; Knox County, Ohio; West, the
Mount Vernon Republican, 126–28, 131–32, 139, 143, 146, 186, 188, 235n4, 240n52. *See also* Republican party
Mount Vernon Republican-News, 182, 81
Music: African, 14–15, 31, 63, 70, 173, 214n25, 225nn21, 23, 245n26, 247n49; blues, 16, 31, 64, 179; brass band, 81, 86, 230n87; instruction in, 19, 70, 87, 91, 93, 98, 168, 223n30, 230–31n102, 231n103; in slavery, 9, 60, 63, 89, 165, 173–74, 176, 180; string band, black, 8, 9–16 passim, 30–31, 59, 62–64, 78, 89, 165, 169, 224–25n18. *See also* Blackface minstrelsy; "Dixie"; Recordings, sound; Snowden Band; Songs; Whistling; *and individual instruments*
"My Last Cigar," 77
"My Old Kentucky Home," 59, 75, 76

Nanjemoy district, Md., 9, 25, 27, 30–32, 173, 175. *See also* Charles County, Md.
Nathan, Hans, 158, 172, 181, 244n11, 245n27, 246n43, 247n54
National Road, 11, 46–49, 54, 178, 221n58
Neilson, Peter, 50, 229n69
Nevins, Richard, 63
Newark, Ohio, 81, 127–28
Newville, Ohio, 148–50
New York City, 3, 6, 17, 57, 80, 81, 160–61, 167, 168, 182
Northwest Ordinance, 9, 10, 237n23
Northwest Territory, 47, 55, 61, 136, 222n71. *See also* Knox County, Ohio; West, the
Norton, A. Banning, 246n39

Oberlin, Ohio, 144, 146
O'Bryan, William, 53–54, 69–70, 222n71
"Oh, Dem Golden Slippers," 77, 91, 161
Ohio. *See* Knox County, Ohio; Northwest Territory; West, the; *and individual locations*
"O How I Wish I Was Singgle Again," 90, 115
"Old Dan Tucker," 6

"Old Uncle Ned," 74, 169
Oliver, Reuben, 90, 161
Oral expression. *See* Irony; Parody; Signification
"Owl Creek Quickstep," 170

Parody, 30, 77, 78, 159, 173–74, 179, 247nn49, 51. *See also* Irony; Signification
Pataskala, Ohio, 63
Payne, James, 87
Payne, John, 87
Payne, Vera, 16–17, 87, 171
Pelham, Dick, 5, 84. *See also* Virginia Minstrels
Piano, 74, 82, 86, 194, 195, 229n87, 231n102
Piersen, William D., 243n72
Planter society. *See* Charles County, Md.; Greer, Alexander; Tobacco
Plummer family, 54–56
Port Tobacco, Md., 40, 221n55
Potomac River, 27–29, 30, 31, 33, 45, 46, 50, 54, 173, 175, 177, 219n35
Propriety. *See* Respectability

Quakers, 56, 143, 240n46
Quillin, Frank U., 126

Race relations, Knox County, Ohio: and churches, 53, 77–78, 138, 145; and demographics, 12–14, 115, 136–37, 143, 144, 199, 238n33; and economic issues, 14, 52, 112, 114, 134–35, 139, 142, 159, 198, 235n3, 238n33; and interracial courtship, 14, 142–44, 148–50, 152, 242nn59, 65; laws governing, 13, 94, 96, 126–33, 135–36, 142, 146, 148, 171, 237n23; and racial discrimination, 13, 48–49, 78, 85, 103, 112, 124, 126, 139, 142–43, 153, 155, 171–72, 201, 238n33; and sentimental culture, 12, 102, 103, 112, 114, 119, 122–23. *See also* Abolitionism; Colonization, African; Democratic party; Fifteenth Amendment; Racism; Republican party; Slavery; Underground Railroad
Racism, 4–5, 7–8, 13, 16, 67, 85, 103, 112, 139, 142–43, 182, 201, 212n8,

213n24, 242n59. *See also* Race relations, Knox County, Ohio
Ralls, James A., 137
Ransom, Reverdy, 136
Recordings, sound, 62–63, 64, 193, 194, 196–97, 224–25n18, 225nn19, 23, 250nn4, 6
Reed-Maxfield, Kathryn, 171
Republican party, 77, 126–29, 133, 135, 143–45, 159, 235nn3, 5. *See also* Abolitionism; Race relations, Knox County, Ohio; Slavery
Respectability, 7, 14, 78, 102–3, 119, 138, 149–50, 178, 228n71, 232–33n23, 233n24. *See also* Sentimental culture
Rice, Thomas "Daddy," 5
Richland County, Ohio, 89, 148
Root, E. D., 63, 89, 148
Root, George, 64, 91, 93
Rourke, Constance, 3, 249n73
Russell, Tony, 5

Sampson, Henry T., 223n5
Sarah (slave), 34, 36, 41
Satire. *See* Irony; Parody; Signification
Scharf, J. Thomas, 55
Schools. *See* Education
Scott, Alta, 67, 90–91, 161
Scott, Alven, 67, 90–91
"Seely Simpkins Jig," 170
Sentimental culture, 12, 19, 75–78, 81, 101–23, 176, 233nn26, 29, 30
Signification, 174, 216n10, 247n52, 248n59
Simmons family, 137, *207*
Simpkins, Seeley, 55, 170, 246n39
Simpson (estate), 32, 175
Slavery: black community life in, 9, 173, 216n13; in Charles County, Md., 25–46; children's life in, 41–42, 52, 177, 180, 215n4, 220nn45–47; church positions on, 53, 56, 143; demographics, Maryland, 9, 30–32, 55–56, 173, 215n8, 216nn13–15; in Frederick County, Md., 55–56; household staff in, 33–39, 41, 177–78, 219n35; minstrel show depictions of, 6–7, 74, 180–82; on the National Road, 47–48; and Ohio politics, 77–78, 134, 143–47, 237n23, 240n48. *See also* Abolitionism; Music;

Slavery (*continued*)
    Race relations, Knox County, Ohio;
    Southampton (Va.) revolt; Underground
    Railroad
Smith's Point, Md., 25, 27–43, 45, 175.
    See also Charles County, Md.
Smith's Tavern, 87, *88*, 205, 251n18. *See*
    also Taverns
Smith, Valerie, 111
Smyrna, Ohio, 112, 183, 199, 201–5,
    250nn10, 11
Snowden, Annie, 11, 59, 88, 91, 92, 96,
    98, 189, 197. *See also* Snowden Band
Snowden Band: instruments, *2*, 14, 19,
    20, 59–60, 63–64, *65*, 73, *86*, 88, 89,
    91, 93, 102, *113*, 129, *141*, *151*, 189,
    214n37; repertoire, 14, 57–80 passim,
    85, 90–91, 96, 102, 114, 129, 161,
    164, 169–70, 177, 192, 226n41; social
    context of, 11–14, 21, 57–93, 102–3,
    114, 135, 141, 148, 161, 164, 165–66,
    205–7, 233n24, 251n18
Snowden, Benjamin (Ben), *2*, 3, 8, 11, 12,
    14, 18–22, 59, 63, 66, 67, 73, 80, 87–
    91, 96, 115, 123, *125*, 129, 131–33,
    148–52, 159–61, 166, 183–92 passim,
    197–99, *200*, 201–7, 244n16, 250n11.
    See also Snowden Band
Snowden, Benjamin (of N.Y.), 119, 146,
    147, 241–42n55
Snowden, Ellen Cooper, 9, 11, 12, 14, 16,
    21–32 passim, 36, 41–54, 56, 62, 68–
    70, 78–80, 94, 96, 110, 118–19, 123,
    133–34, 137, 145, 148–50, 165, 166,
    171, 172–77, 186–88, 197, 199,
    215n4, 228nn63, 68. *See also* Snowden
    Band
Snowden, Elsie, 11, 59, 88, 91, 96, 99,
    189, 197. *See also* Snowden Band
Snowden, Helen, 118, 119, 234n44
Snowden, Lewis (Lew), *2*, 3, 8, 11, 12,
    18–22, 59, 63–67, 73, 80, 86–90 pas-
    sim, 96, 129, *130*, 131–33, 141, 148–
    50, *151*, 152, 159–61, 166, 183–85,
    189, *190*, 192, 197–99, 201, *202*, 203–
    5, *206*, 207, 250nn11, 17, 244n16. *See*
    also Snowden Band
Snowden, Martha, 11, 59, 88, 96. *See also*
    Snowden Band
Snowden, Mary, 109
Snowden, Oliver, 56, 110

Snowden, Phebe, 11, 59, 88, 96, 118. *See*
    also Snowden Band
Snowden Road, 23
Snowden, Sophia, 11, 59, 73, 88–96 pas-
    sim, 101–23, 148, 150, 161, 166, 189,
    197, 232n19. *See also* Snowden Band
Snowden, Thomas, 9, 11, 14, 22, 27, 32,
    41, 54–56, 62, 78, 94, 96, 110, 119,
    133, 135, 137, 145–47, 165, 166. *See*
    also Snowden Band
Sobel, Mechal, 36, 248n58
Songs: black traditional, 30–31, 46, 71–
    72, 77, 138–39, 164, 165, 169, 173,
    176, 180–82, 247n51; minstrel, 3, 5–
    8, 14, 19, 20, 57, 77, 78, 85, 158–65
    passim, 169–71, 175, 177, 179, 180–
    82, 248n63, 249n73, 250n6; popular,
    12, 14, 21, 67, 74–78, 80–83, 98,
    101, 107, 114, 169, 177, 179, 225n29,
    227n51, 231n102, 233n29; religious,
    14, 46, 68–73, 77, 78, 180, 226n32.
    See also Blackface minstrelsy; "Dixie";
    Music; Snowden Band; *and individual*
    songs
Sophia (slave), 27, 32, 34, 38
Southampton (Va.) revolt, 40, 173,
    219n39
Southern, Eileen, 189
Starobin, Robert, 219n34
Stephon (slave), 34, 39–41
Stoddert family, 32, 39

Tambourine, 5, 7, 19, 63, 151, 180, 181,
    229n87
Taverns, 47–49, 60–62, 87, *88*, 178
Tawa, Nicholas, 227n51
Temperance, 77, 78, 178, 242n67. *See*
    also Respectability; Sentimental culture
Theater. *See* Blackface minstrelsy; New
    York City; Woodward Hall
"There Is Danger in the Town," 91
"There's a Meeting Here Tonight," 72, 91,
    161
Thomas (slave), 27, 32, 34, 36, 39–41
Tobacco: as crop, 17, 25–35 passim, 43,
    55, 133–34, 174, 180, 217n17,
    220n48, 237n19; as vice, 77, 116, 150,
    230n95, 242n67
"Tobacco Song," 90, 230n95
Toll, Robert C., 8, 20, 161, 169, 223n5,
    243n5, 246n41

Triangle, 14, 63, *151*, 181
"Turkey in the Straw," 6, 159, 196–97
Turner, Clyde, 19, 20, 87, 197
Turner family, 137
Turner, Frederick Jackson, 124
Turner, Nat, 40
Turner, William, 19, 20

Underground Railroad, 41, 146, 147,
    241nn54, 55. *See also* Abolitionism

Violin, 2, 3, 5, 7, 12, 14, 17, 18, 59, 60–
    64, 73, 81, 89, 102, 129, 153, 160,
    165, 168, 170, 172, 180, 181, 189,
    192, *193*, 194–97, 224–25n18,
    229n87, 231nn102, 103, 246n39,
    250nn4, 6
Virginia, 30, 36, 40, 57, 119, 120, 136,
    143, 146
Virginia Minstrels, 5–6, 7, 8, 84, 158, 191.
    See also Blackface minstrelsy; Emmett,
    Daniel Decatur
Voting rights. *See* Fifteenth Amendment;
    Race relations, Knox County, Ohio

"Walk, Mr. Bookar," 170
War of 1812, 51, 177
Warsaw, N.Y., 118, 146, 241n55
Washington, Ohio, 127
Wayman Chapel (A.M.E.), 137, *138*, 139.
    See also African Methodist Episcopal
    (A.M.E.) Church

"We Are Coming Sister Mary," 76, 169
"We Are Goin to Leave Knox County," 57,
    64, 78, 80, 85, *92*, 93
Welker, John, 51
Welker, Martin, 51–52, 70
West, the, 8–11, 13, 16, 21, 42–47, 50–
    53, 60–62, 67, 76, 80–81, 91, 100, 102,
    124, 136, 197, 207, 222n71, 232n17,
    235n2
Whistling, 60, 157–58, 224n9, 246n39
Whitlock, Billy, 5, 84. *See also* Virginia
    Minstrels
Wintermute, H. Ogden, 18, 214n32
Wintermute, Isabelle, 18, 205, 242n65
Withrew, Refind E., 57, 59, 75, 103
Wolfe, Charles, 64
Women's roles, 91, 93, 101, 103–7, 112,
    114–19, 122, 233n30. *See also* Senti-
    mental culture
Woodward Hall, 81–83, 142, 228n71,
    229n72
Wooten family, 137
Wootton, Ada Bedell, 194, *195*, 196–97
Work, John, 63

Zanesville, Ohio, 61–62, 88, 127, 128,
    129, 134, 235n1
Zerrick family, 166, 167, 188, 189. *See
    also* Emmett, Daniel Decatur
Zouaves, 76, 127–28, 151, 236n7, 242–
    43n71